Shakespeare's Romances Reconsidered

Shakespeare's Romances Reconsidered

EDITED BY

Carol McGinnis Kay
AND
Henry E. Jacobs

THE UNIVERSITY OF NEBRASKA PRESS
LINCOLN AND LONDON

"Romance as Masque" © 1978 by Northrop Frye. This essay was previously published in a somewhat different form in Northrop Frye, *Spiritus Mundi* (Bloomington: Indiana University Press, 1976).

Library of Congress Cataloging in Publication Data
Main entry under title:
Shakespeare's romances reconsidered.

    Bibliography: p. 181
    Includes index.
    1. Shakespeare, William, 1564-1616—Tragicomedies—
Addresses, essays, lectures. I. Kay, Carol McGinnis,
1941-   II. Jacobs, Henry E.
PR2981.5.S5   822.3'3   77-17389
ISBN 0-8032-0958-4

Contents

FOREWORD   vii

1. Norman Sanders
   AN OVERVIEW OF CRITICAL APPROACHES
   TO THE ROMANCES   1

2. Northrop Frye
   ROMANCE AS MASQUE   11

3. Clifford Leech
   MASKING AND UNMASKING
   IN THE LAST PLAYS   40

4. Howard Felperin
   ROMANCE AND ROMANTICISM:
   SOME REFLECTIONS ON *THE TEMPEST*
   AND *THE HEART OF DARKNESS,* OR,
   WHEN IS ROMANCE NO LONGER ROMANCE?   60

5. Cyrus Hoy
   FATHERS AND DAUGHTERS
   IN SHAKESPEARE'S ROMANCES   77

6. Joan Hartwig
   CLOTEN, AUTOLYCUS, AND CALIBAN:
   BEARERS OF PARODIC BURDENS   91

7. Joan Warchol Rossi
   CYMBELINE'S DEBT TO HOLINSHED:
   THE RICHNESS OF III.i   104

8. Charles Frey
   TRAGIC STRUCTURE IN *THE WINTER'S TALE:*
   THE AFFECTIVE DIMENSION   113

9. David M. Bergeron
   THE RESTORATION OF HERMIONE
   IN *THE WINTER'S TALE*   125

10. Charles R. Forker
    IMMEDIACY AND REMOTENESS IN
    THE TAMING OF THE SHREW AND
    THE WINTER'S TALE TEMPEST   134

11. David Young
    WHERE THE BEE SUCKS:
    A TRIANGULAR STUDY OF *DOCTOR FAUSTUS*,
    THE ALCHEMIST, AND *THE TEMPEST*   149

    NOTES   167

    SELECTED BIBLIOGRAPHY
    ON THE ROMANCES   181

    General Works with Significant Sections
       on the Romances   182
    Studies of Romance and of Shakespeare's
       Romances   187
    Pericles, Prince of Tyre   192
    Cymbeline   195
    The Winter's Tale   199
    The Tempest   205

    CONTRIBUTORS   216

    INDEX   218

Foreword

Until recently, only one of Shakespeare's romances, *The Tempest*, had received any great measure of critical or dramatic attention; compared with the remainder of the Shakespeare canon, *Pericles, Cymbeline,* and *The Winter's Tale* were seldom discussed and even more seldom performed. Within the past quarter-century, however, that neglect has been remedied. An increasing number of articles and books about the romances have been published, and perhaps in part as a result of that scholarship, dramatic interest in the plays has increased: within the past ten years all four Shakespearean romances have been staged at the Old Vic, in Stratford-upon-Avon, on Broadway, and at Shakespeare festivals throughout the United States and Canada.

In view of this increasing interest, the Second Alabama Symposium on English and American Literature was devoted to the Shakespearean romances, bringing together scholars and their current explorations of these late plays. Held at The University of Alabama from October 16 through October 18, 1975, the symposium included the presentation of eleven scholarly papers (published here in a somewhat revised form), an informal talk by the Shakespearean actor Morris Carnovsky, and a production of *Pericles* by the University Theatre.

There was no attempt to view the plays from a single perspective; therefore the essays in this volume approach the romances from diverse points of view, and come to varying conclusions about their nature and significance. There are inevitably some common thematic motifs and common critical concerns. But in general the spotlight of attention shifts from essay to essay, resulting finally, it is hoped, in a more complete illumination of the subject.

The first essay, by Norman Sanders, serves as a general introduction to the various types of scholarly work done with the romances.

The next three, by Northrop Frye, Clifford Leech, and Howard Felperin, deal with broad concepts or patterns. Frye discusses Old and New Comedy and the masque in relation to the romances (including *Henry VIII* and *The Two Noble Kinsmen*), with reference to writers from Aristophanes to Tennessee Williams. Leech also deals with the masque, clarifying a pattern of masking and unmasking in early seventeenth-century drama, with concluding emphasis on the romances. Felperin, after a discussion of the nature of romance and Romanticism, compares the demystification and remystification of romance in *The Tempest* with a similar process in Conrad's *Heart of Darkness*.

In the next two essays, Cyrus Hoy and Joan Hartwig examine specific patterns in these late plays. Hoy sees the relationships of fathers and daughters in the romances in the light of such relationships in Shakespeare's earlier plays, and Hartwig discusses the function that the three clown-fool characters—Cloten, Autolycus, and Caliban—serve as bearers of disorder, parody, and corruption.

Each paper in the last group discusses a discrete aspect of an individual play. Joan Warchol Rossi argues that Shakespeare's use of Holinshed in *Cymbeline* was far more pervasive than previously realized. Charles Frey and David M. Bergeron both deal with aspects of *The Winter's Tale*: Frey shows how the dramatic structure of the play manifests the jealousy of Leontes and its consequences; Bergeron suggests dramatic and historical sources that may be linked with the restoration of Hermione, and considers the nature of the statue. The two final essays then treat what is usually held to be Shakespeare's final romance: Charles R. Forker compares the interplay between art and nature, between creating and breaking illusion, in *The Tempest* with an almost reverse process in *The Taming of the Shrew*, and David Young shows how Shakespeare's treatment of magic in *The Tempest* was influenced by two other great Renaissance plays of magic, *Doctor Faustus* and *The Alchemist*.

The volume concludes with a lengthy bibliography of general works that deal, wholly or in part, with Shakespeare's romances, and of articles and books that deal with the individual plays. We hope this will be useful to both undergraduate and graduate students, and to scholars who are doing further work in the field.

We wish to express our appreciation to the many administrators, faculty members, and graduate students at The University of Alabama whose financial and personal assistance made the Shakespeare Symposium, and hence this volume, possible. One final note of sorrow and appreciation is due to Clifford Leech, who died in Toronto on July 26th, 1977. During the Symposium and in his life he embodied the spirits of good scholarship and good fellowship. His works and his friends can attest that he "hath built . . . Such strong renown as time shall never raze" (*Pericles,* III.ii. 46-47).

Carol McGinnis Kay
Henry E. Jacobs

Shakespeare's Romances Reconsidered

1

An Overview of Critical Approaches to the Romances

Norman Sanders

The very existence of a symposium on the romances should serve as a reminder that in one area at least of Shakespeare study a generally accepted conclusion has been arrived at: namely, that the final plays can be considered profitably as a group. Schematizing the works in one way or another has been common practice ever since Hemminge and Condell's initial tripartite division of the First Folio. But most studies which have their basis in some unifying aspect of the canon eventually fall into a sequential analysis of the separate works, because very few schemes can integrate the imaginative experiences offered, say, by *Othello* and *A Midsummer Night's Dream*, or even by *King John* and *Henry VIII*. The romances are the exception. Not only do most critics agree that something is gained by viewing them as a type of play, but many critical analyses of the individual works move from one play's distinguishing details to the patterns, rhythms, and dramatic materials common to them all. One can only assume that their common denominators are not simply critical derivations but are central rather than peripheral to the visions of life they offer—which is why, I suppose, Dowden's notorious "period" (if not his label of "serenity") is still acceptable for the final plays alone.[1]

Behind all such criticism lies historical fact. It is generally believed that these plays were written between 1607 and the beginning of 1612, and Malone, Coleridge, Collier, Dyce, and Furnivall have taught us to view them as collective evidence of an artistic response to life at a particular moment in Shakespeare's career.[2] The fact of chronology is supported by the nature of the plays' content, for they all work repetitively with romance materials: large time-spans, riddles, shipwrecks, the strange loss and recovery of children, rural and court settings, extremes of characterization, happy endings embracing incipient tragedy, and so on. Now, at no point in his career was Shakespeare a waster of his dramatic ideas; in play after play he mined diligently states of mind, character types, social and emotional situations, and theatrical devices. Thus we find Claudius's soliloquy of guilt later treated at play-length in Macbeth, or a career-long worrying of the question of what it is that makes the human heart so hard. But his manner in the final plays is different in kind. In them we find repetition rather than expansive probing, theatrical juggling rather than progressive exploration. Whereas Viola shows us more about denied female affection than does Julia, and Iago tells us things about human evil that Richard III never knew, the resurrections and rebirths of the romances strike us as being variations on a theme.

But these plays pose a unique critical problem. While A. C. Bradley may differ from R. W. Battenhouse who differs from Maynard Mack about what *King Lear* conveys in its final effect, their varying critical accounts at least agree that there is something that the play is about.[3] The romances, rather than raising the question "What do we see in what Shakespeare has wrought?", lead us to ask, "What was he trying to do in the first place?" Such basic critical uncertainty is perhaps one reason that this group of plays has received outright condemnation from critics who have demonstrated exceptional ability to appreciate the rest of Shakespeare's work. The nature of the attacks is best summed up by the maker of the first of them, Ben Jonson, in passages from the prologue to *Every Man in His Humour,* the "Ode to Himself," and the induction to *Bartholomew Fair*:

> Though need make many poets, and some such
> As art and nature have not bettered much;
> Yet ours for want hath not so loved the stage,
> As he dare serve the ill customs of the age,
> Or purchase your delight at such a rate,
> As, for it, he himself must justly hate:
> To make a child now swaddled, to proceed
> Man, and then shoot up, in one beard and weed,
> Past three score years . . . .
> He rather prays, you will be pleased to see
> One such today as other plays should be;
> Where neither Chorus wafts you o'er the seas;
> Nor creaking throne comes down, the boys to please.
>
> (Prologue, lines 1-16)

No doubt some mouldy tale
Like Pericles, and stale
As the shrieve's crusts, and nasty as his fish—
Scraps, out of every dish
Thrown forth, and raked into the common tub,
May well keep up the play-club.
(*Ode*, lines 21-26)

If there be never a servant-monster i' the fair; who can help it? . . . nor
a nest of antiques? He is loth to make Nature afraid in his plays like
those that beget Tales, Tempests, and such like drolleries.
(Induction, lines 127-30)[4]

In these strictures are not only all the features that were later to
provoke Dr. Johnson, Dryden, Shaw, and Lytton Strachey,[5] but
also those which more favorable critics have felt obliged to explain
away. Of course, in recent years such attacks have been less common; since Strachey's day there seems to be a greater readiness to
agree that all Shakespeare is good even in its badness.

The combination of historical evidence and literary impression
has proved irresistible in leading critics to the question: Are these
plays final in more than a chronological sense? Are they not also
in some way a summing-up, the master's statement of his final
position? The answers attempted have fallen into three broad
categories: the biographical, the structural, and the visionary.

The attractions of the biographical approach are obvious.
Plays which bear so heavily the stamp of repetition, which are so
similar, and which interpose between the author and the reader
no seemingly complete public world and array of complex individual characters, encourage critics with the hope of moving easily
through their surfaces and into the playwright's mind. The paths
adopted have been various, the most concrete being the historical.
If Shakespeare was a busy man of the theater, then the contemporary stage must have been a leading force in his creative life, and
therefore much that seems puzzling in the romances could very
well have been due to influences exercised by Jacobean theatrical
conditions. Through the work of men like E. E. Stoll, G. E. Bentley, and Harley Granville-Barker, the various possibilities of
theater pressures have been pursued with subtlety and ingenuity.[6]
So we are offered the master poet in middle age spurred on to
greater experimentation by the emerging competition of the

younger Beaumont and Fletcher. Or both they and Shakespeare were tempted to take advantage of effects offered by the resources of a new indoor Blackfriars Theater. Or perhaps an audience with courtly tastes, reflecting some decline in the national psyche, stimulated the production of a coterie drama with a compulsion toward self-parody and theatrical self-consciousness previously unknown. Naturally there has been resistance from those who wish to protect us from the possibility of viewing the Bard as pure hack from some Bankside Grub Street, and so have reminded us that though a fashion-follower he nevertheless always managed to preserve his moral and artistic integrity.

A far more widespread biographical activity than that of the historical critics is the creation of the poet's soul from the evidence of the works. In the exploitation of this legacy from the Romantics, the finality of the plays is accepted in every sense. They *are* the state of mind of Shakespeare in the last decade of his life; they embody the intellectual state to which his experience of life and the practice of his art have brought him. Everyone is familiar with Edward Dowden's version: the tone of high morality, the all-embracing repentance, reconciliation, forgiveness, love, and peace; the value placed upon nature's unchanging rhythms; the interest in the happy innocence of youth; the ready acceptance of the supernatural; the sense of maturity and wholeness joined with a patronizing regard of the pains and joys of life that had made the playwright a sadder, wiser, and serene man.[7] This benign late-Victorian creation was elaborated many times—and in some ways still is being elaborated. So too are aspects of the inevitable counterblast to it by Lytton Strachey. His late Shakespeare was an old man bored with himself, his art, and people generally, taking refuge in poetic dreams in which etherial songs alternated with outbursts of disgust.[8] This attack, of course, was not on Dowden's critical method but on the conclusion he came to. As the recent Bloomsbury industry has shown us, Strachey never escaped from the Victorian front parlor at all; he remained there all of his life as a rather grubby-minded schoolboy. Yet an echo of Strachey's voice remains in more recent criticism of the plays which lays stress on their strongly puritanical tinge, their tense pairing of asceticism with a sensuous appreciation of beauty, their emphasis on discipline, and the real harshness with which the need for duty, morality, and restraint is conveyed.

There is little chance of a return to Victorian biographical confidence, but perhaps we have moved too far from Dowden in the direction of Samuel Schoenbaum[9] and a biographical method limited to documents and allusions. The biography of any great artist is as much the process of his art as the facts of his life; Shakespeare is what he has been to people since his death as well as what he once was to his family, friends, and colleagues. Whether we like it or not, the First Folio is the record of a spiritual odyssey, and few modern critics have been prepared to take on the task of contemplating the playwright's myriad-mindedness as it is displayed in the complete works. Our inability to hold in the mind anything resembling a total Shakespearean vision is perhaps the source of a further fascination of the last plays. They alone attempt to shape into five acts the mixed materials that Shakespeare had previously been content to parcel out into some combination of Polonius's various dramatic categories.

The second critical solution to the puzzle of the romances is structural, an attempt to perceive Shakespeare's meaning by first defining the plays' kind. Seeing the plays as dramatic examples of romance is such a solution. Howard Felperin, in a recent book employing this approach, puts its attractions in this way:

> Although my first and last interest is in the plays, I discovered (after several frontal and fumbling assaults on them) that I could not fulfill my first obligation without incurring the second; that is, I could not arrive at readings of the romances worth having without venturing into the poetics and problematics of romance.[10]

Here, it would seem, is one solid center to which the plays may be tethered while we examine them. The critical gains of such an approach have been substantial. Some writers, like J. M. Nosworthy in his work on *Cymbeline*, have demonstrated how the revival of interest in romance in the reign of James I was not something new but a reexploration of the old. Others, like E. C. Pettet, have shown how the plays are as much an intensification of a quality present in Shakespeare's work from the beginning as they are a new departure. And others, like Frank Kermode in his edition of *The Tempest*, have woven involved contexts of contemporary interests, native traditions, and literary influences.[11]

Side by side with this investigation of the nature of an age-old narrative tradition to which the plays obviously belong, there has been the study of the generally recognized but often fuzzily grasped pastoral convention. Attempts have been made to bridge the gap which separates the twentieth-century reader of *The Faerie Queene* and *Arcadia* from his Elizabethan counterpart, and our awareness of the literary context of which the plays were once a part is the clearer for them.[12] Yet Shakespeare's originality in all genres should warn us against having too great a confidence in the critical dividends to be derived from contextualism of one sort or another. His treatment of the pastoral convention will surely resemble his handling of history, political values, romantic love, and human limitation in other kinds of plays—that is, it will be a blend of accepted tradition and a unique interpretation of it. No matter how clearly defined in a historical sense is the critics' use of their terms, no matter how broad their knowledge of European literary roots, or romance theory and practice, or the mixed form of tragicomedy, or the varieties of the pastoral mode, the final effect of the plays is always a momentary glimpse of moral perfection and human wholeness which must work theatrically within the unit of the five-act structure. Stage experience has proved that they can indeed work in this way. The puzzles of the study can melt away with the wave of a hand of a Gielgud, an Ashcroft, or a Guthrie. On the boards these plays do strike us as being in some way inclusive of and yet beyond the experiences of comedy, tragedy, and history. There is in them that blend of human curiosity and aesthetic passion that Henry James detected: their unique capacity to have the world as it is, contained in an artistic structure showing a form which it does not have in life for those who are living.

Very few critics of the romances, however, are content to be limited by a study of their form and contexts, for, as John Danby put it, "the externals alone would never explain either Shakespeare's excitement or the individuality of his accent . . . it is the inwardness that is important."[13] That inwardness has provided critics with an almost limitless field in which to search for the third kind of answer, the visionary. To read the inward one must assume and interpret an outward which contains more than it shows. And so allegorists of one sort or another are given a free hand. The very patterns, repetitions, and rhythms which enable us to treat the romances as a group are the qualities that facilitate symbolizing and mythologizing.

There seem to be no limits to the critical imagination when its focus is the final plays. Indeed when one surveys the endless possibilities, one cannot avoid two suspicions. First, if the plays are huge symbolic dramas of other-speaking, then they are singularly unsuccessful vehicles for conveying meaning in anything approaching a manner which encourages broad general agreement. Second, if their symbolism is so complex that it can embrace so many apparent contradictions, are they not, in thus symbolizing everything, drawing perilously close to symbolizing nothing?

Perhaps the best way of grasping the critical variety of such studies is to group them into two large divisions. First, there are those readings which take the plays as restating in terms of dramatic romance some system which is more comprehensive than any play can be in itself. Most prominent among these interpretations are those that employ Christian belief in some form. Basic to this approach is the conviction that, since Christianity is an all-embracing and totally satisfying explanation of the universe and man's place in it, anything so obviously good as the Shakespeare canon must somehow exemplify this system of belief. Thus, if the critic can use the Christian values so obviously present (or detected if not obvious) to prove that the play restates imaginatively the Christian vision, then the play can be shown to be even better than it first appeared. The most complete if not the most ingenious book of this kind on the final plays (because competition is fierce in this field of intellectual gymnastics) is still S. L. Bethell's *The Winter's Tale.* His stance is honestly stated at the outset: "It is not a new mythology that the play presents—not a new interpretation of human experience but the old interpretation [of Christian belief] newly translated into terms of the romance." Behind the unreality of much of the play's surface lies a higher reality, so that Leontes' crime is viewed in terms of original sin, and Apollo's oracle affirms God's beneficent ordering of the world. The natural and the supernatural are interdependent; the love and life force represented by Florizel and Perdita supplants and changes the death forces of their parents' generation; the ending dissolves the old Christian dichotomies as Hermione's resurrection expresses a future life in terms of the present moment as a "carefully prepared symbol of spiritual and actual resurrection, in which alone true reconciliation may be attained."[14]

The second large group of symbolic readings are those which, rather than attaching the plays to some wider view of human life, concentrate instead on those elements in them which bear a marked similarity to other vast patterns and master symbol-systems used by people in all eras in their efforts to attain some understanding of the life process. This kind of criticism is clearly linked closely to both the impact of the work done in modern anthropology and comparative religion, and to some modern literature. Its now familiar terminology of vegetation rites, kingly death and dismemberment, fertility rituals, deaths and births by water, rebirths and resurrections is a part of the Frazerian legacy. Colin Still's study of *The Tempest* was one of the earliest and remains one of the most fascinating of such critical performances. The revised title—*The Timeless Theme*—is indicative of the attitude to art on which it is based. For Still all art deals with "the unchanging facts of mankind's spiritual pilgrimage," and *The Tempest* specifically is "a dramatic representation of the Mystery of Redemption, conceived as a psychological experience and expressed in mythological form."[15] As he works out his interpretation, the richness of his comparisons drawn from preclassical, classical, and Christian mythology is certainly striking, and in his hands the play swells to become a digest of the civilizing efforts of humankind.

Perhaps the best-known and most influential exponent of this kind of criticism is G. Wilson Knight. Knight is not so much a critic of the drama as a gifted plunger into the eternal verities of Nature, God, and Man he sees the plays containing. At the basis of his glittering structures rests the position of all those interpreters who employ mythology, ritual, and religion in differing combinations:

> Fundamental verities of nature, man, and God do not change. . . . The dominating ritual of the Middle Ages was the Mass; it was the one supreme drama, to which other forms existed in strict subservience. The medieval system losing its hold, the way was at once opened for a far more richly varied drama, with manifold dangers but also new possibilities of illumination. . . . A common store of racial wisdom for centuries untapped is now released, as Prospero releases Ariel; and the highly responsible artist has himself to explore and exploit the wide areas of imaginative truth apparently excluded . . . by Christian dogma.[16]

This exploiting and exploring of imaginative truth has been the burden of the bulk of recent criticism of the last plays, even though its conclusions range from D. G. James's estimate of their ultimate failure because Shakespeare is trying to go where art cannot go, to D. A. Traversi's claim that they reveal the possesssion of maturity and a completely balanced vision of human life that is the goal of all human striving.[17]

No one can deny the illumination brought to the plays by these symbolic studies. But as each new book appears to display the meaning of *The Tempest,* one does feel a slight pang of dissatisfaction with the critical method which too often ignores Danby's warning that "one of the most important things an apple can mean is simply itself,"[18] and which also tends to push these magical and potent theatrical pieces back into the mass of common Western European symbolism, in a manner that uncomfortably recalls the efforts some years ago of those diligent sourcerers who proved to us that the vision of the history plays is really all there in Hall, Holinshed, the Homilies, and the Great Chain of Being.[19]

The one point of agreement among these symbolic critics is that the romances (while in no sense superior to *Hamlet* or *Twelfth Night* or *Henry IV*) simultaneously subsume and move beyond Shakespeare's earlier worlds of comedy and tragedy and history. In a sense we are back with a variant form of the biographical approach in that the plays are being seen as the embodiment of the final artistic response to life toward which Shakespeare was moving throughout his career. While there are many variants of this view, no one can represent it better than Northrop Frye, because he has best explored its implications with a Coleridgean fertility and because Shakespeare's romances lie at the center of his critical position about literature as a whole. For Frye the plays take us from reality to illusion, from which we emerge into a recognition of transcendental nature that we could not know other than by the symbols of art. The romances can take us, as myth took our ancestors, beyond tragedy and into the participation in a higher order of reality that all men desire.[20]

As we watch Frye work out his ideas, we are reminded once again of other powers that the final plays possess: their capacity to stimulate original creative imaginations and to move into the personal lives of readers and other poets alike. Like Caliban on his island, we glimpse in them a thing like ourselves made perfect; they impose upon us a necessary labor to understand;

they torment us with a world of which we feel we once had the ownership; they offer us an unreachable vision compounded of showers of gold, etherial music, and harsh reality; and they force us to measure our own powers against those of an unyielding magician.

2

Romance as Masque

Northrop Frye

I. Cyclical Structure of New Comedy
versus Polarity of Old Comedy

The two comic genres of Old Comedy and New Comedy are familiar from Greek literature. The distinguishing feature of New
Comedy, the form predominant from Roman times to the nineteenth century, is the teleological plot, in which, as a rule, an
alienated lover moves toward sexual fulfillment. New Comedy
reaches its *telos* in the final scene, which is superficially marriage, and, more profoundly, a rebirth. A new society is created
on the stage in the last moments of a typical New Comedy, and
is often expanded by a recognition scene and a restoring of a birth-
right. In the common device of the foundling plot, the recognition is connected with the secret of somebody's birth. Simpler
and equally popular is the comedy in which a hero, after many
setbacks, succeeds in doing something that wins him the heroine
and a new sense of identity.

In such a structure the characters are essentially functions of
the plot. However fully realized they may be, they are always
organically related to the roles on which the plot turns—for
example, senex, parasite, bragging rival. The *commedia dell' arte*
indicates with great clarity how a group of stock characters,
related to a stock plot, is the basis of the comic structures of
Shakespeare and Molière, both of whom show many affinities
with it. In Ben Jonson's "humour" theory the New Comedy conception of character as a plot-function is rationalized in a most
ingenious way. A character who is, by definition, essentially
what his context in the plot makes him to be obviously has something predictable at his basis. The humour is also, by definition, a
character dominated by a predictable reaction. But predictability

of response is also one of the main sources of the comic mood, as has been noted by a number of theorists of comedy down to Bergson. Therefore, in a "comedy of humours," comic structure, comic characterization, and comic mood are rigorously unified. A similar unity forms the basis for the "well-made play" of Scribe and Sardou in the nineteenth century, a type of drama well within the New Comedy tradition. Many of Jonson's plays, unhappily, especially the later ones, were so "well made" that they failed on the stage through overelaborateness.

New Comedy developed two main forms, the romantic form of Shakespeare and the more realistic and displaced form of the neoclassical tradition, in which the greatest name is Molière. The more realistic such comedy becomes, the more it is in danger of becoming a sentimental domestic comedy, like the *comédie larmoyante* of the eighteenth century. A combination of realistic treatment and New Comedy structure has a tendency to sentimentality inherent in it, as its theme approximates very closely the favorite rubric of the agony column: "Come home; all is forgiven." Molière focuses nearly all the dramatic interest on a central "humour" or blocking figure, whose particular folly, whether avarice or snobbery or hypochondria, helps to keep the tone well away from the sentimental. In Sheridan and Goldsmith the effort to achieve a dry and witty texture is more of a strain. The domestic virtues do not appear to have attracted the loyalty of a major dramatic genius, unless we wish to call Beethoven a major dramatic genius: *Fidelio* is a bachelor's tribute to domestic felicity, but the extraordinary unevenness of the music perhaps indicates some doubt even in his mind.

Eventually the New Comedy structure deserted the stage for the domestic novel, where a sentimental tone is easier to accommodate. The foundling plot reappears in *Tom Jones* and is a standard feature of Dickens. The conception of characterization in Dickens is very close to that of the Jonsonian humour, except that the looser fictional form can find room for a great number of peripheral characters who are not directly concerned in the central plot. But when English drama revived towards the end of the nineteenth century, the formulas of New Comedy were used mainly for purposes of parody, parody being the usual sign in literature that some conventions are getting worn out. We begin with mysterious-heir parodies in Gilbert and Sullivan, notably in

Pinafore and *The Gondoliers*; then we have Wilde's urbane spoof of the foundling plot in *The Importance of Being Earnest*.

Wilde's contemporary, Bernard Shaw, was well aware of the extent to which some standard New Comedy devices had already been parodied by Ibsen. Shaw's parodies of New Comedy recognition scenes include the ingenious device that enables Undershaft to adopt his son-in-law as his successor in *Major Barbara*, and the discovery in *Arms and the Man* that Captain Bluntschli is of the highest social rank possible in his country, being an ordinary Swiss citizen, besides being made rich enough, by inheriting a hotel business, to upstage his rival Sergius. A more conventional type of New Comedy concealed-parentage plot is parodied in *You Never Can Tell*. In the next generation, the writer who most closely followed the New Comedy structure as laid down by Plautus and Terence was P. G. Wodehouse. In other words, the teleological New Comedy structure seems to have dropped out of the center of "serious" literature in the twentieth century.

In this situation writers of comedy clearly have to do something else, and what they are doing may be easier to understand if we think of Old Comedy not simply as a form used by Aristophanes which died with him—in fact before him—but as in a larger structural sense a permanent genus of comedy, open in any age to writers bored or inhibited by other conventions, or suspecting that their audiences are. When we look at Old Comedy in this way, it begins to expand into *the* alternative genus to New Comedy.

The structure of Old Comedy is dialectical rather than teleological, and its distinguishing feature is the contest or *agon*. This feature makes for processional or sequential form, in which characters may appear without introduction and disappear without explanation. In this form, characters are not functions of a plot, but vehicles or embodiments of a contest. The dramatic contest of Old Comedy is as a rule not simply between personalities as such, but between personalities as representatives of larger social forces. These forces may be those of some form of class struggle, as in Brecht, or they may be specific crises like a war or an election, or psychological drives or attitudes of mind. In Aristophanes they are often the forces associated with demagogues in Athens like Cleon who were obsessed with prosecuting the war against Sparta. Such a form is an appropriate one for introducing historical or contemporary figures. We recall how Socrates and Euripides appear in Aristophanes: in Bernard Shaw, who shows the transition to Old Comedy conventions very clearly, we have the caricatures of Asquith and Lloyd George in *Back to Methusaleh*; and this prepares the way for more recent plays about Churchill, the Pope, and various analogues of Hitler. Such characters may also come from literature: I think, as a random example, of Tennessee Williams's *Camino Real*, which begins with Don Quixote and Sancho Panza entering from the audience, in a way curiously reminiscent of *The Frogs*.

We notice in Aristophanes that while the *agon* may conclude with the victory of something the dramatist approves of, it may equally well be a victory of something patently absurd, as in *The Birds* or *Ecclesiazusae*. A comic structure based on a contest in which absurdity is the victor is clearly antiteleological, and the greatest possible contrast to the more idealistic New Comedy. So, although Aristophanes himself is a high-spirited writer, full of jokes and slapstick, the form he uses, in its larger context, is also an appropriate form for black or absurd comedy. Even in him the hostile personal attacks, while they may have been permitted for what were in origin religious reasons, are not simply all in good fun. Even if we rationalize the guying of Socrates and Euripides on this basis, there is still Cleon. The darker tone latent in Old Comedy was recognized in Elizabethan times: Puttenham says, for example: "this bitter poem called the old *Comedy* being disused and taken away, the new *Comedy* came in place, more civil and pleasant a great deal."[1] It was doubtless the sardonic mood of *Every Man Out of His Humour* that made Jonson speak of it as close to Old Comedy, though it is still within the conventions of New Comedy in its structure. In our day the black comedy is normal, but half a century ago, when Chekhov showed characters slowly freezing in the grip of a dying class, many audiences found it difficult to believe that *The Cherry Orchard* or *The Three Sisters* were comedies at all.

New Comedy may go either in a romantic or in a realistic direction: one typical development of Old Comedy is towards fantasy, which now seems to us a peculiarly modern technique. Where characters are embodiments of social or psychological conflicts, the conception of the individual as defined mainly by the "sane" or waking consciousness of ordinary experience is only one of many possible points of view. In New Comedy we are continually aware of the predominance of the sense of experience: we notice this, for example, in the rigid social hierarchy of Shakespearean comedy, which the action of the play never essentially disturbs. Old Comedy, by contrast, may be called the drama of unchained being. In Aristophanes some of the characters may be gods, as in *The Birds,* or the dead, as in *The Frogs,* or allegories, as in *Peace.* A similar tendency to introduce characters who are not coterminous with the bodies of individuals is marked in the theater of the absurd, especially in Ionesco. One direction of this tendency is the archetypal characterization that we find, for instance, in *Waiting for Godot,* where the two main characters identify themselves with a number of representative figures, such as the two thieves crucified with Christ.

Waiting for Godot is also, in one of its aspects, a parody of the vaudeville dialogues, the long shapeless rigmaroles which used to be packed around the "feature film" in my youth. Such verbal filler occasionally appears in legitimate drama, as in the first scene of Shaw's *The Apple Cart,* which dimly recalls the "well-made play" convention of introducing the story and atmosphere through such devices as a heroine-confidante conversation at the beginning. In fact a good deal of the texture of many Shaw plays consists of a type of cross-talk dialogue which bears much the relation to Old Comedy that the *commedia dell' arte* does to New Comedy. In more sophisticated versions of such dialogue, as we have it in certain forms of night club entertainment (e.g., Nicholls and May), it becomes more clearly a verbal *agon.* When the contest is one of incident rather than words, we may have the loose sequential structure of some of the early Chaplin films, where there is a series of collisions between the hero and a number of unsympathetic antagonists, very similar in form to, for example, the last part of Aristophanes' *The Acharnians.*

In New Comedy the essential meaning of the play, or what Aristotle calls its *dianoia,* is bound up with the revelation of the plot, but such a meaning may be crystallized in a number of sententious axioms that express reflections arising from the various stages of the plot. These sententious maxims are one of the best-known features of New Comedy rhetoric. Old Comedy is less sententious and more argumentative than New Comedy, hence it can find a place for the long harangue or monologue, which tends to disrupt the action of a New Comedy, and appears in it only as a technical tour de force, like the speech of Jaques on the seven ages of man. In Aristophanes we sometimes have a direct address to the audience, technically called *parabasis*; in Shaw the *parabasis* is transferred to a preface which the audience is expected to read along with the play; and many recent comedies not only include but are based on monologue, as in several plays of Beckett and in Albee's *Zoo Story*.

As we can see from Aristophanes' use of a chorus, Old Comedy, because of its looser processional form, can be more spectacular than New Comedy. In New Comedy, once we go beyond the incidental songs that we find in Shakespeare, music and spectacle tend to caricature the complications of the plot, as in *The Marriage of Figaro*. But Old Comedy is in its nature closer to musical comedy; the plays of Shaw, despite their intensely verbal texture, often make surprisingly good musical comedies. Again, the fact that Old Comedy is less preoccupied with the game of love and the rituals of upper- or middle-class courtship make it a better medium for a franker and more explicit treatment of the workings of the sexual instinct. Even the scurrility which is so conspicuous in Aristophanes recurs in *Mac Bird* and similar forms of undercover drama.

Of modern dramatists, perhaps T. S. Eliot shows most clearly the conflict between the two types of comedy. Eliot begins his dramatic efforts with the exuberant and superbly original *Sweeney Agonistes,* subtitled "Fragment of an Agon," where, besides the obvious and avowed influence of Aristophanes, many of the features noted above appear, such as the assimilation to musical comedy and vaudeville forms. When he settles down to write seriously for the stage, however, we get such confections as *The Confidential Clerk,* where the main influence is Euripides' *Ion,* usually taken as the starting point of New Comedy. But *The Confidential Clerk* seems, in comparison with *Sweeney Agonistes,* a somewhat pedantic joke, an attempt to do over again what Oscar Wilde (and, for that matter, Gilbert) had already done with more freshness.

Shakespeare's comedies conform for the most part to a romantic development of New Comedy. But Shakespeare was a versatile experimenter, and there is at least one play which comes close to the genus of Old Comedy as we have been dealing with it here. This play is *Troilus and Cressida.* Here the characters are well-known figures from history or literature; the structure is a simple sequential one, built up on the background movement of Helen from Greece to Troy and the foreground movement of Cressida in the reverse direction; the characters are both embodiments and prisoners of the social codes they adopt, and so far as the action of the play itself is concerned, the only clear victor of the contest is absurdity. There is no fantasy in the play, except in the sense in which the Trojan chivalric code is fantasy, but the characterization is archetypal, with a strong sense that the Trojan War, the beginning of secular history, is establishing the pattern for all the history that follows. We find this in the two tremendous speeches of Ulysses on degree and on time, the two primary categories of life in this world, and in Pandarus's remark: "let all pitiful goers-between be call'd to the world's end after my name; call them all Pandars" (III.iii.200-202). The reasons why this play seems a peculiarly "modern" one, and is often performed in contemporary dress, should be clear by now.

New Comedy, especially in its more romantic or Shakespearean form, tends to be an ideal structure with strong analogies to religion. The sense in which Christianity is a divine comedy is a New Comedy sense: the hero of the Christian comedy is Christ, and the heroine who becomes his bride is the reborn society of the Christian Church. Similar affinities between romantic New Comedy and religious myth may occur outside Christianity, as we see in Sanskrit plays, notably *Sakuntala*. Old Comedy is a more existential form in which a central theme is mockery, which may include mockery of the gods, above or below. The presiding genius of New Comedy is Eros, but the presiding genius of Old Comedy is more like Prometheus, a titanic power involved by his contempt for the gods in a chaotic world of absurdity and anguish.

There are two major structural principles in literature: the principle of cyclical movement, from life to death to rebirth, usually symbolized by the solar and seasonal cycles of nature, and the principle of polarity, where an ideal or attractive world, described or implied, is contrasted with an absurd, repulsive, or evil one. In New Comedy the containing form is cyclical: the teleological action moves toward the new life or reborn society of the final scene. The principle of polarity exists within this, as, say, the opposition of a father to his son's desire to marry the heroine. In Old Comedy, where the contest between two contrasting sets of values is usually very prominent, polarity is as a rule the containing form. That is, Old Comedy suggests some kind of social norm implicitly contrasting with its main action in the audience's mind, something in the light of which the absurdity of that action appears properly absurd. There are glimpses of this in Aristophanes, as in the festival of Dionysus in *The Archarnians,* but there is no consistently idealized picture of life presented in his plays. Similarly in New Comedy, idealized life occurs not so much in the action as in the kind of "lived happily ever after" life that is often assumed to begin at the end of the action.

The comedy of the English Renaissance was confined to New Comedy for many reasons, of which perhaps the simplest and most obvious is censorship, combined with the clerical, and more particularly puritan, disapproval of theaters generally. An age in which *Mucedorus* could be denounced as morally corrupting and *Sir Thomas More* treated like a revolutionary manifesto was clearly not an age for an Aristophanes. *Troilus and Cressida* was one of the least popular plays of an otherwise quite popular dramatist. Yet the rigid New Comedy frame was also a hampering one, and although romance is equally rigid in its conventions, and masque far more so, romance and masque both represent to some extent two directions of dramatic experiment away from the established form.

II. Structural Affinities Between Old Comedy and the Masque

In the masque the organizing principle is that of polarity, the contrast between the two orders symbolizied by the two parts into which it was divided, the antimasque and the masque proper. The antimasque normally came first (Middleton even spells it "antemasque"), and it often depicted the grotesque, the ribald, or whatever the audience was ready to accept as socially substandard. Bacon, in his brilliant little essay on masques and triumphs, lists antimasque figures as "fools, satyrs, baboons, wildmen, antics, beasts, sprites, witches, Ethiopes, pigmies, turquets, nymphs, rustics, Cupids, statuas [*sic*] moving, and the like."[2] The masque proper was a stately and elaborate ceremonial in honor of a distinguished person, frequently royal. The theme was usually allegorical or classical, of a kind that often required a good deal of explanation when printed, especially when Ben Jonson was the author. Such a theme was appropriate to the elitism of the setting, the classical deities clearly having been originally created on the analogy of an aristocracy. The actors of the later and more elaborate antimasques were often professionals; those in the masque proper were more likely to be lords and ladies whose names were proudly listed in the printed versions. Highbrow anxieties about mingling upper and lower classes in the plays of the popular theater were seldom ruffled by a masque, which tended to make social distinctions an essential theme in the spectacle. In Jonson especially the general idea is that the antimasque represents a parody or burlesque of something of which the real form is presented later in direct association with the king, or the most eminent figure present.

The masque thus held up an idealizing mirror to its audience, and not only dramatized its stratified social structure, but also in its imagery reflected the whole religious and philosophical cosmology which rationalized that structure. In this cosmology the world began with an act of creation in which a divine power imposed an order on the turbulence of chaos. The order is often called a harmony and is symbolized by music; the creative power is also the power of love, love being, on the purely automatic level of "attraction," the force that enables the warring principles of chaos to separate into the four elements, each of which keeps to its own place. Creation takes the form of a hierarchy or chain of being, and the hierarchy of Jacobean society, the chain of authority depending from the king, continues the natural order of things in its social and political aspects. At every point there is a political and a cosmological parallel: at the bottom of the chain of being is chaos; at the bottom of society are the corresponding elements of anarchy and unrest.

The king, therefore, not only rules by divine right but is a visible emblem of the authority of God. Considering that Jonson remarked to Drummond of Hawthornden that Donne's *Anniversaries* were blasphemous because he said things about Elizabeth Drury that should only have been said about the Virgin Mary, it may seem strange that Jonson sometimes speaks of King James in terms that would be more appropriate to Christ.[3] In *Love Freed from Ignorance and Folly,* the action turns on guessing riddles of which the right answers are Britain and King James:

the riddles themselves come from some paradoxes of Nicholas of Casanus, where the right answer is God. Similarly in *Oberon*:

> 'Tis he, that stays the time from turning old,
> And keeps the age up in a head of gold.
> That in his own true circle still doth run;
> And holds his course as certain as the sun.
> He makes it ever day, and ever spring,
> Where he doth shine, and quickens every thing
> Like a new nature: so that true to call
> Him by his title, is to say, He's all.
>
> (Lines 350-57)[4]

But what seems like a rather brutal flattery is consistent with the genre that Jonson was working in and did so much to create. We may find it hard to realize what a strain these masques must have been on the people in whose honor they were held, not least the king. He, when present, was always at the center of the whole show, being, like Ariel, an actor in it, however passive, as well as an auditor. It is understandable that the few remarks recorded of James at masques should betray an exasperated weariness at being dragged out to so many such entertainments. It is clear that sometimes he would have given his crown to possess the equivalent of that bastion of democratic liberties, the television button, which can turn the whole foolish noise into silence and darkness, leaving not a rack behind.

Prospero's speech after the masque in *The Tempest*, just echoed, expresses with definitive eloquence another characteristic of the masque: its transience. Like a miniature World's Fair, where a whole city is set up and torn down, the masque was an enormously expensive and variegated performance which glittered for a night and disappeared. Some of the printed texts give a sense of trying desperately to salvage something of the intense experience of the original production. "These things are but toys" is Bacon's opening remark in his essay,[5] and the masque does have something of the cultural quality that Fabergé symbolized in a later age, of elaborate "devices" or playthings for a leisure class. The flickering light of candles and torches must have greatly increased the sense of unreality, almost to a point of hallucination. The masque, in short, irresistibly suggests the imagery of magic or summoned-up illusion.

This was the aspect of the masque that got Jonson down: it seems ironic that an author with so strong a sense of the permanence of literature, who was unique in his day for his anxiety to get his plays into print, should have been associated with a fragile and highly specialized dramatic development that had so little significance outside its immediate setting and occasion. Jonson was proud of his ability to write masques, naturally, but the feeling that Inigo Jones, with his endlessly resourceful stage effects, was the real magician and stole the show from him every time, was hard on his self-respect. To preserve that self-respect he clung to the cosmology which the masque dramatized. For him the masque consisted of a perishable body, created by Inigo Jones, and an immortal soul, the poetry that he could supply. The body was also represented by the antimasque, the epiphany of temporary disorder or confusion obliterated by the real masque, which comes to a focus in the figure in front. The *de jure* monarch in particular, who represents the continuity of order in society, is a visible emblem of permanence, including the permanence of Jonson's fame. Thus in the preface to *Hymenaei*:

> So short-lived are the bodies of all things, in comparison of their souls. And, though bodies oft-times have the ill luck to be sensually preferred, they find afterwards the good fortune (when souls live) to be utterly forgotten. This it is hath made the most royal Princes, and greatest persons . . . not only studious of riches and magnificence in the outward celebration of show . . . but curious after the most high and hearty inventions, to furnish the inward parts. . . .
>
> (Lines 6-15)

Unfortunately for this pious hope, the antimasques, along with the elaborate settings, proved to be more popular in appeal to the audience than the highly allusive allegories, buttressed with documentation and footnotes, which Jonson regarded as the soul of the genre. The audience in general, including King James, preferred dancing to talking, and the principle that the dance was the real soul of the masque had much more authority. In Shirley's *The Triumph of Peace* there is an opening announcement that there is to be no antimasque: this provokes protest from one of the characters, who says that the audience will never stand for such a thing, and something like thirteen antimasques follow. Jonson saw in such proliferation of antimasques the degeneration of the form, and in this he was clearly right. Again, the breakdown of the form presaged the fall of the social structure which supported it: one of many examples of the socially prophetic role of the arts.

To return to the cosmology which the masque reflects: we have a descending movement of order and harmony on chaos, which is the original creative act of God and is perpetuated in human society by the structure of authority. God could have created only a perfect world, and this original creation formed a second or ideal level of reality. It included the Garden of Eden, and all myths of a Golden Age or an earthly paradise are reminiscent of it. All that is now left of it is, or is symbolized by, the heavenly bodies. The fall of man established a third level, and the fall of Satan a fourth one, which now has the third in its grip. In the original creation the Son of God descended to the second level, walking in the Garden of Eden; at the Incarnation he descended to the third, and, after his death on the cross, to the fourth. These descents were followed by a rising movement, through the Harrowing of Hell, the Resurrection, and the Ascension. This rising movement is redemptive, bringing man back from his alienated or fallen state to a condition nearer his original one.

Writers of masques, apart from Milton, are so concerned with the secular occasion that there is little explicit reminder of this cosmology. But the cosmology itself was so firmly fixed in the Jacobean mind that such a form as a masque, where the presence of nobility and royalty suggested in itself a secular analogy to spiritual authority, had to fall into a similar shape. Jacobean Christianity, Jacobean drama, Jacobean masque, all inhabited the same mythological universe. Besides, royalty and nobility were not merely an analogy: they represented, to a very considerable degree, the continuing visible form of spiritual authority, especially in Protestant England, where the Church itself had been put under the headship of the temporal sovereign.

In the cosmology, authority descends from above: any descending movement which is not that of authority represents evil, following its own law of moral gravitation, and sinking through our world towards the demonic level and the bottom of the chain of being. The central symbol for this kind of descent is metamorphosis, in the sense of transformation into a lower state of existence, such as we have in Ovid's *Metamorphoses,* in Apuleius, and in the stories about Circe in the *Odyssey* and elsewhere. This theme often appears in the antimasque, and when it does, the movement to the masque proper thus incorporates a cyclical progression from chaos to cosmos, unorganized energy to new life, within the polarized structure. The main thrust of the movement to and through the masque proper is therefore upward, in the reverse direction from Circean metamorphosis and to higher levels of the chain of being.

Both antimasque and masque present unreal worlds, but the masque has at least the reality of an ideal, a dream of a happy island or paradisal garden of perpetual spring, with its providential parental figures of king and queen inhabiting it like the presences in the rose-garden of Eliot's "Burnt Norton." It is significant how often Jonson associates Britain with the legend of the floating island—Delos in classical myth—which has been caught and fixed for a moment. The magically evoked instant is real for that instant, however quickly it fades. And in that instant Britain is seen as what, according to Christian teaching, it originally was: a green and pleasant land, part of the Garden of Eden or Golden Age of unfallen man. In Jonson the magic which calls this state of innocence into a moment of being is symbolized, in particular, by Mercury and Proteus, gods of magic and metamorphosis, and in *The Fortunate Isles* Proteus says of Britain:

> There is no sickness, nor no old age known
> To man, nor any grief that he dares own.
> There is no hunger there, nor envy of state,
> Nor least ambition in the Magistrate.
> But all are even-hearted, open, free,
> And what one is, another strives to be.
>
> (Lines 508-13)

We have to keep the vertical metaphor of the chain of being in our minds to understand the consistency of masque imagery. The descending movement is from the divine through the angelical, human, animal, vegetable, and mineral worlds down to chaos, and the movement itself, when not voluntary or authoritative, is associated with sinister enchantments and the lowering of intelligence and freedom of movement. Human beings turned into animals,

statues, or flowers, like Narcissus, are typical images of such enchantment. In masques this kind of movement is often reversed,
going through the corresponding disenchantments. In Jonson's
Lovers Made Men, a simplified form in which antimasque and
masque have the same characters, we begin with the lovers in the
world of the dead, led there by Mercury in his role as psycho-
pomp. They are not actually dead, but think they have died for
love. They drink of the river Lethe or forgetfulness, but what
they forget is their death, and they come to life again. Thus the
main movement is that of a freeing from enchantment or metamorphosis and a restoration of the original identity. In Campion's
Lords' Masque we are introduced to Prometheus creating women:
Jupiter, furious, turns them to statues, but after the proper
invocations the statues are brought to life. We recall that "statuas
moving" was a common masque theme for Bacon, though he
associates it with the antimasque. An anonymous *Masque of
Flowers* shows flowers turning into men, in a reversal of the
Narcissus theme.[6]

Most of the imagery of the masque, then, is strung along what
we may call an *axis mundi,* the center of the vertical line of images
held together by the chain of being and going in an upward
direction. This upward movement of *axis mundi* imagery connects
the masque with a very similar family of image-sequences that
appears in alchemical symbolism, where the alchemical processes
symbolize the transformation of the soul from the state of original
sin, the *prima materia,* to the state of original identity, the *lapis.*
Closely linked, also, is the immensely long tradition in ritual and
literature of ziggurat imagery, where the vehicle is the climbing of
a tower or a mountain representing the hierarchies of being. This
latter is as old an archetype as civilization affords: it is the basis
of Dante's *Purgatorio* and is going as strong as ever in Yeats, Eliot,
and Ezra Pound, whose "Dioce" goes back to Herodotus and his
description of the original towers of Ecbatana and Babylon. Its
ancient forms have been studied by Gertrude Rachel Levy in *The
Gate of Horn* and *The Sword from the Rock.*[7] In narrative poetry
the sequence usually goes up some kind of spiral climb, but this
is not very dramatic, and would be difficult to stage even for Inigo
Jones. What is symbolically a going up on the *axis mundi* is often
represented in drama as a going within. The masque is naturally a
proscenium drama, and in the usual arrangement the audience

was seated at one end of a hall, the other end displaying a curtain on which the antimasque scene was painted. The scene normally portrayed something low down on the chain of being, just above chaos, such as the slope of a mountain, or simply rocks, rocks being common enough to be recognized at the time as something of a cliche. Afterwards the curtain parted to exhibit one or two inner scenes, spatially thought of as within the mountain or rocks, but symbolically representing an order superior to or on top of them.

Thus in Jonson's *Oberon* we first meet satyrs, then an inner scene shows us two "sylvans" asleep in front of a palace, sylvans being evidently higher in rank than satyrs; then the palace opens to disclose "Fays" or knights, and the masque ends in panegyric of Prince Henry, in whose honor it was held. In Jonson's *Pleasure Reconciled to Virtue* the scene is a mountain (Atlas), beginning with a "grove of ivy" at the bottom, from which Comus, here the genius of gluttony, comes with an antimasque of tuns or bottles. Hercules in this masque has to choose between Vice (Comus) and Virtue; he chooses Virtue and gets Pleasure as well, both of whom are much higher up on the mountain, along with Mercury and the masque dancers. In Campion's *Lords' Masque* we begin with the "lower part" of a divided scene, with Mania, the goddess of madness, in a cave, and from there we move up to the sphere of fixed stars.

The ascending imagery is accompanied by reversals of the stock symbols of descent. Antimasque scenes often begin in a thick mazy wood, a labyrinth where there is no certain direction. In Jonson's *Masque of Augurs* an antimasque dance is said to be "a perplexed Dance of straying and deformed Pilgrims, taking several paths" (lines 271-72). A symbol of lost direction, the echo song, becomes a standard feature of masques. But there is also a higher labyrinth, the controlled and ordered movements of the stars, and *Pleasure Reconciled to Virtue* introduces a dance imitating these movements of which the coryphaeus is Daedalus. When a man appears on the stage as an actor he had already undergone a form of metamorphosis: in the junctions of actors and audience in the masque, such as the dance in which the masquers "take out the ladies," the actors come back to their original identity.

What we have called ziggurat imagery often features two things on the top: an idealized landscape or garden, and the body of a bride who is united with her lover at this point, and whose body is often identified with the garden, as in the Song of Songs in the Bible. In Jonson's *Hymenaei,* perhaps the most elaborate of wedding masques, where Juno symbolizes the marriage union, the masquers' dance is compared to "the Golden Chain let down from Heaven" (line 320) by Jupiter, and the masque is introduced by the figure of Reason, described as "seated in the top of the Globe (as in the brain, or highest part of Man)" (lines 129-30), indicating that the upward movement through the *axis mundi* has an analogy to the human body also. Then again, the strong association of the masque with magic, and perhaps also the link in imagery with alchemy, help to make occult themes prominent in Jonson; perhaps it is not an accident that Jonson's greatest play is about an alchemist, however much of a scoundrel. In *Mercury Vindicated from the Alchemists* we move from an alchemist's laboratory presided over by Vulcan to "a glorious bower, wherein Nature was placed, with Prometheus at her feet" (lines 196-97). In *The Masque of Augurs* we move from an antimasque said to have no connection with the main theme to the gods Apollo and Jupiter, the true augurs in the service of the king: again there is a sense of lower and higher mysteries. The Ovidian and Chaucerian image of the House of Fame or Rumor is employed as a symbol of the confusions of the lower states of being: we may compare the dialogue of Truth and Opinion in *Hymenaei.* In *The Fortunate Isles* we are introduced to a credulous Rosicrucian, teased by an "aery spirit" who reminds us of Ariel, and who promises him visions of "gardens in the depth of winter" and a journey from the depths of the sea to the height of the Empyrean. Eventually he is declared to be a gull, but his dreams of an earthly paradise are satisfied by the Britain of King James.

We noted that occasionally the rising of the chain of being is expressed in a cyclical movement from darkness to dawn, winter to spring, age to youth. The fact that Britain is an island in the far west, a land of the region of sunset, enables the action of some masques to begin in a dark world, as in *Love Freed from Ignorance and Folly.* Here the antimasque presents a sphinx who has kidnapped the "daughters of the Morn," journeying from east to west, and also holds Love a prisoner. As mentioned, Love has to guess riddles of which the answers are Britain and King James. The antimasque is danced by "twelve she-fools," and ends with the recognition of James the sun-king, the rising dawn that puts ignorance and folly to flight. A somewhat similar imagery is employed in *The Masque of Blackness,* with its sequel *The Masque of Queens.*

Milton's *Comus* is, of course, not typical of the court masque, but for that very reason it indicates the kind of thing that could have been done with the form to make it a solid and durable dramatic genre. For one thing, Milton is much less preoccupied by the secular occasion and more aware of the cosmological structure of masque symbolism. It has often been noted that the descent of Peace in the "Nativity Ode" is reminiscent of masque devices, and the "Nativity Ode" is based on the same Christianized cosmology that informs the masque, its theme being the descent of a principle of order and control, of divine origin and repeating the creation, which is symbolized by the harmony of music. The Incarnation opens up a polarizing contrast between the paradisal model world of God's original creation, now entering the third level of human life for the first time since the fall of Adam, and the world of the dark demons infesting that fallen order, who represent what corresponds to the antimasque in the poem. The Christ-child is the rising sun that puts these demons to flight, like King James in Jonson. I have spoken elsewhere of the masque-like arrangement of the opening books of *Paradise Lost,* with the vision of hell followed by the blaze of light in heaven.[8] In *Arcades* we have a classical version of the paradisal order that God originally created, its protection symbolized by the Genius of the wood, the objective counterpart of the lady in whose honor the masque is given.

In *Comus* we begin with the same protected order, symbolized by the Attendant Spirit, who belongs to a world above our own and directly beneath heaven, like the Garden of Eden. *Comus,* however, like *Arcades,* is written in a classical tonality, and the Attendant Spirit's home is associated rather with the Gardens of Adonis (in the background is the easy-going etymology that derives "Adon" from "Eden"). The fact that the Lady's chastity is identified with virginity means that she is less explicitly Christian than a vestal or pagan saint like the nun in *Il Penseroso* or the ideal poet in the Sixth Elegy, just as the "divine philosophy" of the two brothers is less Christian than Neoplatonic.

The Lady and her brothers descend into a labyrinthine forest symbolizing the lower world, where they lose their way and the Lady sings an echo song, after which we are introduced to the antimasque of Comus and his rout. Comus is the son of Circe, and is consequently not Jonson's fat slob but the presiding genius of the world of descending metamorphosis. He and his followers are demonic fire-spirits like the *ignis fatuus,* parodies of the circling heavenly bodies which they profess to imitate, and which symbolize the higher labyrinth of heavenly order. Comus and his band are connected, like the false gods of the "Nativity Ode," with everything "fallen" that we associate with the word natural, on its lower or physical level, the level of animals and plants. The Lady's chastity is what is natural to her on the upper, paradisal and originally human level of nature. The emblems of Comus, the cup and the wand, are sexual symbols representing the aspect of the natural in which man tends to lose his human identity. The argument is hardly intelligible without some understanding of the hierarchic cosmology, both Christian and Neoplatonic, in which there are two contexts for the word "nature."

At the end the Lady returns to her own stage of higher nature, and is presented, along with her brothers, to her parents. Here we have the junction of audience and actors that is characteristic of the masque form, except that the symbolism is more concrete. The Lady and her brothers are the only human beings in the play: everyone else is a spirit of the elements of the nature into which the Lady has descended. The action of her descent, like that of Christ in the "Nativity Ode," polarizes them into the good and the bad, the Attendant Spirit and Sabrina being benevolent spirits of air and water like the Genius of the wood in *Arcades,* the fire-spirits Comus and his followers (along with some earth-spirits, parenthetically referred to in the text) remaining demonic. We notice too the symbolism of a night-world in the far west which we met in Jonson: the setting, near the Welsh border, reminds us also of the sunset world of the Irish Ocean and the mouth of the Dee in *Lycidas.* The release of the Lady by Sabrina, the spirit of the Severn river, belongs to the archaic cyclical symbolism of the dead waters of winter succeeding to the living waters of spring, for even after the Lady has been rescued from Comus she is still "frozen."

The familiar features of Old Comedy, as we have it in Aristophanes—the ribaldry, the sense of an unstructured or substandard society, the fantasy, the dancing—are all features reappearing in the antimasque. The antimasque, as Enid Welsford has noted, goes back to something far older than the masque itself—in fact older than Aristophanes, and an ancestor of his form also.[9] It has affinities with the satyr play which was the embryo of tragedy, and in Elizabethan tragedy, when the mood turns fantastic or grotesque, we get scenes reminding us of antimasques, especially when the theme includes magic. The witches in *Macbeth* are an obvious instance, and in *Macbeth* we also have other illusions, like the moving wood, which were common masque features. For all the obvious differences, the structural affinities of the masque are closer to Old Comedy, being polarized and based on spectacle, than to New Comedy, which is cyclical and based on plot.

III. Structural Affinities between the Masque and Shakespearean Romance

In Shakespeare's romantic comic form the structure is taken from New Comedy, but the presence of what I have elsewhere called a green world makes the polarizing element in his comedy much more prominent, being a collision and eventual reconciliation of two opposed worlds or orders of experience rather than of groups of characters.[10] We make a distinction between Shakespeare's comedies and the romances of his final period, implying that this distinction is generic, or has a generic aspect. In terms of what we have been saying, it seems to me that the "comedies" are plays in which the New Comedy scheme maintains itself to the end, though in its own distinctively romantic way. In Terence or Molière the hero and heroine wriggle out of the obstacles and prohibitions of the blocking figures and arrive at marriage and a festive ending within the social order that the blocking figures have set up. In the romantic comedy of Shakespeare and of some of his contemporaries and predecessors, those central characters approaching marriage who have the audience's sympathy are placed in a different symbolic setting, or what we might call, in this strange world of the nineteen-seventies, a separate reality, usually represented as a forest, which permeates and finally transforms the more "realistic" world of the blocking figures. Here the two worlds have an approximate relation to the worlds of wish-fulfillment dream and of waking consciousness, the former being strong enough to mold the latter into something like its own shape, and hence ultimately more real.

In the romances the two worlds are more sharply opposed: the blocking worlds are an intense contrast to the comic spirit, often forming tragic actions in themselves, as in *The Winter's Tale* particularly. Something in these worlds has to be condemned and annihilated, not simply reconciled or won over, before the festive conclusion can take place. What is annihilated is the state of mind, the jealousy of Posthumus or Leontes, the intrigues of Cymbeline's Queen or the Court Party in *The Tempest,* rather than the people in those states, though some of the people get eliminated too, at least in *Pericles* and *Cymbeline.* The structure of the romances thus approximates the complete polarity of the antimasque and masque. The dramatic romances of Shakespeare and his contemporaries, whatever the circumstances of their original performance, have their roots in the popular theater with its unselected audience. The masque, driven by a steadily narrowing class-consciousness into a brittle spectacle as ephemeral as a firework display, nevertheless has features that make it possible for us to think of romance as a kind of democratized version of the same form, a people's masque, as it were.

In Shirley's *Love's Cruelty* there is a frequently quoted passage about masques: "in the instant as if the sea had swallowed up the earth, to see waves capering about tall ships, Arion upon a rock playing to the Dolphins . . . a tempest so artificial and sudden in the clouds, with a general darkness and thunder . . . that you would cry out with the Mariners in the work, you cannot scape drowning."[11] The explicit reference is to Jonson, but the modern reader will think of *The Tempest* or *Pericles.* In fact Shakespeare, who, as far as we know, never looked at a Quarto proof and left his plays to be gathered up after his death, may have been temperamentally closer to the masque than Jonson was. In any case the romances show an ascending movement from chaos and absurdity to peace and order very like that of the masque, and an actual masque, or masque-like scene (the epiphany of Diana in *Pericles,* the dream of Posthumus in *Cymbeline,* the sheep-shearing festival in *The Winter's Tale,* and the wedding masque in *The Tempest*) appears at the peripety of the action. In drama later than Shakespeare, the most ambitious dramatic romance dealing with themes of redemption and the recovery of original identity, along with a good many alchemical themes, is perhaps the second part of *Faust,* and we can see how that poem flowers out of the two gigantic masques, which dramatically are rather antimasques, of the scene at the Emperor Maximilian's court and the classical Walpurgis-Night.

As I see it, there are six romances in the last period of Shakespeare's production: *Pericles, Cymbeline, The Winter's Tale, The Tempest, Henry VIII,* and *The Two Noble Kinsmen.* The first and last are clearly works of collaboration, and are not in the Folio, but collaboration does not mean that the plays lack unity. Shakespeare in any case would have been the senior collaborator, more likely to be responsible for the general design and scheme of the play. We may look first at *Henry VIII,* now an unpopular and rarely performed play, so often said to be largely the work of Fletcher that the statement has come to have the force of an established fact, though it is not one. If we look at it objectively, without worrying about whether it was really the right sort of play for Shakespeare to be ending his career with, we can see how different generically it is from the other histories. It is, in the first place, a pageant: tremendous parades of nobility take place, to such an extent that one contemporary complained that it made greatness too familiar. The coronation of Anne Bullen in the fourth act is the spectacular climax. When the play was performed at Stratford, Ontario, some years ago, the production was gorgeously costumed, with many resources beyond anything that Shakespeare himself could have commanded; but even Stratford gave up on this scene, and had it simply described as taking place offstage. The spectacular nature of the play is perhaps the reason for the low-keyed quality of the writing. The greater the extent to which spectacle is visually provided, the greater the violation of decorum in having obtrusively magnificent poetry in the text accompanying such spectacle.

The hero of *Henry VIII* is not so much the king as the Wheel of Fortune. The first turn of the wheel brings down Buckingham, the second turn Wolsey, the third Queen Katherine and others. If we like, we can see a rough justice or even a providence operating: Wolsey's fall is the nemesis for his treatment of Buckingham, and Queen Katherine, though innocent, has to go in order to get Elizabeth born. For this reason it is unnecessary to apply moral standards to King Henry: whether we think him resolute or merely ferocious, we cannot be sure if he turns the Wheel of Fortune or has simply become a part of its machinery. Certainly in the crucial event of the final scene, the birth of Elizabeth, there is a factor independent of his will, even though he takes the credit for it, as befits a king. In this final scene there is a "prophecy" by Cranmer about the future greatness of England under Elizabeth and her successors, which generically is a very masque-like scene, a panegyric of the sort that would have normally accompanied the presence of a reigning monarch in the audience.

The only difficulty is that this scene shows the final triumph of Cranmer and of Anne Bullen, and the audience knows what soon happened to Anne, as well as to three of her successors, and eventually to Cranmer. It also knows that the reign of Elizabeth was preceded by that of Queen Katherine's daughter, whose existence Henry appears to have forgotten: "Never before/ This happy child, did I get any thing," he says (V.iv.64-65). The parade of dignity and nobility, the exhibition of power and greatness controlled by a king who is not in the audience but confronting us on the stage, has few of the conventional elements of the masque, but it does leave us with a sense of transience, a world of "shadows, not substantial things," to quote Shirley again, that soon disappears and gives way to what is in its future and the audience's present. Another episode in the play that suggests the masque is the dance of spirits around the dying Katherine, where there seems to be a glimpse of something transcending history. What impresses us most strongly about the play is the reversal of the ordinary standards of reality and illusion. Nothing could be more immediately real than the ups and downs of fortune in King Henry's court, nothing more illusory than a prophecy of a future three reigns away, or the sick fancies of a dying woman. But what the play presents is a sense of reality and illusion quite the opposite of this.

The Prologue insists on the seriousness of the play and the suppression of all buffoonery in it. Nothing of the very little that we know or can guess of Shakespeare's own political attitudes would lead us to believe that those attitudes were revolutionary or even liberal: there is no reason to suppose that he would have shrunk from Jonson's flattery of royalty if that had been part of his job. It is the integrity of the dramatic spectacle itself—and

Henry VIII has, I think, far more integrity than it is usually given credit for having—that turns the whole solemn parade into a gigantic perversion of real social life, no less of one than Shelley's *Masque of Anarchy.* What Shakespeare was aware of as a dramatic craftsman, on the other hand, his sense of what the play needed, is sometimes shown by the incidents and characters he adds to his sources, and in *Henry VIII* this consists mainly of the two episodes, Queen Katherine's vision and Cranmer's prophecy, that have some standard features of the masque.

What emerges from a deeply serious, even tragic, play is an irony so corrosive that it has almost a comic dimension. The higher one is in social rank, the more one becomes bound to a formalized upper-class ritual. With a ruthless king as master of ceremonies, this ritual becomes a kind of sinister sacrificial dance, in which the most conspicuous figure becomes the designated next victim. In *The Two Noble Kinsmen* the sense of ritual compulsion is carried a step further. This play begins with the ritual of Theseus's wedding, and Theseus himself is possessed by the anxiety of ritual: "Forward to th' temple. Leave not out a job/ O' th' sacred ceremony" (I.i.129-30). There are two similar commands later in the same scene. The ritual, however, is interrupted by a counter-ritual: three queens in black, one kneeling in front of each of the three chief figures, urge Theseus to war instead of love. The theme of death taking precedence over marriage is repeated in the climax of the play, when Arcite wins the battle with Palamon but dies. And just as death takes precedence of marriage, so a destructive and enslaving passion destroys the freedom of friendship. This is true not only of Palamon and Arcite, but also of Emily. Emily's emotional life revolves around an early friendship with another woman: she has no interest in marriage, much less in marriage to the survivor of a fight to the death over her, but the rigid class code leaves her no choice. The source of the play is Chaucer's *Knight's Tale,* and Chaucer also has a clear sense of the compulsive and mechanical quality of these deadly ritual games. But *The Two Noble Kinsmen* exhibits a kind of sleepwalking commitment to them that seems almost Aztec, especially in the fact that all those who have volunteered to assist Palamon and Arcite will lose their lives if their principal does. The action of the play is dominated by Venus, who is not Homer's laughter-loving Aphrodite but a goddess as menacing as the Indian Kali, flanked by her lover Mars, the god of war, and her child Cupid, the Eros who is fulfilled only by Thanatos or death.

In two of the earlier comedies that most closely resemble masques, *Love's Labor's Lost* and *A Midsummer Night's Dream,* there is a burlesque interlude that corresponds to the antimasque: the pageant of worthies in the former and Peter Quince's play in the latter. In both plays, however, the effect of the burlesque is not to bring out the superior dignity of the upper-class figures, but to throw an ironic light on their lack of self-knowledge. The gentlemen in *Love's Labor's Lost* are "worthies" who have dedicated themselves to a heroic cause which they abandon at the first distracting stimulus; Theseus in *A Midsummer Night's Dream* has had his own will and his conception of his duty quietly overruled by fairies in whose existence he does not believe. A much grimmer and starker burlesque appears in *The Two Noble Kinsmen,* in the form of a morris dance, an actual antimasque imported from a masque of Beaumont's, where the leading figure is a madwoman, "the jailer's daughter." This is a girl who fell in love with Palamon when he was her father's prisoner and set him free. It is the only "natural," spontaneous, and apparently free-willed action in the play, and a totally disastrous one for her: her humiliation is so complete that she does not even have a name. After looking at this Venus-ruled play, we can perhaps understand why the action of *The Tempest,* which goes in the opposite direction, should culminate in a masque in which, although it is a wedding masque, one of the main themes is the exclusion of Venus.

I spoke of *Troilus and Cressida* as Shakespeare's closest approach to the dialectical and processional structure of Old Comedy. This again shows us the Trojans as victims of the heroic ritual code to which they have bound themselves. In such a situation someone more "realistic," like the ruthless Achilles or the wily Ulysses, comes out on top. In *The Two Noble Kinsmen* there is nothing corresponding to the Greeks of the earlier play, and in *Henry VIII* nothing corresponding to the Trojans, but the two plays taken together illustrate different aspects of the self-imprisoning human will to live in a world of illusion and call it reality. In the four better-known romances the movement of the action is more conventionally comic, but it is a movement towards a separating of the two orders of reality and illusion, the orders symbolized, says G. Wilson Knight, by music and the tempest.[12]

This takes us back to masque cosmology, as music and tempest are the two poles of the chain of being, the tempest the chaos at the bottom of existence and music the order and harmony imposed from above.

I spoke of *The Two Noble Kinsmen* as a play dominated by Venus: in the comic romances the god or goddess who acts as a providence for the action corresponds to the figure in the audience of the masque for whom the action takes place. Thus *Pericles* is the play of Diana, *Cymbeline* of Jupiter, *The Winter's Tale* of Apollo. The providence of *The Tempest* is a human magician, but his magic creates a wedding masque in which Juno appears, Juno being especially the patron of marriage, as in Jonson's *Hymenaei.* These deities are, so to speak, on the opposite side of the stage from the audience, but in the epilogue to *The Tempest* there is a strong hint that the magic and illusion of the play is in large part the creation of the audience. The audience has to release Prospero just as Prospero has to release Ariel, and for the same reason: he has been working for them, and now he wants his liberty. Similarly the gods who direct the action of *Pericles, Cymbeline,* and *The Winter's Tale* to a serene conclusion are working for the audience, who recognize this conclusion as "right."

In the fine craftsmanship of Ben Jonson's verse there is something almost plastic, something that makes his own metaphor appropriate when he speaks of "the well joining, cementing, and coagmentation of words; when as it is smooth, gentle, and sweet, like a table upon which you may run your finger without rubs, and your nail cannot find a joint."[13] Such solidity of technical skill goes with the directing of the masque towards the central figure in the audience: all the illusion points to the waking and conscious reality in the recognition of that figure. But Shakespeare's verse is continually approaching the boundaries of conscious verbal expression, the area where conventional language begins to merge into the rhythms and sounds of a realm of experience we know nothing about, though magicians may claim some knowledge of it. This is the kind of verbal music that takes us beyond drama, with its antithesis of actors and spectators, beyond masque, where the actors sometimes rejoin the spectators, into a world where the distinction of actor and spectator no longer holds, where reality is what the word itself creates, and after creating, sees to be good.

In New Comedy the normal action is the victory of a younger

generation and its erotic ambitions over the older people who block them. They block them, normally, because they want to keep on possessing them, and they want to possess them because the illusion of possession is the only way of concealing from themselves the fact that they are possessed. When they are baffled or reconciled we have a sense of rebirth, as the palsied grip of the elders on the comic society is relaxed and new energies take over. This New Comedy structure is incorporated into the romances: Imogen marries Posthumus and Perdita Florizel despite parental opposition, and Marina and Miranda are also joined with their lovers. There is also a cyclical pattern of renewal as the "winter's tale" of Leontes' jealousy gives place to a new spring, or as Imogen (whose story is closely related to another "winter's tale," the Snow-White story familiar from Grimm) waits out her winter until her stepmother dies and her obsessed father (and, later, her lover) can be brought to see the light. But the main theme in all plays is the reintegrating of the older generation, Pericles with Thaisa, Cymbeline with Caesar, Leontes with Hermione, Prospero with the King of Naples and his own Milan inheritance. It is a fully mature life that becomes transformed, and such a theme is symbolically connected not with rebirth but with resurrection, which in a sense is the opposite of rebirth, a vertical thrust upward from death to a life which is no longer subject to cyclical rotation. Thaisa and Hermione are in effect raised from the dead, a power Prospero also claims, and the prayers said by Leontes over Hermione's grave are paralleled in the great song over the grave of "Fidele" in *Cymbeline* and in the false epitaph set up for Marina in *Pericles.*

This theme of illusory death and genuine resurrection is parallel to what we described in connection with the vertical movement up the *axis mundi* or chain of being in the masque. Changing a person into a statue would be an image of metamorphosis, or descent to a lower state of being: the "statuas moving" that Bacon mentions as frequent in masques, and which we found in Campion's *Lords' Masque,* is an image of restored identity. The crisis of *The Winter's Tale* is the changing of the alleged "statue" of Hermione into the real Hermione: a similar image of resurrection is employed when Pericles is roused from his stupor by Marina, and when Imogen recovers from the narcotic drug. We also noticed that in the masque what is higher on the chain of being is often represented by what is inside the antimasque curtain. Without going into the complicated question of the Elizabethan inner stage, we notice how frequently the "higher" place in the romances is represented by an inner one: the cave of Belarius in *Cymbeline*, Paulina's chapel in *The Winter's Tale*, Prospero's cell in *The Tempest*.

Music is the symbol of the higher or paradisal world for many reasons. It represents the original order and harmony that are being regained, as in the traditional music of the spheres. Its rhythm, again, symbolizes the higher quality of time in the regained world, a world where time is an expression of inward energy and not of objective fatality. This aspect of renewed time is often represented by the dance, as in Sir John Davies' poem *Orchestra*, and though Jonson spoke contemptuously of the "concupiscence of jigs" in Shakespeare's romances,[14] the dances are there for structurally much the same reason that they are in Jonson's masques. The text is emphatic that music plays the decisive role in bringing Thaisa and Hermione to life, and supernatural harmonies surround Belarius and Prospero. There is also a different function of music, represented by the songs of the rascally Autolycus and the mischievous Ariel, in which it has a hypnotic effect, riveting the attention but putting the consciousness to sleep. Here it is working in the opposite direction of charm or paralyzing of action. We may compare the aubade "Hark, hark, the lark," sung to Imogen, after she has spent a night with Iachimo in her room, by order of the degenerate Cloten, whose obscene comments on the lovely song form one of the most extraordinary passages of bitonal counterpoint to be found even in Shakespeare. We take the song to be appropriate to the innocence of Imogen and her remoteness from the kind of thing represented by Iachimo on the one hand and Cloten on the other, but Cloten intends the song to be an aphrodisiac stimulant propelling her in his direction.

The fact that music is found on both sides of the polarizing action reminds us that the obvious genre in which to continue these romance and masque features is the opera, especially such an opera as *The Magic Flute*, with its fairy-tale setting (in what Gurdjaieff would call "pre-sand Egypt") and its polarizing action in which hero and heroine are pulled upwards from a dark realm to a light one. It is a rare soprano who can bring out the curiously inhuman quality of the Queen of Night's first great aria, which sounds as though written for a flute solo rather than a voice. The reason is that the Queen of Night is a magic flute too, and she has her own kind of music, though a kind in harmony with the songs of sirens, not the music of the spheres. There are many similar contrasts in Wagner and elsewhere, but they would take us too far afield.

The romance differs from comedy in that the concluding scene of a comedy is intensely social. The emphasis is thrown on the reintegrated community; there are multiple marriages, and the blocking characters are reconciled or have been, like Shylock, previously excluded. In the four comic romances there are glimpses of something beyond this, something closer to the imagery of pastoral, a vision of a reconciliation of man with nature, in which the characters are individualized against nature, like Adam and Eve in the solitary society of Eden. In *The Winter's Tale* the sense of "great creating nature" as an integral part of what man's life ought to be comes to a focus in the sheep-shearing festival, a masque scene in which the dance of the twelve satyrs forms the antimasque. In *The Tempest* the corresponding focus is in the masque of Prospero, where we meet the goddesses of earth, sky, and rainbow in a world from which the deluge of the tempest has receded, where the rainbow, as in the Biblical deluge story, is the sign that the curse has been lifted from the ground.

The virginity of Perdita and Miranda, which is central to both scenes, is a state traditionally associated both with innocence, the primal state of man, and with magic. It is a state not expected to last: both girls are eager for marriage. Prospero's fussing about preserving Miranda's virginity to the last moment is not morality but magic: all magic, like all music, depends on timing, and it must be the right time when Ariel is released, when the world of magical illusion is dissolved, and when Miranda enters her brave new world. Perdita's dislike of grafted plants is not a hereditary nervousness about bastards, but a sense of the virginity of nature, of nature as a virgin mother who needs no fathering art. Both masques are interrupted, one by Prospero's speaking and the other by the "whoobub," as Autolycus calls it, of Polixenes, churning up the illusions of the lower world. The interruption is a part of the sense of the transient quality of the masque, but that transience gives us an insight into what, perhaps, all dramatic and ritual spectacles are about. Human kind, as Eliot says, cannot bear very much reality: what it can bear, if it is skillfully enough prepared for it, is an instant of illusion which is the gateway to reality.

Masking and Unmasking in the Last Plays

Clifford Leech

To put a bold front on things, to dupe the observer even when he knows or guesses at the fact, to pretend—these are among the things we customarily live by. Plain dealing is alleged to be a jewel; Hamlet tells his mother he knows not "seems" when she suggests that his mourning for his father is a piece of showing-off; Manly in Wycherley's *The Plain Dealer* is sure that truth is always on his tongue and in his act. But Hamlet loves the theater, a place of major pretense, and Manly passes himself off, in Olivia's bed, as the apparent boy she has taken a fancy to.

In extreme cases the theater literally makes use of masks, but these (apart from certain modern echoings, as in O'Neill) have a major significance only in Greek tragedy and comedy and in the Japanese No. "Let's pretend" is here carried to an extreme, but we need only Aristotle to make us realize that the Greek audience felt drawn into the spectacle, living thus more intensely than was customary with the persons and stories of legend, and occasionally history, that for most of them were surely a deeply embedded part of their experience. Mary Renault in her novel *The Mask of Apollo* has made us feel that, for the great actor, the mask paradoxically supplied a way of truly entering into the imagined character.[1] The "anti-illusionist" theater of Brecht, the expressionists, and their successors works at its best when illusion, apparently against the odds, takes its old command. What I shall be primarily concerned with here is trying to show how Shakespeare, and other writers of his time, could use the masque as another way of pushing "Let's pretend" to a limit, and even occasionally to a manifestly ironic limit.[2]

We may think first of the structure of the masque as it was performed at the courts of James and Charles: a presenter's speech; the appearance of the masquers; the masquing dance; and the "revels," which was the taking into the masque of persons of opposite sex who had previously been among the audience—or rather the full penetration of the masque into the ambience within which it was performed. This was followed by a going-out, a withdrawal of the masquers from the great hall into which they had come as alleged strangers. The masquers entered, mingled, and withdrew. But not indefinitely. When the "revels" took place, the masquers were manifestly part of the company around them, as Henry VIII was in Shakespeare's play when he danced with Anne Bullen and kissed her. After the masquers had withdrawn, there was always a hope for more reveling either soon or later. The antimasque, which will be important in my argument, was an invention of Jonson in *The Masque of Queens* (1609), though there is a hint of it in *The Masque of Blackness* (1605): it commonly came right at the beginning or after the presenter's speech, although in Shirley's *The Triumph of Peace* (1634) there is a thirteenth antimasque between the masquers' "main dance" and the "revels."

At this point it may be useful to clarify the Jacobean and Caroline uses of the terms "masque" and "entertainment." The masque, despite all the complications that grew upon it in the reigns of the two monarchs, is centered on the great formal dance performed by the disguised masquers and then on the "revels." The entertainment is an amorphous thing, usually employing the song and dance and allegory characteristic of the masque but without the formal line which the masque never totally lost sight of. In other respects, too, the entertainment has its special character. Not tied to the great hall, it may be performed in the tilt-yard or elsewhere in the open air. The entertainments doubtfully attributed to Lyly in the 1590s are among a substantial group clearly written for outdoor performance, and as late as *Arcades* we have another clear example of this: the references to the "smooth enamell'd green" and the "shady roof/ Of branching Elm Star-proof" leave the matter beyond doubt.[3] Indeed the entertainment is to be linked with the pageantry of the streets, as in the London Lord Mayor's Shows and the welcoming pageants for James when he entered London after his journey from Scotland, and in many continental analogues known to us through pictorial representations. The masque was a special development, unique in its alternation of disguise and unmasking, of first separateness from and then mingling with the gathering for which it was presented. It can indeed be seen as an offshoot of the entertainment, intended for special occasions in great halls.

The distinction between the two forms can be illustrated by a brief reference to *Arcades* (1632) and *Comus* (1634). Milton called *Comus* "A Maske," whereas *Arcades* is described as "Part of an entertainment presented to the Countess Dowager of Darby." *Arcades,* with a slight stretching of the term, can be seen as a miniature masque adapted to the resources available on the occasion, lacking both a dance by the members of the Countess's family, who enter at the beginning, and the revels. The "Noble persons" do approach the Countess's "seat of State" and offer their homage to her. But this shadow of a masque is only part of the total entertainment presented, which was doubtless made up of a variety of things. *Comus,* on the other hand, is a highly sophisticated variant of the masque proper. It builds up to the presentation of the three children to their parents; apparently revels were included, for at the end of the presentation we read: *"The dances ended, the Spirit Epiloguizes"* (line 975.s.d.); and there is the antimasque of Comus and his rout, which is closely worked into the total structure. Of course there are things here which give a special character to this masque. The didacticism is more "sage and serious" than is customarily found, although different in tone rather than in kind. Further, there are the tightness of the plot-structure and the use of a prologue and epilogue, a device that links *Comus* with common theater-practice. But even prologue and epilogue are not unprecedented: they appear in Jonson's *Masque of the Gypsies Metamorphosed* (1621). Thus Milton, while being truly adventurous, had in certain respects been anticipated by other masque-writers of the time.

The variations from the regular pattern of the masque that will now be noted are due sometimes to the author, sometimes to the whim of the sovereign, who, by exercising the privileges of his position, could dictate an impromptu change. In Beaumont's *Masque of the Inner Temple and Gray's Inn* (1613), James so much liked one of the antimasques—it was the one largely borrowed for inclusion in *The Two Noble Kinsmen* of the same year—that he asked for it to be repeated when the whole masque was over. He would have done the same with the other antimasque if one of the performers had not already got *"undressed."*[4] Such an "encore" would of course be damaging to the pattern that has here been insisted on as essential to the masque. James did the same thing the following year at the presentation of *The Masque of Flowers,* of uncertain authorship, where he not only asked for the antimasque to be repeated at the end but invited the masquers to the *"banquet"* that was to follow the performance.[5] As for variations provided by the author, we have already noted Shirley's use of what we can call "an interrupting antimasque" in *The Triumph of Peace*; and in Jonson's *The Gypsies Metamorphosed* the antimasquers, having *"chang'd,"* become the masquers proper.

When we turn to masques incorporated in plays, we should expect to find greater variation. A masque at, for example, the Blackfriars theater could give an idea of what happened at Whitehall or in other banqueting places, but it could not reproduce as a whole what some of the actors and spectators had seen in a masque proper. For one thing, there was not enough time. A major part of an evening was given over to a masque at court, and in Shirley's *The Triumph of Peace* we are told to imagine, as the masque ends, that the first hint of morning is in the sky. Since the performances were given in February, this was surely dependent on imagination, but they must have gone on long enough to make the assembly highly conscious of a long passage of time. Secondly, it was difficult to give on either a public or a private stage a proper suggestion of the revels, or of the paying of a formal tribute to a sovereign or other great personage. Shakespeare does use the revels in *Henry VIII* (1613), as he had done in *Romeo and Juliet* (ca. 1595), but this seems rare. Moreover, the great personages in whose honor the masques-within-plays were performed were, after all, only players. What we shall be looking at now are thus truncated masques. Moreover, they are commonly given an ironic twist peculiarly their own. Only a few examples can here be noted.[6] I shall use a rough chronological order, occasionally departing from it to bring together some similar variations.

Jonson's *Cynthia's Revels* (1600 or 1601), written before he became a masque-writer, uses the masque for satiric purposes. The various follies represented in Cynthia's court are the masquers who come in their disguises to do homage to her. At the end she commands their unmasking, and then delivers her stern judgment on them. Manifestly there could be no revels here. Instead of the oneness between masque and the person honored (however great their difference in "degree") and instead of the close mingling which the revels give, we have here rebuke and a temporary banishment. Jonson was to find his ambience as a masque-writer mainly at Whitehall, and one may wonder if, in his tributes to James there, he ever thought back to the satiric presentation of the masquers in *Cynthia's Revels*. After all, the Whitehall masquers cannot all have been paragons.

Something similar is to be found in Middleton's *Your Five Gallants* (ca. 1605). Katherine is expected to choose a husband from the gallants who come as masquers. But they are made to reveal their true characters, and the Latin mottoes they carry, which they do not understand, manifest them as they are. Even the gift they bring to Katherine is shown to be stolen from Katherine herself.

It is a different thing when the masquers take a major initiative, killing the sovereign instead of paying homage. Examples are of course to be found in Marston's *Antonio's Revenge* (ca. 1600) and in *The Revenger's Tragedy* (ca. 1606). The author of the latter play, always willfully and often splendidly overdoing things, has two sets of masquers with the same murderous purpose: the second set find Lussurioso already dead and are reduced to using their swords on each other; regrettably, there has to be one survivor, but he is an obscure and anonymous person. We can perhaps deduce a tiredness with the formal compliment that the masque proper presented.

In Marston's *The Malcontent* (ca. 1603) we have again something different, although the notion of masquers as assassins is still present. The entry of the masquers is given thus:

> *Cornets: the song to the cornets, which playing, the mask enters:*
> MALEVOLE, PIETRO, FERNEZE, *and* CELSO, *in white robes, with dukes' crowns upon laurel wreaths; pistolets and short swords under their robes.*
>
> (V.vi.68.s.d.)[7]

Astonishingly, the revels follow immediately, as the masquers take out their appropriate ladies. As they dance, two of Malevole's assistants use the occasion to further their suits, which are not intended towards matrimony. This undercuts the "happy ending" of the play: the court is still the loose and corrupt court that had banished Malevole. Then the masquers are seen *"bending their pistols"* on Mendoza, the temporary duke (V.vi.113.s.d.). He is not killed, but merely ejected from court. So the affair ends in comedy, but Malevole's words—

> O, I have seen strange accidents of state:
> The flatterer, like the ivy, clip the oak,
> And waste it to the heart; lust so confirmed,
> That the black act of sin itself not shamed
> To be termed courtship.

> (V.vi.137-41)

—may remind us of the Duke's speech near the end of *Measure for Measure* (the plays may have been written in the same year,[8] and both Malevole and Vincentio were disguisers on the grand scale), but we are even more directly reminded that what Malevole says here has, without his knowing it, close reference to the goings-on in the preceding revels. Marston's reversal of the normal order brings out the irony more strongly.

A comparable variation on the accepted ordering of things is the masque in Dekker's (and perhaps Marston's) *Satiromastix.* This was acted about 1601, so perhaps belongs to the same year as *Cynthia's Revels,* to which it has some resemblance. It is remarkable that, before the flowering of the masque at James's court, there should be such manifest undercutting of the form in the theaters. The king in *Satiromastix* is presented, not with a tribute, but with the appearance of Caelestine, whom he lusts after and whom, on the unmasking of her, he finds to be apparently dead. Her subsequent resurrection brings things into harmony. Inga-Stina Ewbank has suggested that the "untrussing" of Horace just afterwards is "a kind of antimasque."[9] Although this description may be a little forced, it is true that solemnity is here followed by an exhibition of the comic. There is a pulling down instead of a building up, which James himself showed a liking for when he required a repetition of an antimasque after the whole show was technically over. But that was several years later: again we find that the theater anticipated what happened at Whitehall.

One of the most daring variations occurs in Webster's *The Duchess of Malfi* (1613-14), Shakespeare's *The Two Noble Kinsmen*

(1613), and Ford's *The Lover's Melancholy* (1628) and *Perkin
Warbeck* (ca. 1629-34). Here the antimasque substitutes for the
masque. In this, as in many things, *The Duchess of Malfi* is savage:
in Act IV a servant enters to tell the Duchess that Ferdinand
"hath intended you some sport" and that the Pope, when "sick
of a deep melancholy," was cured by being shown "several sorts
of madmen." The masque is indeed turned on its head: the presenter, a servant, does not ask permission for the masquers to
enter; he merely says: "the self-same cure/ The Duke intends on
you" (IV.ii.38-44).[10] The Duchess responds: "I am chain'd to
endure all your tyranny." The sovereign is chained to her chair;
not for her the power to vary the pattern in James's way. The
presentation that follows is clearly an antimasque, beginning with
song, turning to dialogue in which the madmen exhibit their
special kinds of derangement, and ending with a dance. There
are no revels and no tribute. The next entry is Bosola's in his
old man's disguise, preparing the Duchess for death.

In *The Two Noble Kinsmen,* on the other hand, the effect
would be wholly comic were it not for the presence of the jailer's
daughter among the antimasquers. We have seen a good deal of
her before; we know of her love for Palamon and his lack of
interest in her. The country people, led by their Schoolmaster,
see that she is mad and feel sure therefore that she will prove a
strong addition to their team. But she is presented very differently from the antimasquers in *The Duchess of Malfi.* Our sympathies
are strongly with her, as they hardly are with the simple people
of the country. It may be better, though less pleasant, to be mad
with her than to be wise with the Schoolmaster. Yet in the dance
that follows, the printed text makes no mention of her as an
individual, nor does she receive any mention from Theseus, the
most courteous of sovereigns both here and in Chaucer, however
glib his words and actions can sometimes seem. This section of the
play is among those commonly attributed to Fletcher, and, with
what I have called elsewhere his "sceptical shrug,"[11] he may have
been characteristically content to let the girl merely pass by.
Shakespeare would probably have lingered for a moment on the
personal situation.

John Russell Brown in his Revels edition of *The Duchess of
Malfi* thinks the most likely date for that play is the spring or
autumn of 1614, or perhaps the winter of 1613-14.[12] If he is

right, *The Duchess* followed quite soon after *The Two Noble Kinsmen,* and we may guess that the use of an antimasque by itself indicates an indebtedness. Nevertheless, the differences are fairly extreme. The self-subsisting antimasque of *The Two Noble Kinsmen* takes place in the open air, as do the entertainments presented to a sovereign or other great person mentioned above. The grim but equally self-subsisting antimasque in Webster's play is thrust upon his great lady in her own palace.[13] And the atmosphere is indeed claustrophobic. Of course, in a sense the atmosphere at Whitehall was claustrophobic too. The banqueting hall was not large, nor was the great hall of Ludlow Castle where *Comus* was first performed. But at Whitehall the sovereign was present, and England, Scotland, Ireland, Virginia (and nominally France) were his possessions. When the masques involved the idea of civic harmony, it was thus a wide-ranging one, and in imagination the walls expanded. For the Duchess the walls close in.

The plays by Ford, *The Lover's Melancholy* and *Perkin Warbeck,* present the antimasquers as masquers in a different way. In the earlier of the two, the physician Corax stages an antimasque of madmen (Ford knew his Webster), quite genuinely believing that it could cure the mental sickness of Prince Palador.[14] Again, this is an antimasque by itself. So too in *Perkin Warbeck* the marriage of Perkin to Lady Catherine is saluted by a masque introduced thus:

> *Enter at one door four* Scotch Antics, *accordingly habited; enter at another four wild* Irish *in trowses, long-haired, and accordingly habited. Music. The Masquers dance.*
>
> (III.ii.111.s.d.)[15]

But there is no hint of a masque proper; the antimasque in this variation is neither threatening, as in *The Duchess of Malfi,* nor comic with a tinge of sadness, as in *The Two Noble Kinsmen.* Rather, it is given as an exhibition of the national differences between the Scottish and the Irish. It has a point in the story in indicating that Perkin now has Scottish as well as Irish supporters (with perhaps a hint that neither group is much to be relied upon). The antimasque is otherwise without dramatic impact.

William Blissett has suggested that *Bartholomew Fair* is itself a grand antimasque and that its accompanying masque is the court at which it was presented. He draws attention to the Prologue and

Epilogue addressed to James and to the fact that the play was performed at court immediately after its first showing at the Hope. "Here," it is implied, "are the masquers (not disguised on this occasion, except in so far as we are all disguised all the time), with their sovereign among them; now we shall present an anti-masque displaying the fooleries of the puritans and other subjects of the king."[16] Perhaps Blissett is correct, for James was ready enough to believe that he and his court were near to the ideal which the masquers always presented. But could the audience at the Hope have a glimpse of this? Admittedly, the Prologue and Epilogue were designed for the court, so Jonson may have had in mind the masque-antimasque relation that Blissett envisages. A good point is made in drawing attention to something that it is not possible to find a precedent for—that the court performance may have been planned along with the performance at the Hope. This suggests that in writing *Bartholomew Fair* Jonson had in mind not merely two performances but in effect two differently oriented plays. One of them, if we accept the case cogently argued by Blissett, was dependent on yet another variation in the use of the antimasque, and a further way of taking up the masque in a new fashion.

But perhaps we should not leave *Bartholomew Fair* at that point, if the performance at court suggests that the courtiers should be seen as masquers, with the king as in a masque accepting the tribute of their presence, and if we assume that the grotesque opposite is given by the people of the fair and their visitors (aiming, as the antimasque always did, at the king's "true delight"), we must remember too the puppet show of Lantern Leatherhead and John Littlewit. This is a play-within-a-play, made ridiculous through its use of puppets, but leading to the chastening of Zeal-of-the-Land Busy. When Overdo invites everyone home to supper, Bartholomew Cokes (who insists that the Fair is *his* fair, bearing his name) demands that the puppets shall go along and entertain them all. The fool's play, the Fair, survives. The puppet play can be seen as a variation on the antimasque, oddly placed near the end of the play proper, and, we are promised, continuing thereafter. We have seen that the antimasque could triumph at court, with the king demanding an encore. Here there is a special triumph, for Jonson's antimasque within an antimasque will not be parted with at all. And the puppet master has been seen as a caricature of Inigo Jones, the great designer of masques and plays at court. This antimasque, twice removed from the masque proper (the king seated in state, with his court around him), is thus presented as the work of the man who, along with Jonson, gave to the Jacobean masque its highest authority.[17] But if Leatherhead's antimasque triumphs, are we not to infer that the grand anti-masque which is the play as a whole triumphs over the alleged masque of the king and court? This irony is developed so discreetly that neither the Master of the Revels nor James would have seen the point. Jonson had been in trouble enough before.

When we turn to Shakespeare we perhaps rightly begin with *Timon of Athens*. The date is uncertain. A quarter of a century ago I argued that it was not to be seen as close to *Lear* but rather as immediately preceding *Pericles*. There I was at one with E. K. Chambers.[18] The play seems to mark the end of Shakespeare's tragic writing and, because it reached an impasse, to lead into his new development in the last plays. And, as we generally find in what follows, it includes a masque. In Act I Timon is exhibiting his generosity at a banquet. A servant enters to say there are "certain ladies most desirous of admittance" (I.ii.116). Then Cupid, the presenter proper, follows with these words:

> Hail to thee, worthy Timon, and to all
> That of his bounties taste! The five best senses
> Acknowledge thee their patron, and come freely
> To gratulate thy plenteous bosom. There,
> Taste, touch, all, pleas'd from thy table rise;
> They only now come but to feast thine eyes.
> (I.ii.122-27)

The syntax is indeed odd, though it could be clarified on the stage. If the Folio reading "There" is correct, it would be accompanied by a gesture at the dinner table and its guests, "They" by a gesture towards the entrance from which the ladies are coming. There is an irony here, for the "ladies," habited as Amazons, are clearly enough whores. Apemantus in an aside calls them "madwomen" (line 133), "a sweep of vanity" (line 132), and sees their madness as the true nature of "the glory of this life" (line 134). By "sweep" he is not referring primarily to the sweeping movements of the dance, as the New Arden editor suggests,[19] but to what will be swept up when a metaphorical spring-cleaning has been done.

After the ladies have danced, we have this stage-direction, which, in view of the general state of the text, we can take to be Shakespeare's:

> *The Lords rise from table, with much adoring of Timon, and to show their loves, each single out an Amazon, and all dance, men with women, a lofty strain or two to the hoboys, and cease.*

(I.ii.145.s.d.)

In view of Apemantus's words, we are surely bound to take these revels as at least as titillating as those that we have noticed in *The Malcontent.* Yet Timon, still playing the kind host, says that the ladies have added "worth" and "lustre" to his party (line 149), and invites them to an "idle banquet" offstage (line 155). It may be stretching things too far to see him as the homosexual always polite to women, but they are not invited to the men's dinner table. Yet if here in his prosperity he is politely remote from women, he later turns brutally on Phrynia and Ximandra, the camp-followers of Alcibiades, using to them the insulting word "beagles."[20] Now he sees women as the enemy of man, bringing venereal disease in her crotch. Later, in *The Winter's Tale,* Shakespeare was astonishingly to show Leontes and Polixenes as thinking of marriage as what brought them out of a virginal innocence.[21] There is a further touch of acid in that the women who grace Timon's banquet are presented as Amazons, one-breasted women who fight against men. Running through the last plays there is a thread suggestive of hostility to women, complicated by a stress on a father-daughter relationship in which the father clings to his authority. The hostility is brutally presented in *Timon,* and in a more complex way in *Lear.* There is of course a variation in *Coriolanus,* where the mother-son relationship is overtly disturbing.

Inga-Stina Ewbank has properly reminded us of the contrast between Timon's two feasts: in the first there is lavish hospitality, with a sensual masque included; in the second Timon throws water on his guests.[22] His own drink from now on will be Nature's water. Ewbank does not talk here of an antimasque. The function of the antimasque, at least at court, was to give a *point d'appui* from which the main masque was to develop. The second feast here is no simple reversal of the first, being too far away to be more than an ironic contrast. Moreover, there is simply one man acting on the men whom he is now rejecting: he is taking on something of James's role as manipulator. We may hazard a final conjecture: perhaps the guests at the second feast become antimasquers in a way when they go out hurriedly, their dignity shredded.

And now to the last plays proper. Throughout his career Shakespeare had used disguise and undisguising, from *The Two Gentlemen of Verona* (ca. 1594) onwards. Boy-player wearing a girl's costume, then disguised as a boy, then undisguised as a girl (but actually a boy)—this goes back to Lyly and before him. Shakespeare's enemy Robert Greene used it in *James IV*. We pretend and then give up pretense, though all the time remaining what we are. The boy-girl-boy-girl-(boy) pattern in several of Shakespeare's early plays and the interestingly unknowing assumption of another man's being in *The Comedy of Errors* (ca. 1592) indicate a readiness to see that pretense, conscious or unconscious, is part of the way we live. At the end of such plays pretense is apparently given up, and we are invited to accept a happy ending. But a doubt remains. Is pretense so easily to be abandoned? If it is a condition we necessarily live with, we can hardly say Yes. *Twelfth Night* shows us Orsino wanting to see Viola in woman's dress before he can accept her as his "fancy's queen," for he can hardly be persuaded by what he is told. His eyes, and doubtless his other organs of sense, must be satisfied.

In an article I wrote some years ago, I suggested that the last plays, in contrast to the tragedies, presented a drama of "cycle" rather than "crisis."[23] The endings of the last plays seem to leave the issue open, while the tragedies truly end. We do not much care what happens to the Britain of *King Lear* (which is why the occasional debating about who was to be king after Lear appears nugatory), or to the Cyprus of *Othello,* or even to the Scotland of *Macbeth* and the Denmark of *Hamlet.* I have been told that we should see these things in relation to our own time. But for us, as for the people in the plays, there is no going back to the condition we once knew: the same mistakes lie in wait. Yet in both tragedies and "romances" there is a future, which may not be totally cyclic. Our own experience tells us that we do make improvements in the smaller things. Shakespeare in his tragedies did not offer such consolations: he was not primarily concerned with politics in those plays, but only with the dreadful endings of the people he valued most. Like many of us today, he was anguished about men and women, not about the state, which was near his heart (though with reservations) in his early and middle histories. Nor did he in his last plays give a firm promise of regeneration. He may well have had his doubts about the notion of communal harmony that the masques at court generally insisted on.

But he also knew that pretense and disguise and undisguising were part of life, and these things dominate the last plays, replacing the sharp facing of indomitable evil that was his concern in the tragedies. Pericles does not recognize Marina when she first appears before him on his ship. How could he, for he had seen her only as a newborn baby? But the revelation occurs in due time. T. S. Eliot in "Marina," his poem derived from the play, may appear to end on a note of hope, but Pericles says:

> What seas what shores what granite islands towards my timbers
> And woodthrush calling through the fog
> My daughter.[24]

There are threats here in "granite" and "fog," for which the call of the woodthrush and the barely recognized daughter do not quite atone. More explicit is the full recognition in Shakespeare: Marina becomes a masque figure doing homage to the Prince her father. And afterwards in his dream Diana appears to Pericles. She is disguised in being a dream figure, but as a goddess can give commands. All ends in reunion—and retribution. We may indeed remain unsatisfied with the punishment of the wicked Antiochus and his daughter, the malignant wife of the Governor of Tarsus, and even the comparatively innocent Governor. Is it possible to make so simple a distinction between good and evil characters? Within the framework of this play we can, for Pericles and Thaisa and Marina are almost inhumanly free from guilt. Lysimachus, Governor of Mytilene, is a more dubious case, but we can allow for his reformation. Even so, dare this satisfy us that the world has been put right? Ultimately, the quasi-masque-figure Diana seems to be nibbling at the edges of things, as we all do. As a goddess, she might perhaps do a bit better. But that was not Shakespeare's affair here.

Her appearance to Pericles is similar to Jupiter's to Posthumus in the next play, *Cymbeline* (ca. 1609). Jupiter is accompanied by the ancestors of Posthumus, but the group can be seen only as masquers in reverse, perhaps like the court in William Blissett's interpretation of *Bartholomew Fair*. But if the masque is not here, revelation is. Iachimo is made to recognize his guilt, Posthumus his wife's fidelity and his own unworthiness; the wickedness of Cymbeline's queen and her son Cloten are made manifest. How seriously are we to take it all? "Who is't can read a woman?" is the grotesque epitaph that Cymbeline bestows on his wife (V.v.48). The disguised people are brought into the light. It is true that the last plays suggest a future in a way that the tragedies do not. But it is the future that the masque presents too: a banquet, and then a morning with a headache and a dry tongue.

Shakespeare had the masque very much in mind when he wrote *The Winter's Tale* (ca. 1610). The supreme masque is one that happens off-stage and is fully described by Cleomenes and Dion when they enter at the beginning of Act III and indicate how impressed they have been by their visit to Apollo's oracle. They are strangers who come to the oracle's shrine, but they are not disguised while the god himself is. The masque is not only invisible to the theater audience but again inverted. This scene is commonly omitted in performance, but is needed for a full recognition of Apollo's power, the power that was to kill Mamillius and that gave to Leontes a riddling message about his future, similar to the one Jupiter gave to Posthumus. But we have a new departure in the "invisible masque," all the more impressive through being invisible, just as later Apollo's power is made transcendent through his continuing invisibility. Diana in *Pericles* and Jupiter in *Cymbeline* are of small account compared with Apollo in *The Winter's Tale*; and perhaps the most splendid of masques is always one that we see only in our mind's eye.

In *The Winter's Tale* we also have the coming to life of the apparent statue of Hermione, and her descending to pay homage to her lord Leontes. Again there is a reversal, for the sovereign is the one who comes with his court, the disguised figure the one who accepts (and reciprocates) his devotion. Incidentally, Paulina is clearly the "presenter" in this echo of the masque.

In *The Tempest* (ca. 1611) there is only one god, Prospero, and he is simultaneously an imperfect human being. He takes delight in getting all his enemies within his power. He uses magic (a dubious matter even when "white") to reduce them to numbness, and he is the maker of a masque. His irascibility may owe something to Jonson's; that would be a joke which Shakespeare, though hardly Jonson, would have enjoyed. But of course there is more to Prospero than this; in another aspect he can legitimately be seen as Shakespeare, writing his last independent play. The goddesses in his presentation—Iris, Juno, Ceres—are not goddesses at all, but, as he frankly tells us, are spirits at his beck and call. We have always known that disguised masquers, whether at court or in plays, are merely players, or courtiers and known as such. But here the situation is made overt; Ariel admits to having presented Ceres, which is a sophisticated underlining of the theater's pretense. The "spirits" belong to a different world from that of Prospero and Miranda and Ferdinand. Clearly such spirits could not take part in a revels with the boy and girl whose betrothal was being celebrated. It was forced upon Shakespeare that this masque must be interrupted. The excuse is that Prospero suddenly remembers that Caliban and his confederates have a plot against him, which he must deal with. This excuse is implausible, for with his power how could he forget and why should he be worried?

We may also notice that the dance of *"certain Reapers"* follows the appearance of "certain Nymphs" whom Iris has summoned. This antimasque, following the abortive introduction of a masque proper, is strongly reminiscent of the ending of an antimasque at court: *"to a strange, hollow, and confused noise, they heavily vanish"* (IV.i.138.s.d.). It is right, in a profound sense, that Prospero should put an end to the antic affair and should proceed to his famous speech on the mutability of all things. This speech puts all masques, all human ambition and pretense, into a small place within the frame of the All, even if that All is only sleep. We dream our special masques, as Cleomenes and Dion made us dream in *The Winter's Tale.* And yet a new and more vicious antimasque follows, for as long as we live we relapse. Caliban and his new masters, whom he now despises, enter *"all wet,"* and it is evident that Caliban is the only man of sense among them. The spirits are no longer goddesses but dogs:

A noise of hunters heard. Enter divers SPIRITS *in shape of dogs and hounds, hunting them about; Prospero and Ariel setting them on.*
                                          (IV.i.254.s.d.)

We may remember that in Shakespeare's time the atheistically inclined sometimes reversed the spelling of "god." In any event, the sovereign of the island slips a little when he acts as presenter of this antimasque. If, as cautiously suggested above, Prospero was meant to remind us of Jonson, there is an element of fun in the interruption of the masque and in the ferocity of this antimasque.

The two remaining plays have both been referred to already. In one of them, probably in both, Shakespeare worked with John Fletcher, who was to be his successor as leading dramatist for the King's Men. Nevertheless, Shakespeare's impress is in some measure upon them. He looks back to his own early plays and early days, as he had already done in *Pericles* and *The Winter's Tale.* In his choosing of Ephesus as a final locality, *The Comedy of Errors* cannot have been far from his mind. In his adapting of Greene's *Pandosto,* the memory of his old enemy's attack must have occasioned a wry and perhaps quite amused smile. There is, however, a contrast between *Henry VIII* and *The Two Noble Kinsmen.* The history aims at a fairly faithful representation of events that may have occurred in the lifetime of some of the spectators' grandparents. The names of many of the characters, and of other people who are merely mentioned (most notably More), must have been household words in the spectators' own time. It is, in fact, a reconstruction of a past still living in its immediate effects upon the present of 1613. This makes it different from the histories of the 1590s, even though the Wars of the Roses could not be forgotten by the people who lived under the *soi-disant* heirs of York and Lancaster. Appropriately *Henry VIII* includes a careful reconstruction of the typical Tudor masque, with a presenter's speech, a main masquing dance, and a revels. Shakespeare makes full dramatic use of this, making English history take a leap into the dark when Anne Bullen is chosen as Henry's partner in the revels and he kisses her. Only in *Romeo and Juliet* did Shakespeare make his masque so functional in the plot and so accurate a reproduction of what went on in high places.

In *The Two Noble Kinsmen* we have seen an example of the antimasque as masque, as in plays by other dramatists that followed. This play also has its theophanies, where the gods remain invisible, as in *The Winter's Tale,* and act in the riddling way of Jupiter and Apollo. The writing here is surely Shakespearean, and deeply ironic. The human beings who offer homage are all left

puzzled: the gods seem to have come together in a grand deception.

We have no evidence whether or not there was an approach
to the masque in *Cardenio* (ca. 1612), for by the time Theobald's
version appeared, the masque was ancient history and no longer
to be understood. The nearest that the eighteenth century got to
the masque was the singing of "God Save the King" at Drury Lane
in 1745; its nearest approach to the antimasque was the harle-
quinade, which in later years of pantomime was to follow the
fairy tale.

We have already noticed that, without the formal use of a
masque, the endings of *Pericles* and *Cymbeline* and *The Winter's
Tale* present an unmasking. So in *The Tempest* does the emergence
of Miranda and Ferdinand when they leave their game of chess
(itself a nice comment on a marital relationship, particularly in
Miranda's accusation of cheating) and do homage to Prospero
and Alonso. There is a sense of shock here, for Prospero had implied to Alonso that both boy and girl were dead. There was an
effective performance of *Pericles* at Stratford, Ontario, where
one saw the look of incredulity on Thaisa's face as Pericles approached Diana's temple. A similar astonishment comes upon
Leontes when he sees the apparent statue of Hermione move, and
feels her warm to his touch. These moments have of course their
connection with the unmasking of masquers, but with an important difference. In the masque proper the social gathering knew
that the masquers were from among themselves, England's privileged class, but in *Pericles* and *The Winter's Tale* the husband or
wife could not anticipate the meeting. The players here are much
more "real" than the court-masquers could ever be, for a priestess
of Diana and a statue become living women, loved despite the
passing of the years. The love is stronger than that almost anyone
felt for James. And yet they are all players, all pretenders.

So in the end the masque was not good enough, though Shakespeare humanized it in these last plays. His use of it provided, as
we have seen, a reminder of the court masque, brought the stately
frolics of Whitehall to the Blackfriars and the Globe, and supremely recalled to us that all theater is pretense, that disguises belong
to our lives too. Even so, the masque's contrivance is not a close
analogue to the shock of recognition that we all are aware of,
when suddenly the scales flake off, as when we know, for good

or ill, our own particular Iachimo or Hermione for what he or she is.

There were other ways in which Shakespeare's audience could be reminded of the theater's essence—the play-within-the-play and the dumb show. Shakespeare used both of these freely: the dumb show as late as *Pericles* as well as, mischievously, in *Hamlet*; the play-within-the-play from his near-beginning, in *The Taming of the Shrew*, and again in *Hamlet*. Neither of these devices was forgotten by his successors. But around 1610, when the King's Men were established in the Blackfriars, the masque was inevitably prominent in his mind. Although we do not know him as a masque-writer at court, he had at least a friendly relation with Jonson, who brought the masque to fruition. As a member of the company that enjoyed James's patronage, he must have been frequently at Whitehall. And although his attitude to the masque seems at times to be as ironic as that of any of his contemporaries, he saw in the masque's pretense a quasi-ultimate expression of what the theater was doing. "Let them come in," says the chief person of the house, for strange guests must be made welcome even in our days. Of course, James knew that they were not really strange, merely his courtiers, or friends, as today the neighbors' children appear on Halloween. Similarly, at court and at the theater Burbage and his company became the friends of their audience, who saw them so often at the Globe and Blackfriars.

This is something more subtle than anything Shakespeare gave us in his early histories. The early battles are a form of dumb show, although the satiric indications of battle in *2 Henry IV* and *Henry V* made the idea of battle horrible despite the absurdity of the mimetic act. *Henry VIII* is a history without a battle. Instead, we have an ironic account of the Field of the Cloth of Gold, like the invisible masque in *The Winter's Tale*, though there the irony is muted. Here we see two sovereigns, each dragging homage out of the other, each being "all dressed up" to impress. "Dressed to kill," in fact. Meanwhile at home an execution could take place, a queen could be repudiated, and a major change in affairs of state could result from the sovereign's kissing a woman he had not seen before. Not that there is anything very wrong about that, but it is better to leave it till the second meeting.

So the masque remained absurd but fascinating, and Shakespeare, while making full use of it in his last plays, gave it an

appropriate undercutting as Jonson did in *Cynthia's Revels,*
with many of their contemporaries and successors following the
example. We may wonder what Shakespeare would have thought
of Shirley's *The Triumph of Peace.* That masque is commonly
contemned as a mere atonement to Charles for the wayward behavior of Prynne. But this view does, I think, an injustice. We
have already noticed the passing of the night which is brought
home to us in the stage-direction that follows the revels:

> *The Revels being past, the Scene is changed into a plain champaign*
> *country which terminates with the horizon, and above a darkish sky,*
> *with dusky clouds, through which appeared the new moon, but with a*
> *faint light by the approach of the morning; from the farthest part of*
> *this ground, arose by little and little a great vapour, which being come*
> *about the middle of the Scene, it slackens its motion, and begins to*
> *fall downward to the earth from whence it came; and out of this rose*
> *another Cloud of a strange shape and colour, on which sat a Young*
> *Maid, with a dim torch in her hand. Her face was an olive-colour, so*
> *was her arms and breast, on her head a curious dressing, and about her*
> *neck a string of great pearl. Her garment was transparent, the ground*
> *dark blue, and sprinkled with silver spangles, her buskins white,*
> *trimmed with gold. By these marks she was known to be the fore-*
> *runner of the morning, called by the ancients Amphiluche, and is that*
> *glimpse of light which is seen when the night is past, and the day not*
> *yet appearing.*
>
> (Lines 731-45)[25]

Amphiluche, after a song from her, ascends to her place above
and the masquers *"are called from their Revels by other voices."*
The masque ends with *"Amphiluche hidden in the heavens, and*
the Masquers retired." Dawn is felt to be imminent, the assembly
is tired, day awaits. But we also remember that we are in the year
1633, a mere nine years from the beginning of the Civil War, and
several years after Charles had first faced a hostile Parliament. An
unpleasant dawn was on its way, and is not this what we feel at
the end of every masque, though never so manifestly as here?[26]
The revels are indeed ended. It is not surprising that in the theaters
Shakespeare and his contemporaries played tricks with the
masque, sometimes feeling more at home with the antimasque,
sometimes presenting a masque proper, as in *Timon* and as far
back as *Cynthia's Revels,* in a way that makes us feel the irony of
it all.

There was perhaps another reason why the antimasque was so frequently used in plays while the masque proper was commonly neglected or transformed. Although the antimasquers at court were probably in most cases professional players, Stephen Orgel in his editions of *Ben Jonson: The Complete Masques* and *Ben Jonson: Selected Masques* imagines that the King's Men could themselves be masquers.[27] Surely this goes against all we know of the situation at Whitehall. The antimasque, we can assume, was the professional player's "thing." Therefore, when it came to a serious revelation of identities, it was good to avoid the pure masque-structure, while bearing it still in mind, and to present Pericles and Thaisa, Imogen, Hermione, and Prospero (a kind of presenter to the carefully delayed revelation of Ferdinand and Miranda at chess) as what we can take for the moment as "real" people—husbands and wives—reunited after a long interval, a betrayed woman ready to forgive, and young lovers lovingly quarreling over a game. The masque itself was a game, but a game that bites into us. It gives an image of what revelation is, something far more disturbing than the unmasking of masquers.

Charles Maturin, in his curious novel *Melmoth the Wanderer* (1820), has this to say:

> Where art assumes the omnipotence of reality, where we feel we suffer as much from illusion as from truth, our sufferings lose all dignity and all consolation.[28]

Of course he is wrong. Painting and sculpture and music and nondramatic poetry, when they affect us as powerfully as anything in our experience, do not take away from our dignity or our consolation. At their best they remain firm through the centuries and command our homage always. But perhaps the greater part of dramatic writing, and the masque above all, do take something away. Here we are being put upon. Nevertheless, the irony, sometimes explicit, sometimes delicately implicit, makes us laugh at ourselves in for a moment taking them with full seriousness. And surely the masque-writer and the dramatist often laugh too. As, when we remember them, and guess at their meaning, we commonly laugh at our dreams.

4

Romance and Romanticism: Some Reflections on The Tempest *and* Heart of Darkness, *Or When Is Romance No Longer Romance?*

Howard Felperin

> Da suche und finde ich das Romantische, bei den ältern Modernen, bei Shakespeare, Cervantes, in der italienischen Poesie, in jenem Zeitalter der Ritter, der Liebe und der Märchen, aus welchem die Sache und das Wort selbst herstammt.
>
> [I seek and find the Romantic in the older moderns, in Shakespeare, in Cervantes, in Italian poetry, and in that age of knights, love, and folktales from which Romanticism and the term itself originate.]
> —Friedrich Schlegel, "Brief über den Roman"
> ["Letter on the Novel"]

The recent quickening of interest in Shakespearean, Spenserian, and medieval romance may be seen as part of a broader movement within criticism at large, an attempt to rediscover the roots of our modern literary consciousness in the romance forms of fantasy, play, and dreaming that we are all, so to speak, born into. While this recovery of older romance traditions proceeds in a serene and scholarly fashion, a more speculative and polemical side of the same critical project is emerging in the field of Romanticism, conceived no longer as an isolated period or movement within literary history but as a continuing artistic crisis. Despite the contrasting moods of recent criticism in romance and in Romanticism, the one calm and objective and the other worried and introspective, their concerns are as intimately related as their common etymology suggests. For it is precisely the apparently untroubled sublimity of the native tradition of high romance embodied in the work of Shakespeare, Spenser, and Milton—a gorgeous and spontaneous abundance as of nature itself—that conditions a crisis of anxiety for the post-Renaissance poets who endeavor to resume that tradition and bring forth their own second nature. Or so several recent theorists of Romanticism would have us believe.[1]

That is of course a simplification of the relation between the older literary mode of romance and the modern literary movement of Romanticism. But there is a sense in which each field of study reinforces the prevailing conceptions and misconceptions of the other, and it has to do with certain shared assumptions governing the way we conceive literary history. Students of Romanticism tend to regard the romance literature of the Middle Ages and Renaissance as a well-traveled world, with large historical and structural contours that are by now familiar and safe. They imply that our maps of those earlier literary periods, somewhat like actual Renaissance maps of the known world, are in more or less reliable agreement, while the adventure of charting dark regions is in the area of Romantic and post-Romantic studies, where every man is his own mapmaker and no two maps conform. At the same time, scholars of that older romance literature implicitly accept and reinforce the terms of this myth of Romantic modernism. We largely ignore all that is dark and unsettling in our subject as if it properly belonged to a later age, and we retreat into a nostalgic humanism with its bland and idealized orthodoxies of "the great chain of being" and "the Elizabethan world-picture." In so doing, we complacently avoid the unsettling modernity that characterizes all great works, however culturally exotic or temporally remote. For this myth of modernism and the pastoralization of the past that goes with it are themselves Romantic constructs, under which we all more or less unwittingly labor. And not until we attempt to work ourselves out from under them can we hope to understand either romance or Romanticism more fully, no more than a man can understand his own society without somehow leaving it.

The work of Northrop Frye, evenly divided as it is between those earlier and later literatures and equally influential in both fields, will serve to illustrate the literary-historical myth I have begun to describe. "Romanticism," he writes, "is a 'sentimental' form of romance, and the fairy tale, for the most part, a 'sentimental' form of folktale."[2] Frye's terms are directly adopted from Schiller's famous essay, "Über naive und sentimentalische Dichtung," though "naive" here means simply "primitive" or "popular" and is not historically identified, as it is in Schiller, with "classical," while "sentimental," as in Schiller, means "later" or "sophisticated." In adopting Schiller's terms, however, Frye has also adopted, though less obviously, Schiller's historical scheme. In the theory of modes that opens *Anatomy of Criticism,* Frye divides western literature into a scale descending from "myth" through "romance," "high mimetic," and "low mimetic" to "irony," a scale which is correlated to the historical periods in which each mode successively dominates: classical, medieval, Renaissance, eighteenth century, nineteenth century, and modern. Like Schiller's starker contrast of the "naive" or classical poet in touch with the natural world and the "sentimental" or Romantic poet alienated from it by modern civilization, Frye's logical and chronological scheme conceives literary history as a process of disintegration or displacement away from the natural integrity and univocality of myth and toward the self-conscious distancing and discontinuities of irony. This history of literature moves, following hard upon an enlightenment conception of cultural history that derives as much from Rousseau as from Schiller and Friedrich Schlegel, from the anonymous universality of myth to the individuality or eccentricity of modern fiction. Frye systematically avoids valorizing this "progress of poetry" in any of the ways it has been successively valorized by various schools of ancients and moderns, classics and romantics, over the past three centuries. Yet he nonetheless repeats the historical scheme that underlies and generates these schools and their quarrels in the first place. It may turn out that the weakness of Frye's rehabilitation of romance is not his avoidance of history, as is commonly charged, but his inability to do without a version of it.

Romance for Frye is thus a "displacement" in a human and secular direction, and Romanticism a further displacement, from the original unity of a putative mythic source. "The redemption myth in the older [Christian] mythology," he writes, "emphasized the free act of God in offering man grace, grace being thought of as essentially the transformation of the human moral will. Such grace proceeded from a divine love or *agape.* Romantic redemption myths . . . throw the emphasis on an *eros,* or love rooted in the human sexual instinct. Such an *eros* develops a distinctively human idealism, and for such idealism, the redeeming agent is also human-centered."[3] The characteristic self-consciousness of modern, i.e., Romantic, art, which Friedrich Schlegel pointed out at the beginning of the nineteenth century, is for Frye, as for Schiller and Schlegel before him, the measure of its historical and cultural distance from a naive mythic source, though that source is no longer seen as the mythology of classical antiquity but rather the Judeo-Christian Scriptures. Since Scriptural Christianity still retains during the Middle Ages and Renaissance a "canonical" status, for the romancer of those earlier periods a reunion with his source and concomitant authorization of his vision is still within reach. Dante, Milton, and Spenser all project the basic movement of Scriptural romance from paradise lost to paradise regained, and their work becomes the prototype, or at least the metatype, of earlier romance. From Frye's viewpoint, it could be fairly inferred, there are no secular romances in the Middle Ages and Renaissance, since whatever displacement from Christian myth has occurred is not enough to prevent recognition of the mythic shape they still retain.

Nothing is more remarkable in Frye's writings on earlier romance than the absence of any suggestion that this recuperation of pristine mythic shape may be incomplete or problematic and may be presented as such by the romancer himself. Even Shakespeare, though generally considered a secular poet, ends his final romance—which for Frye represents the "mythos of summer" at its height, a text "not simply to be read or seen or even studied, but possessed"[4]—with a masque echoing the covenant of seedtime and harvest, an apocalyptic vision of dissolution and recreation, and a prayer echoing the Christian imperative: "As you from crimes would pardoned be,/ Let your indulgence set me free" (Epilogue, lines 19-20). After all, while Shakespeare may be a secular poet, he is also a "folk poet," a popular dramatist profoundly at one with a culture in which Christian forms and institutions are still dominant. *"The Tempest,"* Frye acknowledges, "is not an allegory, or a religious drama,"[5] since Prospero's renunciation of his magic and vision of apocalypse do not imply a divine will and an eternal world, but the art that so pervades the play is at least the human counterpart of divine grace, a medium of upward transformation to a more perfect and pristine human nature and community, which is the order of romance. The assumption is that the erring inhabitants of the historical and daylight world of Milan have been sufficiently reformed as a result of Prospero's art, and that they will bring back with them something of the heightened nature of the golden or moonlit world of the island. What emerges from *The Tempest* is at least a silver world, an archetypal romance order of an old world inhabited by old men undergoing renovation. It is only fair to Frye, as well as important to my argument, to point out that this reading of *The Tempest* and of earlier romance is not unique to him; it is more or less explicit in the work of Knight, Barber, Tillyard, Traversi, and most of the more recent studies of Shakespearean romance and pastoral.[6] Frye's is only the most lucid, systematic, and influential statement of what has become a commonplace of Shakespearean criticism.

There are, however, some unsettling features of the play, particularly of its final act, that simply do not conform to this, by now orthodox, view of it. Among them is the fact that, as Frye himself observes, Prospero "appears to have been a remarkably incompetent Duke of Milan, and not to be promising much improvement after he returns. His talents are evidently dramatic rather than political."[7] Few commentators have cared to delve too curiously into this matter, preferring instead to pursue innocent analogies between Prospero's art and that of his creator or to position that art within a Renaissance dialogue between the claims of nature and nurture. But Prospero's relation to his art is deeply ambivalent and goes to the heart of the play's romance status. The passion for theatrical magic that Prospero displays on the island is wholly continuous with the passion for magic and the liberal arts that caused him to lose his dukedom in the first place. The loss was not simply a result of overindulgence in his studies; rather, those studies carry within them an amoral, even hedonistic, potential which may pull their practitioner away from the ethical and political world or move him to attempt to impose their structures upon it. These dangers, while they might not be serious in a member of the citizenry, would be in a duke, and Prospero's career illustrates both dangers in the extreme. He fluctuates, as a duke, between the poles of benign neglect and benevolent despotism.

From the beginning of the play there is a quality of excess, of overcompensation on Prospero's part in exercising on the island the power he had formerly failed to exercise in the historical world. This testiness is too salient and consistent a feature of Prospero's characterization to be explained away, as Frye and others do, as the nervous tension that accompanies the magician's role or the traditional crankiness of the *senex iratus* of New

Comedy. In his opening harangue of Miranda, in which Prospero irritably recounts the history of the Milanese *coup d'état,* his own self-insulation in art is conveniently whitewashed and the blame for his banishment projected outward onto those "potent ministers" of evil, Antonio and Alonso (I.ii.275). Prospero's division of the world into simple and self-flattering contrasts of black and white, a technique of romance-making at its most naive, is repeated in his vision and treatment of Caliban, whose faltering aspirations toward humanity he now denies categorically, just as he had once credited them categorically. Similarly, his show of superior and unnecessary force in humiliating Ferdinand is based on nothing shown to exist in Ferdinand, and is not designed to benefit him. Rather, it seems designed to display Prospero's power, and like his other austerity measures, seems to arise out of his own guilty conscience, out of his own complicity in having created the social disintegration he is now bent on overcorrecting. Prospero's art is something less than the purely ethical instrument it is usually made out to be, just as he himself is less than an exemplar of disciplined virtue.

Similarly, the romance order of the final act is something less than it is usually made out to be. Several of the cast do indeed succumb to the spell of Prospero's magic and proclaim the correspondence of their experience to the romance model Prospero would like it to be. Ferdinand concludes from the betrothal masque that "So rare a wond'red father and a wise/ Makes this place Paradise" (IV.i.123-24). Miranda, in what is perhaps the most famous line of the play, labels the society that emerges from it a "brave new world" (V.i.183). And Gonzalo, who has already demonstrated his own limited talents at romance-making, chorically sums up what he takes to be the meaning of events: "Prospero [found] his dukedom/ In a poor isle; and all of us, ourselves,/ When no man was his own" (V.i.211-13). Were *The Tempest* the archetypal romance it is supposed to be, the play would end right here on this uplifting note, which would accord with the dramatic reality we have seen. But Gonzalo's summing-up is clearly wishful thinking. It glosses over Antonio's stony silence and Prospero's curt dismissal of him. It glosses over, too, Prospero's almost cynical rejoinder to his daughter's exclamation of naive wonder and joy: " 'Tis new to thee" (V.i.184). Perhaps more significantly, the temptation to assimilate the close of *The Tempest* to the rising rhythm of Gonzalo's speech ignores what one critic has termed the mood of disenchantment of the final scene, the "collapsed spirits" in which Prospero refers to his impending retirement and delivers his epilogue, as well as the prolongation, even procrastination, with which he projects his renunciation and return: "Four times, beginning with 'our revels now are ended,' he bids farewell to his art and the island, and prepares to leave (IV.i.148, V.i.29, 34, 64). Four times he reminds Ariel that he'll soon be free (IV.i.261, V.i.5, 95, 241). On three different occasions he promises to tell his story later (V.i.162, 247, 302), which is a way of attenuating the absoluteness of the break, and extending the experience into the future."[8] The final act is suffused with an awareness, culminating in the epilogue, that Prospero's efforts at romance-making have somehow failed but may yet be recuperated by one last fling.

Such a demystifying approach to the romance ending of the play, while it redirects our attention to ironic elements usually overlooked, cannot, however, be accorded the last word. Though Prospero is reluctant indeed to abandon the art in which his power over others resides, however imperfect it has proved, the fact remains that he does abandon it and does so with an expressed awareness of its "vanity" and "roughness." His all too human vacillation, disenchantment, and eventual renunciation might be said to constitute the central romantic triumph of the play, even if it is something of a departure from the exultations of archetypal or conventional romance. After all, his attempts to protect himself behind a shroud of romantic wonder and project himself as a godlike source of power and wisdom, of masques of judgment and masques of mercy, had been an extension of his original squeamishness toward the mere worldlings whose baser motives he had never been entirely above, for all his masquing. While Prospero's exalted role-playing escapes the criticism of those in the play whose capacity for high designs answers to his own, Caliban's irreverent insistence on his usurpation and tyranny serves throughout to underscore the unattractive parallels between Prospero's situation and behavior and those of the worldlings and groundlings he contemns. In the final act, Prospero's awareness of his common bond with the Milanese courtiers he has punished extends even to the meanest of the cast, to the darkest of the alter-egos he had formerly repudiated but now acknowledges as "mine." In depedestaling himself and reappearing "as I was sometime Milan" (V.i.86), Prospero undergoes his own sea-change, a self-humiliation into humanity that redresses his earlier self-exaltation in art. The epilogue, in which he appears on a bare peninsula of the stage, divested of his magic robe, and utters a subdued plea for our indulgence, represents the final stage of this reformation, the mood of collapsed spirits, the intimations of failure paradoxically only reinforcing the effect of romance.

It is important to note, however, that this triumph takes the form of a demystification of romance, a stripping away of illusion and a repudiation of art. We are at the furthest remove possible from the spells, magic, spectacle, and wonder of a naive romance consciousness. Such coercive theatricality has, in fact, been explicitly repudiated by Prospero as the condition of a new ethical integrity. It would seem that, far from returning to its mythic source in religious awe and wonder, *The Tempest* has broken irreparably with its mythic source and entered the realm of an ironic secularity, a world in which illusions of bravery are seen as illusions and the social order is seen not as a divine but as an all too human and precarious construct. Yet this final act of personal demystification on Prospero's part, and the demystification of romance it entails, is simultaneously a remystification, a building up of a new illusion, more subtle and perhaps more potent. For Prospero has exchanged a naive and literal magic for a sophisticated and figurative one. He has even metaphorically fulfilled one of the primal dreams of human art at its most romantic and Faustian: to create a man. What is the effect, after all, of Prospero's decreation of himself as a magus and artist except his new creation of himself as a man? The cast-off role of magician becomes a foil against which a fragile human self is formed and defined. Of course this latest remystification of romance on Prospero's part is also subject, in turn, to further demystification. For it too is an act of illusionism, the human image that we are left with at the end being the product of an artful sleight of hand that can represent the human and the real only by the negative means of foils and contrasts, by showing what they are not rather than presenting the things themselves. The repudiation of art and magic in favor of humanity and reality that closes the play is only another manifestation of art and magic, opening Prospero's final act to charges of slumming and mock-humility. *The Tempest* remains true to its romance form only by acknowledging the artificiality of its romance form. The play can neither reunite with its romance archetype nor leave it altogether behind, in much the same way that Prospero himself can neither remain the artist nor quite become the man; he delays and prolongs his abandonment of art only to promise to return to it after the end of the play to retell his story to the cast. The play and the protagonist are caught up within an endless and dizzying dialectic between self-mystification and self-demystification, to which no final or stable synthesis seems possible.

It becomes increasingly clear that *The Tempest* can in no way be seen as a "naive" romance in Schiller's or Frye's sense, but exhibits an ironic sophistication in relation to its romance models that is nothing if not "modern." The play is hopelessly displaced, by all the distance of theatrical self-consciousness that Prospero and ultimately Shakespeare bring to it, from the ritually sanctioned forms of romance espoused by Gonzalo. If this example of naive romance turns out not to be so naive, however, what can be said of later examples of the mode? For according to the scheme of literary and cultural history we are examining, it is only with the Enlightenment that elements of irony, distance, and sophistication invade the pristine integrity of the romance realm, and a major displacement from the ritual origins of romance occurs. Only now does the joy of reunion with a mythic source become problematic or unavailable in its original purity. Even here, however, there is no suggestion of loss in Frye's work, especially by contrast with that of such Romantic revisionists as Harold Bloom, or W. J. Bate, who share the same historical scheme, albeit more openly. After all, the dominant mode of modern literature, as we all know, is not romance but irony, and since all modes are, in Frye's view, created equal, there is no cause for alarm.

Yet in his historical, as distinct from his theoretical, scheme all modes are *not* created equal, since literature depends for its authority on its proximity and conformation to the religiously and culturally sanctioned source which is myth, and myth is not literature. Literature, that is, cannot supply its own authority. Schiller and Schlegel at least felt the need to rescue Romantic (i.e., modern) literature from invidious comparison with ancient literature in a way that balanced acknowledged loss with gain.

And more recently, Harold Bloom has developed the same historical scheme of Romanticism as an ongoing process of revisionist
displacement, and, in a tonality of rich gloom, he has fixed the
high cost of Romantic belatedness in the dangers of solipsism or
epigonism that beset the modern writer.[9] The absence of a sense
of loss in the work of a critic whose literary-historical scheme
commits him *a priori* to a sense of loss can only suggest that
Frye, at some level, does not accept the consequences of his own
scheme. In this respect, Frye may be wiser than he might appear
and a better literary historian than he is sometimes said to be. For
Frye's historical equanimity reflects the undiminished admiration
many of us retain, against all our own historicist training and
bias, for a Romantic tradition that fully rivals its Renaissance
models in richness and intensity while repeatedly asserting its own
belatedness and lamenting its own loss.

The distorting tendency of that literary historicism that conditions our dealings with romance can be more fully illustrated if
we turn to a great latter-day example of the mode. Conrad's
Heart of Darkness, we are used to hearing, is an unrelieved "night-
journey," a quest-romance turned upside down or perhaps inside
out, the ultimate modernist ironization of the romance form it
adopts.[10] Indeed, the tale opens with an extended analogy between the darkening flood of the Thames estuary that will be the
point of departure for Marlow's adventures and the Thames of
earlier days and brighter tales:

> It [the Thames] had known and served all the men of whom the nation
> is proud, from Sir Francis Drake to Sir John Franklin, knights all,
> titled and untitled—the great knights-errant of the sea. It had borne all
> the ships whose names are like jewels flashing in the night of time,
> from the *Golden Hind* returning with her round flanks full of treasure,
> to be visited by the Queen's Highness and thus pass out of the gigantic
> tale, to the *Erebus* and *Terror,* bound on other conquests—and that
> never returned. It had known the ships and the men. They had sailed
> from Deptford, from Greenwich, from Erith—the adventurers and the
> settlers; kings' ships and the ships of men on 'Change; captains, ad-
> mirals, the dark "interlopers" of the Eastern trade, and the commis-
> sioned "generals" of East India fleets. Hunters for gold or pursuers of
> fame, they all had gone out on that stream, bearing the sword, and
> often the torch, messengers of the night within the land, bearers of a

spark from the sacred fire. What greatness had not floated on the ebb of that river into the mystery of an unknown earth! . . . The dreams of men, the seed of commonwealths, the germs of empires.[11]

It is impossible, from this point on, not to view the movement of *Heart of Darkness* against a background of Renaissance travel literature—not only Drake's circumnavigation of the world but all those tall tales of exploration and discovery in collections like *Purchas' Pilgrimages* that so engaged the imagination of Coleridge, for one, and further back, Shakespeare himself in *The Tempest*.

That this is the narration of a spellbound or naive romancer, however, is only too clear from the unwitting disparities between the scene he has just set and the nostalgic paean he launches into. For the "knights-errant of the sea" who populate the gigantic tale of his recollection have been displaced on the darkening Thames by the bourgeois crew of company-director, lawyer, and accountant aboard the cruising yawl *Nellie*; the unitary vocation of Renaissance merchant-adventurer by the modern discontinuity of business and pleasure; the mythological splendor of the *Golden Hind* by the barnyard homeliness of the *Nellie*. We are repeatedly struck by the narrator's apparent unawareness of the ambivalence of his own language: "Hunters for gold or pursuers of fame," "bearing the sword, and often the torch," "the germs of empires." These opening ironies of situation and language do not bode well, to say the least, for the tale's chances of reunion with or recreation of a naive mythic source.

This demystification of romance becomes even more explicit when Marlow takes up the narrative burden. His account of the Roman conquest of Britain further debunks the first narrator's naively romantic account of the national past, and with it all hope of a historical "progress" or continuity of romance, since not even its original or mythic form ever existed in history but in "the idea only":

> It [the Roman conquest] was just robbery with violence, aggravated murder on a great scale, and men going at it blind—as is very proper for those who tackle a darkness. The conquest of the earth, which mostly means the taking it away from those who have a different complexion or slightly flatter noses than ourselves, is not a pretty thing when you look into it too much. What redeems it is the idea only. (P. 7)

Marlow, the middle-aged mariner and latter-day quester, presents himself to us, in contrast to the initial narrator, a Sunday-sailor who has never left home, as a consciousness demystified from the start. It is not that he never shared the narrator's passion for gigantic tales, but rather that he would seem to have outgrown them and left them behind:

> Now when I was a little chap I had a passion for maps. I would look for hours at South America, or Africa, or Australia, and lose myself in all the glories of exploration. At that time there were many blank spaces on the earth, and when I saw one that looked particularly inviting on a map (but they all look that) I would put my finger on it and say, When I grow up I will go there. The North Pole was one of these places, I remember. Well, I haven't been there yet, and shall not try now. The glamour's off. . . . But there was one yet—the biggest, the most blank, so to speak—that I had a hankering after. (P. 8)

The mystified state of mind, the romance consciousness that Marlow implicitly claims to have left behind, he now identifies with childhood, as he does at several later points with womanhood, so that his account of his launching out into an actual Congo that "had ceased to be a blank space of delightful mystery—a white patch for a boy to dream gloriously over" (p. 8) is presented from a ruthlessly demystified point of view. His appointment by the company is the result, not of providence or divine mission, but of the "glorious affair" of the chance killing of a "supernatural being" named Fresleven and the intervention of an "enthusiastic" aunt (p. 9). Not even the romantic figure of Kurtz at this point holds any magic for Marlow: ". . . now and then I would give some thought to Kurtz. I wasn't very interested in him. No. Still, I was curious as to whether this man, who had come out equipped with moral ideas of some sort, would climb to the top after all, and how he would set about his work when there" (p. 31). It is only work, in fact, that escapes the unflattering light of Marlow's intelligence: "I don't like work—no man does—but I like what is in the work, the chance to find yourself. Your own reality—for yourself, not for others—what no other man can ever know" (p. 29). The kind of work Marlow has in mind, dramatized in his efforts to repair his boat and keep it going up river, is the opposite of heroics. And yet his language endows it with the same purpose and value that the heroics of earlier quest-romance had once held—the goals of hard-won self-realization, reward, and revelation. It may be that the state of demystification Marlow claims to have achieved and repeatedly demonstrates in his narration may itself be a mystification; with every ironic use of the language of quest-romance, he may be demonstrating the impossibility of ever really leaving behind quest-romance, returning to a source in the very moment he thinks he is leaving it behind.

To leap to such a conclusion, however, would be premature, since the novella's work of demystification has at this point barely got under way. Just as the initial narrator's voice had seemed naive in contrast to the undeluded voice of Marlow, so Marlow's seems naive in contrast to the desperate voice of Kurtz. For Kurtz has undergone the same process of mystification and demystification in his own romantic quest as Marlow has in his, only in a heightened and intensified—one is tempted to say a mythic and archetypal—form. In his descent upon the African darkness under the aegis of the International Society for the Suppression of Savage Customs, Kurtz has cast himself as an apostle of European enlightenment, the counterpart within the tale to those romantic "knights-errant" of the narrator's opening recollection. Far from being dead, the romance of commerce and Christianization, of the sword and the torch, is alive and well and living in the Congo—at least for a time. Kurtz has recreated that role on nothing less than a mythic scale. His mission is directly patterned on that of those Renaissance voyagers, so much so that he seems less a particular modern man or character in a novel than a timeless composite or collective figure—hence his utility for Eliot in the epigraph to "The Hollow Men." Marlow in fact demonstrates in genealogical detail that "All Europe contributed to the making of Kurtz" (p. 50). The myth he embodies has been in the making long before Columbus, for as Marlow points out, it is as old as imperialism itself. Kurtz's treatise on "The Suppression of Savage Customs" aspires to the un-self-questioning status of a sacred text, a myth in the sense not of a story about a god but of a story *by* a god:

> He began with the argument that we whites, from the point of development we had arrived at, "must necessarily appear to them [savages] in the nature of supernatural beings—we approach them with the

might as of a deity," and so on, and so on. "By the simple exercise of our will we can exert a power for good practically unbounded," etc., etc. From that point he soared and took me with him. The peroration was magnificent. . . . It gave me the notion of an exotic Immensity ruled by an august Benevolence. It made me tingle with enthusiasm. This was the unbounded power of eloquence—of words—of burning noble words. There were no practical hints to interrupt the magic current of phrases, unless a kind of note at the foot of the last page, scrawled evidently much later, in an unsteady hand, may be regarded as the exposition of a method. It was very simple, and at the end of that moving appeal to every altruistic sentiment it blazed at you, luminous and terrifying, like a flash of lightning in a serene sky: "Exterminate all the brutes!" (P. 51)

Kurtz's treatise—up to its lethal gloss—is a kind of anatomy of romance-making, and the impression it leaves on Marlow of "an exotic Immensity ruled by an august Benevolence" is an astute definition of romance at its most naive. The existential project out of which it grows, at once so topical and so anachronistic, of creating a brave new world of religion and commerce, is of course a failure, one that recapitulates the previous failures of the Renaissance voyagers themselves: those men who, like Kurtz, had assumed the prerogatives of gods toward the natives they encountered; who fell often into practices more savage than those of the "savages" themselves; and whose efforts at civilization, i.e., Christianization, lagged fatefully behind their efforts at colonial exploitation (the former being a pretext for the latter). The last irony is beautifully pointed in Marlow's comparing Kurtz's head to an ivory ball. But the crucial difference between Kurtz's repetition of past romantic texts and pretexts and its earlier models is that at some point he realizes his own failure, and that way madness lies. He recognizes that the encounter with alien cultures necessitates the examination of one's own cultural presuppositions, but he cannot save himself from the consequences of a maddening intersubjectivity. For Marlow, however, the encounter with Kurtz is a timely and saving encounter with his own archetype. Kurtz is a vertical quester, whose "exalted and incredible degradation" (p. 67) precipitates an analogous, if less dangerous, self-demystification in the horizontal quester Marlow. This demystification enables him to ironize his own earlier ironic stance and thereby recover a goal for his questing: the goal of absolute demystification.

Kurtz's self-convicted nihilism, expressed in his darkly lucid gloss and deathbed pronouncement of "The horror! the horror!" (pp. 71, 75, 79), carry for Marlow an authoritative clairvoyance that makes his own fugitive ironies seem frivolous and defines a further horizon of self-knowledge to be pursued for his own quest.

It still appears, however, that in *Heart of Darkness* we are dealing with an ultimately ironic or "satanic" (p. 68) quest-romance, the furthest displacement imaginable, in Frye's literary-historical terms, from the ideal vision of earlier quest-romance. After all, Conrad's replacement of Christian revelation as the goal of romantic questing with that of an absolute demystification, and the wisdom-figures of hermit or Christian tutor (like Spenser's Contemplation) with a desperate nihilist, should result in the ultimate ironization of the mode itself. But a curious reversal has taken place, one that has been implicit from the outset. Like Dante, who in moving through the deepest stages of his infernal descent discovers that he has already begun his ascent, Marlow's confrontation with the negativity of Kurtz takes the form of an almost pure affirmation:

> I went no more near the remarkable man who had pronounced a judgment upon the adventures of his soul on this earth. The voice was gone. What else had been there? . . . If such is the form of ultimate wisdom, then life is a greater riddle than some of us think it to be. I was within a hair's-breadth of the last opportunity for pronouncement, and I found with humiliation that probably I would have nothing to say. This is the reason why I affirm that Kurtz was a remarkable man. He had something to say. He said it. . . . He had summed up—he had judged. "The Horror!" He was a remarkable man. After all, this was the expression of some sort of belief; it had candour, it had conviction, it had a vibrating note of revolt in its whisper, it had the appalling face of a glimpsed truth . . . he had made that last stride, he had stepped over the edge, while I had been permitted to draw back my hesitating foot. And perhaps in this is the whole difference; perhaps all the wisdom, and all truth, and all sincerity, are just compressed into that inappreciable moment of time in which we step over the threshold of the invisible. Perhaps! I like to think my summing-up would not have been a word of careless contempt. Better his cry—much better. It was an affirmation, a moral victory paid for by innumerable defeats, by abominable terrors, by abominable satisfactions. But it was a victory! That is why I have remained loyal to Kurtz to the last, and even beyond, when a long time

after I heard once more, not his own voice, but the echo of his magnificent eloquence thrown to me from a soul as translucently pure as a
cliff of crystal. (Pp. 71-72)

Romance, it seems, does not die so easily as Marlow had once
thought or as many commentators on this tale seem to think.

The progressive demystification of romance we have traced
throughout *Heart of Darkness,* culminating in the absolute demystification of the mythic poet-quester Kurtz, has been in the service
of a remystification of romance all along. This countermovement
is implicit in Marlow's desire to set out for the Congo in the first
place despite his foreknowledge that "the glamour's off"; in his
romanticization of the most unromantic kind of work; in his
paradoxical recognition of Kurtz's "exalted and incredible degradation"; and finally in his confrontation back in Brussels with
Kurtz's "Intended." Throughout he has referred to her, as to
women in general, as inhabiting a benighted world of romantic
illusions, so that when he refers to her in the passage above as "a
soul as translucently pure as a cliff of crystal" it comes as something of a surprise or *volte-face.* Yet when Marlow finally meets
Kurtz's lady, that presiding figure of his romantic questing, the
scene is far from one of unmitigated irony. Irony itself is here
ironized to maintain the spell of romance! ". . . bowing my head
before the faith that was in her, before that great and saving
illusion that shone with an unearthly glow in the darkness, in the
triumphant darkness from which I could not have defended her—
from which I could not even defend myself" (p. 77). And so
Marlow, once again turned romancer, lies. Not to do so would
have been "too dark—too dark altogether" (p. 79), a regression
from the level of enlightenment Marlow claims to have achieved.
To tell the simple truth would be to lie, to subvert the experience
of Kurtz into a simple act of demystification when it has been
presented all along as a complex interaction of demystification
and remystification. Marlow nonetheless appears in the scene to
claim an ironic advantage over the Intended and to draw us into
thinking we share that ironic distance. But Conrad is quick to
ironize Marlow's irony and restore the balance of remystification
through the Intended's naive response: "an exulting and terrible
cry . . . of inconceivable triumph and of unspeakable pain" (p.
79). The phrase in its ambivalence is the truest reaction possible

to Marlow's story, which is at the same time both naively romantic and ironically sophisticated. It illustrates the inability of latter-day romance ever to regain its mythic form or to shed that form completely, ever to reunite with its source or to leave that source definitively behind. To consider *Heart of Darkness* as a "myth of modernism" is to reveal the mythic status of modernism itself.

In his *History of English Poetry* (1781) Thomas Warton asserts that during the Elizabethan age there still existed a "degree of superstition sufficient for the purposes of poetry, and the adoption of the machineries of romance," that "the reformation had not yet destroyed every delusion, nor disenchanted all the strongholds of superstition," that "Reason suffered a few demons still to linger, which she chose to retain in her service under the guidance of poetry," and that "the national credulity, chastened by reason, had produced a sort of civilized superstition, and left a set of traditions, fanciful enough for poetical decorations, and yet not too violent and chimerical for common sense."[12] Such a view of literary history since the Renaissance as a progressive demystification or displacement or ironization or secularization or internalization of romance is still very much with us and, in fact, underlies and conditions our criticism of romance and Romantic texts alike. Yet such a historical scheme cannot be reconciled with the two extraordinary, but not unrepresentative, romances we have examined. Both *The Tempest* and *Heart of Darkness,* though separated by three centuries of literary and cultural history, reveal a dialectic between the demystification and remystification of their own romance mode that is implicit at every point in their dramatic and narrative structures. In such phrases as "Some vanity of mine art," "O brave new world. . . . 'Tis new to thee" and "his exalted and incredible degradation," "her exulting and terrible cry," phrases in which the full niaveté and the full irony of these texts is self-consciously present, the entire argument of this essay lies compressed. It is naive to place these great romances within a historical sequence of progressive demystification moving from myth to irony, since each is demystified from the start. To do so is at once to patronize the past by oversimplifying it and, paradoxically, to idolatrize the present by making it the source of complexity. The consequences of this procedure are not only bad literary history but also bad literary interpretation.

5

Fathers and Daughters in Shakespeare's Romances

Cyrus Hoy

Behind all the fathers and daughters in Shakespeare's romances are the most affecting father and daughter he ever drew, Lear and Cordelia. Shakespeare's tragedies are the necessary prelude to the romances; the romances are inconceivable without the tragedies; and among the tragedies, *King Lear* stands out for a number of reasons, not the least of which concerns its protagonist's relation to women. Lear is a father with daughters, not a son with a mother (as in *Hamlet* or *Coriolanus*), or a husband with a wife (as in *Othello* or *Macbeth*), or a lover with a mistress who is both more and less to him than a wife (as in *Antony and Cleopatra*). Of all the possible relationships of man and woman, that of father and daughter seems finally to have been the one that moved the dramatist most, for from it he derives the mysterious rhythms of suffering and grace, of loss and restoration, that sound throughout the last four plays. The fates of Pericles and Marina, Cymbeline and Imogen, Leontes and Perdita, Prospero and Miranda, encompass patterns of error and pain and ultimate deliverance which the imagination of the dramatist obviously found comfort in contemplating, and on which all his creative energies were focused in the effort to endow the patterns with formal shape in the romances. With its poignant representation of peace after long suffering which Lear all too briefly attains with Cordelia, *King Lear* represents the beginning of the imaginative way that will lead to *Pericles, Cymbeline, The Winter's Tale* and *The Tempest.*

    Cordelia is not, of course, Lear's only daughter. She has two sisters who are as false as she is true. The finality of the distinction drawn between Cordelia's faith and Goneril and Regan's treachery suggests the degree of idealization that has gone into Cordelia's creation. She is a model of the heights to which human nature can rise when actuated by a rare integrity and selflessness; Goneril and Regan are the more commonplace examples of the depths to which human nature can fall when governed by hypocrisy and greed. The ideal that Cordelia embodies cannot be sustained in the tragic world of *King Lear,* and one suspects that Shakespeare was attracted to the romance form at least in part for the freedom it gave him to create an atmosphere in which other idolized daughters—Marina, Imogen, Perdita, Miranda—could endure. But the image that Cordelia projects—of idealized virtue closed round by sinister forces—is one that persists into the romances: Marina in the brothel; Imogen at the mercy of sundry nefarious plots hatched by a scheming stepmother, a brutal stepbrother, and a deceived husband; Perdita cast out at birth to whatever chance might befall her. Only Miranda, as the consequence of her father's peculiar powers, lives in anything like security, and even she has been the object of an attempted rape by Caliban. Cordelia's role in the design of *King Lear* is paradigmatic of that of all the daughters in the last plays: they are distressingly vulnerable to a host of evils, but they are incorruptible, and they all in one way or another redeem the father figure. In *King Lear,* Cordelia is reconciled with her father, who begs her forgiveness and who is, in effect, restored to life by her ministrations in a memorable scene (IV.vii) which would comprise the play's finale if *King Lear* were a romance. As it is, the tragedy sweeps on to its catastrophe, but the sort of recognition scene Shakespeare composed for Lear is recapitulated with ever-increasing brilliance in *Pericles, Cymbeline,* and *The Winter's Tale,* where it serves as the appropriate occasion for demonstrating the daughter's redemptive powers: the restorations of Marina and Perdita to their fathers serve to restore their fathers to life after prolonged periods of mourning, even as the restoration of Imogen to her father serves to restore him to his senses after a prolonged period of foolish blindness. The finale of *The Tempest* is differently managed, as we shall see, but the redemptive quality of Miranda is affirmed from the outset of the play. Prospero calls her the cherubin who preserved him when he was exiled from his dukedom (I.ii.152-53).

Fathers and daughters had, of course, been present in Shakespeare's plays since the early years of his career, when old Baptista shrewdly made the marriage of his sweet Bianca dependent on the provision of a husband for his curst Katherina, in *The Taming of the Shrew.* Usually the fathers in early Shakespeare are the stock figures of romantic comedy, whose daughters decline to marry the suitors of their choice, as Silvia rejects Thurio in favor of Valentine in *The Two Gentlemen of Verona,* or as Hermia declines Demetrius for Lysander in *A Midsummer Night's Dream,* or as Anne Page manages to avoid Dr. Caius and win Fenton in *The Merry Wives of Windsor.* There is a tragic version of this familiar situation in *Romeo and Juliet* when old Capulet insists that his daughter, secretly wed to Romeo, should marry Paris. *Much Ado About Nothing* gives us the pathetic figure of Leonato in his indignation at the shame visited upon Hero his daughter, falsely accused of infidelity on the eve of her marriage; and in *As You Like It* we have the clever Rosalind following her father into exile in the Forest of Arden. But the relation of father and daughter does not become problematic until, inevitably, in that most problematic of plays, *Hamlet,* where we are confronted with Ophelia and Polonius. Their one scene together (I.iii) turns on the familiar subject of the man on whom the daughter has placed her love. Since her suitor is Hamlet and a prince, his intentions toward her cannot be honorable because she is not his equal; this is the line that Ophelia's brother has been taking with her when the scene begins, and it is the line that her father continues with her—in even stronger terms—in the last half of the scene, after the brother takes his leave. When she tries to state her belief that Hamlet loves her in honorable fashion, Polonius pours scorn on the notion. The "holy vows" with which the prince has "given countenance" to his declarations of love are, according to Polonius, "springes to catch woodcocks." Because he knows what young men are like, Ophelia is to be guided by his knowledge. She is, to her undoing; among the ballad stanzas that she sings in her madness is one that bears witness to what a forcible impression her father's counsel has made on her imagination: "Young men will do't if they come to't" (IV.v.60). Polonius is Shakespeare's first considerable depiction of the father as an insensitive blunderer who, persuaded of the soundness of his own judgment, is blind and deaf to all signals that he may be wrong, and impervious to the violence he may be doing in the pursuit of his own will. The type will recur in Shakespeare, though daughters will never again be as docile as Ophelia.

The next daughter whom Shakespeare drew was Desdemona,

whose gentle modesty exists side by side with an independence
of will and a courage to follow where love leads that surprise and
disconcert her father. When she is brought into the council
chamber before Othello and Brabantio, she enunciates with great
clarity and force a principle of duty which places her directly
in the tradition shared by daughters in the later plays:

> My noble father,
> I do perceive here a divided duty:
> To you I am bound for life and education;
> My life and education both do learn me
> How to respect you; you are the lord of duty;
> I am hitherto your daughter. But here's my husband;
> And so much duty as my mother show'd
> To you, preferring you before her father,
> So much I challenge that I may profess
> Due to the Moor, my lord.
>
> (I.iii.180-89)

This is the position on which Cordelia will take her stand in
King Lear:

> Good my lord,
> You have begot me, bred me, lov'd me: I
> Return those duties back as are right fit,
> Obey you, love you, and most honor you.
> Why have my sisters husbands, if they say
> They love you all? Happily, when I shall wed,
> That lord whose hand must take my plight shall carry
> Half my love with him, half my care and duty.
> Sure I shall never marry like my sisters,
> To love my father all.
>
> (I.i.95-104)

One must resist any tendency to oversimplify tragic actions as
profoundly subtle as those which comprise the plots of *Othello*
and *King Lear,* but in both instances the daughter's role as victim
of the tragedy is unmistakably clear, and the father's share in con-
tributing to her victimization is delicately but firmly woven into
the tragic pattern. When Brabantio, Desdemona's father, says to
Othello: "Look to her, Moor, if thou hast eyes to see;/ She has
deceiv'd her father, and may thee" (I.iii.292-93), he is sowing a
seed of suspicion that will later, under Iago's nurture, come to

monstrous flower in the husband's imagination. And Lear's rejection of Cordelia is a piece of monumental folly that leads to his destruction and to hers. She is his youngest and most loved daughter, and he has no more expected to be crossed by her than Brabantio has expected his daughter to elope with a Moor. As for the daughters themselves, they leave the fathers whom they have had to disappoint in order to be themselves, and they attempt to make new lives for themselves elsewhere. But they have been enmeshed in a fate that will not finally permit this escape. Since, for purposes of the tragedy, Desdemona is first and foremost Othello's wife and only secondarily Brabantio's daughter, the implications of her death are significantly different from those which surround the murder of Cordelia, who for dramatic purposes is primarily Lear's daughter and only secondarily the wife of the King of France. The tragic spectacle which ends each play makes this clear: Desdemona dead in the arms of her husband, Cordelia dead in the arms of her father. For all her declaration—in her speech defining her duty—to the effect that she shall never marry like her sisters, to love her father all, Cordelia after her marriage does in fact continue to love her father all; she leaves her husband to return to her father and to go about his business, and finally to die for him. Offstage, in the background to the closing scene of *Othello,* there is a dead father to Desdemona, brought to his grave through grief at her marriage, but we are concerned with him only in the moment when we hear Gratiano say that he is glad Brabantio is not alive to know of his daughter's murder (V.ii.204 ff.). For the marriage bed loaded with the corpses of Othello and Desdemona, the end of *King Lear* gives us Lear with the dead body of Cordelia in his arms, and the sad spectacle is redolent both of a father of sorrows bending over the child who has tried to save him, and a lover bending over the body of a beloved destroyed by forces he himself has unleashed.

All Shakespeare's work from *Lear* to the end of his career seems to be generated by the tension between two powerful imaginative efforts: on the one hand, to free the self from bondage to the kind of female monsters most horrifically embodied in Goneril and Regan, and on the other hand to replace the sense of female monstrosity with a sense of female purity that will have the effect of saving the imagination from despair—of sweetening it, as Lear might say, when he calls to an imaginary apothecary for an ounce of civet. The imagination at work in the romances can still produce some monstrous growths: Dionyzia in *Pericles* and the stepmother Queen in *Cymbeline* are further examples of female evil. But the romances also give us two memorable examples of women, Imogen and Hermione, who are wronged by unjust masculine suspicions, while giving us as well two extraordinary treatments of the masculine imaginations that have wronged them, namely Posthumus and Leontes, their husbands and fiercest accusers. Prior to the romances, however, all the protagonists of Shakespeare's later tragedies display a need to escape from the domination of women: Lear from Goneril and Regan, Macbeth from Lady Macbeth, Coriolanus from Volumnia, Antony from Cleopatra. The areas of tension differ widely from play to play. The shades of unrelieved evil in which Goneril and Regan are drawn make plausible the fierce tirades which Lear launches against them. There is something almost poignant in Macbeth's recognition that, in his inurement to crime, he has far outdistanced his wife, who once had to urge him to it. Coriolanus resists his mother's tutelage without ever altogether recognizing what it is that has him in its power. Antony knows that he must break his strong Egyptian fetters if he is successfully to fulfill his role as one of the triple pillars of the world, but he never manages to do so.

Lear had given us an idealized figure—Cordelia, with her truth-telling—to counterbalance the vicious sisters, with their glozing lies, but such a figure has disappeared in all the later tragedies, at least in its female embodiment. Vestiges of what she has represented remain, notably in the person of Coriolanus, where Cordelia's refusal to compromise and her expulsion are recapitulated. The expulsion of one who speaks uncomfortable truths—or declines to speak comforting lies—is treated again in the person of Alcibiades in *Timon of Athens,* a play that is particularly interesting for what it does not contain. The idealized figure of Cordelia is obviously necessary if the imagination (either of Lear or of the dramatist who created him) is to be saved from despair; just how necessary is evident from the example of Timon, who does in fact give way to despair.

Timon of Athens is in all essential respects a womanless play; women appear in only two scenes, and it is not without significance that in their two appearances, they are brought on first (in I.ii) in a masque of Amazons led by Cupid, and later (in IV.iii) as two whores in the company of Alcibiades. The impression of women as mannish whores is a legacy of *King Lear,* where they have been fully represented as such in the persons of Goneril and Regan; it is the only impression left to the imagination of the dramatist when such an ideal of woman as that represented by Cordelia is no more. Timon the protagonist is neither father nor son, husband nor lover; he is relentlessly, irremediably alone, first in the society of his troops of seeming-friends, then in his distrust, his sense of betrayal, his misanthropy. This is especially noticeable in the dramatic treatment of Alcibiades, that proto-type of the male beloved. He offers Timon his friendship, but Timon will have none of it. When in Plutarch we read of how the Athenians covered the faults of Alcibiades "with the best wordes and termes they could, calling them youthfull, and gentlemans sportes,"[1] we find ourselves back among the emotional equivoca-tions of Shakespeare's sonnets, for example, number ninety-six, addressed to the poet's young friend and beginning "Some say thy fault is youth, some wantonness,/ Some say thy grace is youth and gentle sport."

But the crucial fact about the role of Alcibiades in *Timon of Athens* is that he is determinedly kept at arm's length from the protagonist. In the play's desolate world, the idealized image of a Cordelia (destroyed at the end of *Lear*) is not likely to be revived; and the idealized image of a male beloved, however much it might once have sustained the imagination of the poet-dramatist, seems now to have outlived its usefulness. The imagination of the drama-tist—to judge from the world it created in the tragedies that follow *King Lear*—is not yet capable of reviving the idealized Cordelia in the vigor and purity of Marina and Imogen, Perdita and Miranda; all it can do is dwell on the forces that drive the male protagonists who present themselves to the dramatist's vision, and the forces are all embodied in the female sex. When Shakespeare tries to ignore this fact, as he did in *Timon of Athens,* he produces a dramatic fragment from which any profound incitement to passion is lacking: an effect without a cause. In the other plays of these years (1605 to around 1607), the imagination considers the possible sensual-erotic bonds that might conceivably tie a man to a woman, and addresses itself in Lady Macbeth, Volumnia, and Cleopatra to the depiction of the woman who will be both wife and mother, who will spur the man on to surpass himself and comfort him when he fails, in whose arms he will be content to die but from whose fierce determination he will also struggle to be free, whose hold on him will in some mysterious way drive him to crime in the eyes of the world.

This is the psychological climate which produces the romances. The dramatist is engaged in a quest to free the imagination from all the shrill mistress-wife-mother figures who have inhabited the late tragedies, and to create in their place an ideal of femininity on whom the imagination can bestow its tenderest sentiments, without the distractions of sexual desire. Thus the need to make the feminine ideal a daughter. Quests are of course native to the romance form, and the dynamics of the four last plays are all directed to the revelation of a radiant young woman whose purity and integrity have the effect of bringing light to the darkness in which fathers are plunged as a consequence of the world's evil or their own folly or both. With their simplicity, courage, and healthy integrity, Marina, Imogen, Perdita, and Miranda move through their plays like redemptive graces. The impression made by these daughters is the more remarkable when we consider that the first of the romances opens with a scene in which we—along with Pericles—suddenly find ourselves in the presence of a father and daughter who are guilty of incest, the ugliest relationship that a father's love for a daughter may imply. Here, at the outset of the romances, we are confronted for just a moment with the disturbing possibilities which it will be a principal endeavor of the dramatist's art to suppress in the plays ahead. Like Pericles, the dramatist gazes at full upon the guilty love of father and daughter, and then flees; but he will never forget what he saw. The romance quest in all the four last plays will be aimed at replacing the guilty passion with a pure affection, with creating an ideal of femininity which the imagination can hover over and cherish without guilt.

The discovery of evil in the King of Antioch's incest with his daughter leaves its mark on the dramatist's treatment of father and daughter relations in everything that follows. This is particularly evident in the treatment of fathers in the romances. Each is a distinct dramatic creation and they are not to be lumped together, but no one who has studied the romances will have failed to notice the wariness with which fathers are treated in their relations with their daughters in the first three plays. For one thing, fathers have remarkably few scenes with their daughters in *Pericles, Cymbeline,* and *The Winter's Tale.* Through most of these plays, the daughters are lost to their fathers in one way or another. Pericles' loss of Marina is presumably but one more feature of the pattern of painful adventures—which also includes loss of wife for a season—to which even so good a man as he is subject in this mutable world; his is much the least complicated case of all those on exhibit in the last plays. He has done nothing to deserve separation from his daughter. Nonetheless, they are separated until very late in the play when, sunk in years and grief, he finds her again in a scene which is clearly modeled on Cordelia's restoration to Lear. The parallels are explicit in the "fresh garments" for the long-suffering father and the music that sounds as he recognizes his daughter.

Imogen's relations with Cymbeline are more complex. He presumably loves her, but he seems bent on destroying her, perhaps from that same obscure fear of incest which causes him to try to forbid her marriage to Posthumus, bred like a son in his household. He objects to her marriage with Posthumus as strenuously as Brabantio has objected to the marriage of Desdemona and Othello. Imogen is superbly indifferent to his anger. She tells him:

> I beseech you, sir,
> Harm not yourself with your vexation,
> I am senseless of your wrath; a touch more rare
> Subdues all pangs, all fears.
>
> (I.i.133-36)

Her father has banished her husband, and that is her one concern. Long before Imogen is literally lost to her father—during that period in the last half of the play when no one but the audience knows of her whereabouts—she has been lost to him in their estrangement. He has a second wife on whom he dotes and who, with her son (the wretched Cloten), has the management of the affairs of his kingdom. Cymbeline's character consists in not seeing. For all his kingly role, he is a cipher, in the play no less than in his realm. This is evident from the long and highly elaborate final scene where the complicated plot is untangled and where the king, who might be expected to have a chief function in bringing the truth to light (as, for example, the Duke does in the final scene of *Measure for Measure*), is in the demeaning position of having to have everything explained to him. When he is told of the queen's death-bed confession, he is surprised to learn of her wickedness but sees no reason to reproach himself for not having previously suspected it:

> Mine eyes
> Were not in fault, for she was beautiful;
> Mine ears, that heard her flattery, nor my heart,
> That thought her like her seeming. It had been vicious
> To have mistrusted her . . . .

But if he sees no reason to reproach himself, he admits that his daughter might. He continues:

> yet, O my daughter,
> That it was folly in me, thou mayst say,
> And prove it in thy feeling. Heaven mend all!
>   (V.v.62-68)

At what ought to be an emotional high point of the scene—the reunion of father and daughter—even Cymbeline is not so dim as to fail to recognize that he is playing an undignified second-fiddle. He says to Imogen, who is locked in the embrace of Posthumus:

> How now, my flesh? my child?
> What, mak'st thou me a dullard in this act?
> Wilt thou not speak to me?
>   (V.v.264-66)

Only then does Imogen kneel to him and ask his blessing. It is the daughter's reunion with her husband that is the emotional high point of the scene, and the point reinforces what is clear enough in the play as a whole: that Imogen is first a wife and then a daughter. The passion which she arouses is safely and conventionally exhibited in her husband and not in her father, who looks on uncomprehendingly.

The distancing of father from daughter is continued in *The Winter's Tale*. The estrangement of the two is here the more violent, for Leontes is literally determined to destroy his wife's presumed bastard; he decrees the infant Perdita's exposure to the elements. Her eventual restoration to her father proceeds along significantly different lines in *The Winter's Tale* from the course it takes in Greene's *Pandosto,* Shakespeare's source. The denouement of Greene's novel is managed as follows: Fawnia (Perdita) is brought with her beloved Dorastus (Florizel) into the presence of Pandosto (Leontes), and he, not knowing the girl to be his daughter, is promptly enflamed with a lust for her which he seeks to satisfy in a succeeding series of alternating promises and threats. She of course steadfastly refuses him, and when at last her true identity is made known, the incestuous passion he has felt for his daughter causes the already abundant cup of his shame to run over. Greene's novel closes:

> but Pandosto, calling to mind how first he betrayed his friend Egistus [Polixenes]; how his jealousy was the cause of Bellaria's death [i.e., the death of Hermione, who in the novel is not restored to life]; that, contrary to the law of nature, he had lusted after his own daughter— moved with these desperate thoughts, he fell in a melancholy fit and, to close up the comedy with a tragical stratagem, he slew himself.[2]

It required a strong-minded dramatist to resist such a finale as this in 1610-11, the very period when Beaumont and Fletcher were captivating audiences with the exquisite anguish of Arbaces and Penthea, the brother and sister in *A King and No King.* They struggle against a passion that threatens to be bigger than they are until they are delivered from their incipient shame by the discovery that they are not, in truth, related. But this is a subject which, to the imagination that produced Shakespeare's romances, does not bear conscious thinking on, however powerful a hold it might have exercised on the unconscious workings of that imagination. Shakespeare not only suppressed all reference to a father's incestuous love for his daughter, he declined as well to dramatize the scene in which father and daughter discover each other. In *The Winter's Tale* the recognition scene takes place offstage and is recounted by three gentlemen. The whole weight of the finale is thus given over to the scene with Hermione's statue, its metamorphosis to the living woman, and her restoration to her husband and daughter. Just as, for dramatic purposes, Imogen makes her principal impression as Posthumus's wife rather than as Cymbeline's daughter, so Leontes is chiefly memorable as Hermione's conscience-stricken husband rather than as Perdita's father.

In each of the first three romances, a scene is carefully furnished with a father and a daughter whose reunion is a prominent feature in the comic resolution of all three plays. The treatment of the relationship, however, seems straitened, as if observed from a distance, and it is never developed in terms exclusively its own. The dramatist seems at pains to keep the full emotional weight of a play from falling on a father and daughter's love. So Pericles and Leontes have wives who are lost and found again, even as their daughters are; and Imogen has a husband and Perdita a beloved who exercise that claim on their duty of which Desdemona and Cordelia have spoken, and which takes precedence over duty to a father. In *Pericles, Cymbeline,* and *The Winter's Tale,* the imagination of the dramatist is fascinated with the relation of a father to a daughter; it circles around the subject ever so tentatively; it returns to it repeatedly. But it is only on the fourth return, in *The Tempest,* that the imagination is prepared to deal with the subject directly, to imagine the hitherto unimaginable, to think the unthinkable.

Among the unthinkable conditions that *The Tempest* is prepared to set before us (such as getting all one's enemies in one's power) is a father's dream of having his daughter entirely to himself from her infancy through the twelve years that bring her to the verge of womanhood, and on a desert island too. Incestuous impulses are rigorously banished, and the foreground of consciousness is occupied with the need to protect chastity from rape. Prospero's feelings for Miranda are the feelings of a father for a daughter whom he idealizes, whose innocence he would preserve against the sinfulness of the world in general, and whose chastity he would safeguard against the particular violence of men, who will do to her what he did to her mother in order to beget her. He knows his sex, as Polonius might say. It is all very poignant because it is all so natural and so hopeless. Miranda must be allowed to marry; she is ready to and she wants to. With the appearance of Ferdinand, the wheel of amorous questing has come full circle from the opening scene of the first romance to the middle scenes of this last one. Pericles, when he thought to win a beautiful lady from her father, found himself exposed to the guilty secret of their incest. Ferdinand, led into the presence of Prospero and Miranda by Ariel's music, discovers a stern father who will set him sundry tests but who is not in the end unappeasable, and a daughter whose ardor charmingly matches his own. She is spirited, and one can imagine her, if pressed far enough, roundly declaring to her father that so much duty as her mother showed to him, preferring him before her own father, so much must she now challenge that she may profess due to Ferdinand. It is to Prospero's credit, and a measure of his wisdom and his humanity, that he never forces her to say anything of the sort. Though he may not be so glad of their union as they are (as he says in soliloquy at III.i.92), he recognizes its inevitability when he recognizes Ferdinand's worthiness, and he gives it his blessing. As Prospero, when he finds his enemies repentant, is prepared to forego his natural inclination for vengeance and have mercy on them instead, so in a parallel movement, when he finds that Ferdinand has satisfactorily endured the trials he has put him to, he is prepared to forego his all-too-human inclination to keep his daughter to himself and to give her in marriage instead. He has lost his daughter, as he tells Alonso late in the play (V.i.147-48), but he is resigned to her loss for he has recognized its inevitability; Miranda was straining for her freedom every bit as avidly as Ariel was.

Part of the triumph of *The Tempest*—both the triumph dramatized in Prospero's magnanimity and Shakespeare's triumph in depicting it—resides in what the dramatist has won through to in this play: the representation of an ideal of femininity which the masculine imagination at last manages to secure for itself. Miranda is what the imagination finally succeeds in conceiving in place of the Gonerils and Regans, the Lady Macbeths and Volumnias and Cleopatras from whom, rightly or wrongly, it considers itself to have suffered. As a product of the imagination, she is very much the father's child. We hear nothing of a wife to Prospero; he has nurtured her; she has sustained him in his moment of anguish. The imagination is here able to envision a relationship between father and daughter that is not marred on the one hand by the father's jealousy or his efforts to play the petty tyrant, nor on the other by the daughter's rebellion against or indifference to his will. Least of all is it tainted by any unnatural sexual attraction on either side. The blind and foolish fathers like Cymbeline and Leontes are replaced at last by the wise and magnanimous Prospero, even as the passionate and clamorous women of the late tragedies give way to the gentle but ardent figures of Imogen and Perdita and Miranda. The son and husband and lover of the late tragedies becomes the father of the romances, a role that he does not at first accept with perfect equanimity. Cymbeline clings to his role of husband with a vicious second wife who turns him into a doting fool, to the neglect of the best interests of his daughter. And Leontes indulges a raging jealousy on behalf of his wife, to the near destruction of their daughter. Only Prospero is set before us as a father and nothing more.

As is regularly noted in accounts of the romances, their principal figures have a way of recapitulating dramatic fates from earlier plays, but in a nontragic key. Thus both Posthumus and Leontes are Othellos who have not in fact killed their Desdemonas, and Cymbeline is a weaker Lear who has succumbed to the Goneril/Regan-like authority of his second wife, but who is ultimately delivered from the same by the not-untimely deaths of her and her son. Prospero's earlier avatar is the Duke in *Measure for Measure*: he conducts *The Tempest* as the Duke presides over the action of his play, though with a surer hand and to deeper ends. But it is the relation of both ducal figures to their play's feminine leads that is most striking. The Duke in *Measure for Measure* hovers protectingly over Isabella and presumably at the end of the play will take her in marriage, a prospect that has not always pleased audiences, however much scholars of the play may be edified by its moral-allegorical implications. Matters are more rationally—one is tempted to say more decorously—managed in *The Tempest*. Prospero's solicitude for Miranda is, appropriately, the solicitude of a father (as the Duke's solicitude for Isabella ought to be but apparently is not). And having protected and cherished the idealized figure of feminine chastity which has saved him from despair, Prospero, recognizing that Miranda can no longer appropriately be his, gives her up, along with his staff and his book.

Cloten, Autolycus, and Caliban:
Bearers of Parodic Burdens

Joan Hartwig

Not everyone would automatically categorize Cloten, Autolycus, and Caliban as musicians; it might even take a while to notice that they create similar effects in each play. Autolycus is easily recognizable as a musician because he enters *The Winter's Tale* singing; but how do Cloten and Caliban, figures more bestial than human, rank in the same category? I think that they qualify, but primarily in a negative sense.

Cloten hires a group of musicians to serenade Imogen in the morning, a device to win her favor. Does it work? No more than Cassio's "wind instrument" aubade works to soothe the disturbed nuptial morning of Othello and Desdemona.[1] But Cloten, and Cassio, at least know enough to *try* to use music to win favor, though neither understands that music has its own integrity and must be played from appropriate motives (and with appropriate instruments) in order to represent what it conventionally may—that is, concord in human relationships that signifies harmony with the larger cosmic order. Seen as a limited, manipulable tool, as Cloten obviously does see the aubade, the music's figurative, metaphysical values are not only unrealized, they are parodied.

For his part, Caliban offers a poetically inspired praise of the island's music, and he offers it to an inept and drunken audience—only to Stephano and Trinculo, as far as he is aware:

> Be not afeard, the isle is full of noises,
> Sounds, and sweet airs, that give delight and hurt not.
> (III.ii.135-136)

In this speech, Caliban demonstrates a musical or at least an aesthetic sensitivity. He had earlier corrected Stephano in his song of "Flout 'em and [scout] 'em" for having sung it to the wrong tune, at which point *"Ariel plays the tune on a tabor and pipe"* (III.ii.121.s.d.124); and it is in response to this tune played by "the picture of Nobody" (III.ii.126-27) that Caliban reassures his companions not to be afraid of the island's noises. Such musical sensitivity cannot be heard in his drunken song of freedom in an earlier scene:

> No more dams I'll make for fish,
>   Nor fetch in firing
>   At requiring,
> Nor scrape trenchering, nor wash dish.
>   'Ban, 'Ban, Ca-Caliban
> Has a new master, get a new man.
>
> Freedom, high-day! high-day, freedom! freedom, high-day, freedom!
>
> (II.ii.180-87)

Stephano responds to his drunken exhilaration with, "O brave monster! lead the way" (II.ii.188), and, as they leave the stage, the drunken trio visually parody the entire concept of rational leadership. In both the "sweet airs" speech and the drunken "freedom" song, Caliban provides a musical reference for his new companions and, through the inversion of his awareness, suggests that he carries a musical burden for the whole of Prospero's art.[2]

The last part of Act I in John Marston's *The Malcontent* evidences specifically the relationship between the Fool and the main character of the play in terms of a similar musical counterpoint. Malevole asks Passarello, "Canst sing, fool?" Passarello responds:

> Yes, I can sing, fool, if you'll bear the burden: and I can play upon instruments, scurvily, as gentlemen do. O, that I had been gelded! I should then have been a fat fool for a chamber, a squeaking fool for a tavern, and a private fool for all the ladies.
>
> (I.viii.2-6)[3]

According to William Chappell in *Popular Music of the Olden Time,* "the burden of a song, in the old acceptation of the word, was the base, foot, or under-song. It was sung throughout, and not merely at the end of the verse."[4] A fascinating linguistic history involving the confusion of "bourdon" and "burden" is detailed in the *OED*, under "Burden," IV:

> The earliest quotation for BOURDON[2] shows that the word was already confused with this. Apparently, the notion was that the bass or undersong was "heavier" than the air. The *bourdon* usually continued when the singer of the air paused at the end of the stanza, and (when vocal) was usually sung to words forming a refrain, being often taken up in chorus; . . . . As the refrain often expresses the pervading sentiment or thought of a poem, this use became coloured by the notion of "that which is carried" by the poem: its "gist" or essential contents.

Shakespeare's own interchangeable use of the two terms appears in *The Tempest,* I.ii, in Ariel's first song to Ferdinand. Ariel calls for the "sweet sprites" to bear the "burthen," and with anti-masquelike clumsiness the *"Burthen, dispersedly"* follows: "Bow-wow. . . . Cock-a-diddle-dow," a song which might make the modern ear wonder at Ferdinand's reaction: "Where should this music be? . . . sure, it waits upon/ Some god o' th' island" (I.ii.380-90). He is probably referring, as he says, to the sweeter part of the air, but he includes the crude refrain, or undersong, as worthy of the gods. In II.ii, Caliban enters *"with a burthen of wood"* (the other sense of the word "burden"), and his entrance seems clearly to prepare in parodic terms for Ferdinand's entrance in the next scene *"bearing a log"* (III.i).

It will be evident by now that I am using two words, "parodic" and "burden," with insistent frequency. The latter word has the double sense I have just indicated; the former is also a word with musical associations. In Greek drama, the "parode" referred to a side entrance into the orchestra, as well as to the "first ode sung by the chorus after entrance" (*OED*). As a song sung beside or against the central action, which took place in front of the proscenium, the Greek parode balances that which it is set against: for example, at the beginning of Aeschylus's *Agamemnon* the questioning by the Chorus beside the silent figure of Clytemnestra both literally and symbolically focuses on the Chorus's quest for truth which she and others consistently frustrate throughout the play.

Because of these musical origins, the word has an earlier and broader suggestiveness than that usually accorded it—a suggestiveness that Samuel Johnson includes in his definition of parody as "a kind of writing, in which the words of an author or his thoughts are taken, and by a slight change adapted to some new purpose."[5] Though in the modern sense, or in the "strict sense," as Leo Salingar terms it,[6] parody ridicules that which it imitates—reducing the original to literal and usually demeaning proportions—it seems to me that in the mind of the listener another almost simultaneous process occurs: when the original work is recalled through the reduced terms of its imitation, the original regains authority and fresh meaning because it is so far from the level of its burlesque imitation. The parody emphasizes similarities between the original (usually serious) and the imitation (usually comic); yet, because the contrast between levels of enactment is so great, parody also tends to polarize the imitated action. Thus, in my use of the term, parody heightens and expands, even as it qualifies and diminishes the meaning of the action which it imitates. I am emphasizing the musical derivations of both "parody" and "burden" in order to suggest a structural relationship between Cloten, Autolycus, and Caliban, and their plays.

Cloten is the least likeable of the three, less tolerable than Caliban possibly because he purports to be human and not a monster. They both smell bad, but Cloten's refusal to change his shirt reflects his obliviousness to human sensitivity, whereas Caliban's odor suggests a natural affinity with earth and sea. Upon Cloten's initial entrance, the First Lord tells him: "Sir, I would advise you to shift a shirt; the violence of action hath made you reek as a sacrifice" (I.ii.1-2). Cloten's offensive smell is the direct result of his unnatural attack upon the exiled, departing Posthumus; and Cloten's reply, "If my shirt were bloody, then to shift it" (I.ii.5), indicates the combination of violent intentions and comic obliviousness to decorum that characterizes him throughout *Cymbeline.* Caliban's smell, described by Trinculo who takes cover from the storm under Caliban's garments, is the result of his fishlike qualities: "What have we here? a man or a fish? dead or alive? A fish, he smells like a fish; a very ancient and fish-like smell" (II.ii.24-26). Both characters seriously threaten the welfare of people we care about; for both of them, the fool's bauble becomes an instrument of attempted rape, rather than the instrument for ladies' lustful dalliance, as Passarello and even Edgar's Poor Tom define it.[7] But in Caliban's case, Prospero controls the monster's potential deeds earlier and more obviously than the providential power in *Cymbeline* contains Cloten's attempts upon Imogen (III.v.137 ff.). Nonetheless, at first Cloten is amusing, and we must feel some gratitude that there is a worse fool than Posthumus to elicit our disfavor.

Shakespeare employs a subtle strategy of displacement in his introduction of Posthumus (already exiled at the play's beginning) and Cloten, his on-the-scene "understudy." The two Gentlemen who begin the play immediately draw a comparison between Cloten and Posthumus:

> He that hath miss'd the Princess is a thing
> Too bad for bad report; and he that hath her
> (I mean, that married her, alack, good man!
> And therefore banish'd) is a creature such
> As, to seek through the regions of the earth
> For one his like, there would be something failing
> In him that should compare.
>
> (I.i.16-22)

The initial contrast between the "thing/ Too bad for bad report" and the "creature" that surpasses hyperbolic praise continues through the minimal presentation of Posthumus. Although he has but a moment to exchange love tokens with his bride before taking his leave, he fulfills the formulaic expectations of a romantic lover-hero, whereas Cloten, the would-be lover-hero, is persistently present but thoroughly inept. What we hear about in glowing terms is Posthumus; what we see in his place is Cloten. What more convincing contrast is possible to affirm Imogen's choice of a husband? Shakespeare presents this contrast in several ways; for example, Imogen's response to her father represents the thorough disdain with which all the reasonable characters in the play look upon Cloten in comparison with Posthumus: "I chose an eagle,/ And did avoid a puttock" (I.i.139-40). Immediately thereafter, Cloten makes his first appearance, and we must agree with Imogen that he is a foolish figure, unworthy of entertaining any notions of her as a mate.

Thus far, we are filled with Posthumus's good reports, and with Cloten's obvious foolishness. The scene moves to Rome with reiterations of Posthumus's good report by Philario and the others, excepting Iachimo; and then, incredibly, we watch Posthumus fail to match his good report. He *agrees* to allow Iachimo to test Imogen's fidelity. To this point, Shakespeare has carefully paired Posthumus and Cloten as exact opposites on a scale of potentially heroic nobility; now he begins to bring them together through the disintegration of the delicate equation between Posthumus's external reputation and internal integrity, so that we can eventually see *with* Imogen the same noble frame in Cloten's headless corpse. This is a remarkable bit of psychological stagecraft.

The realization that Imogen's description of Cloten's headless corpse is a factual, if idealized, description of the body of the man she loves beyond life itself is stunning. Cloten, the fool, turns out to be identical with Posthumus in external terms, as he has boasted all along he was:

> . . . the lines of my body are as well drawn as his; no less young, more strong, not beneath him in fortunes, beyond him in the advantage of the time, above him in birth, alike conversant in general services, and more remarkable in single oppositions; yet this imperceiverant thing loves him in my despite. What mortality is! Posthumus, thy head, which now is growing upon thy shoulders, shall within this hour be off.
>
> (IV.i.9-17)

Many readers of the play, and even some who have seen it in live performance, fight Imogen's identification of Cloten with Posthumus to the bitter end. They say that she is, at this moment, uncharacteristically a foolish girl, misguided by her love for an unworthy man, dazed by the hardships of her wandering in Wales, and by her sleeping potion, not to mention Pisanio's report of Posthumus's rejection of her. So she cannot be held responsible for her assumption that this corpse is in fact Posthumus:

> A headless man? The garments of Posthumus?
> I know the shape of 's leg; this is his hand,
> His foot Mercurial, his Martial thigh,
> The brawns of Hercules; but his Jovial face—
> Murder in heaven? How? 'Tis gone.
>
> (IV.ii.308-12)

It certainly seems to be an uncomfortable moment in the play for the audience.

But if we examine the implications involved in our continuing acceptance of Imogen as a reasonable heroine, we are forced to acknowledge that, paradoxically, bodies have little to do with love. Cloten is transformed in death because of his headlessness into the physical twin of the man Imogen loves. And precisely because Posthumus has lost his head—his reasonableness—he is the figure that Cloten represents. We know that there is a substantial, though elusive difference, but we are chagrined by the blunt, comic confutation of our knowledge in this scene. What occurs in the way of our readjustment is fascinating. Because we must retain our respect for Imogen, we modify our disgust for Cloten, and as a by-product, Posthumus seems to recover some of the respect he has lost. A psychological tendency is to compensate for a compensation, and because we must give an inch to Cloten's former boast in order to exonerate Imogen's mistaken view of his headless corpse, we are eager to give a mile to Posthumus, whom we wanted to like from the start, but who has proved so unlikeable. It seems to me that this is a masterly maneuver of a playwright intent upon changing his audience's point of view from complacent morality to disturbed compromise.

We know that Shakespeare failed on occasion to change narrower and more secured perspectives. Samuel Johnson, in his famous denunciation of the "unresisting imbecility" of the play's artifices,[8] was not the last to voice discomfort with the play. I suggest, however, that Shakespeare here challenges a new kind of potential in his audience's awareness. We are asked *not* to look at Posthumus as a romance hero, although he starts out according to formula; *not* to see the plot as a romance (nor as a history); *not* to be confined by formulas of any kind, be they comic, satiric, pastoral, or tragic. Instead we are asked to accept evidence that life is a continuing dilemma-ridden confrontation with perplexities. In the use of an absurd figure like Cloten to represent literally a potentially noble figure like Posthumus, Shakespeare takes the technique of parodic parallel further than he has in earlier plays. What started out as parody ends as identification. When we accept the identification, as Imogen has, it is possible for Posthumus to be reborn out of the visibly present corpse of his counter-person, his fool who carried the burden. After the removal of the parodic fool, Posthumus regains the stage and gains as well a new, if not entirely regenerated, perspective on life, love, and the pursuit of tolerance.[9]

Cloten, like the fool in *Lear,* disappears halfway through the play's action. Autolycus, on the other hand, appears only after the catastrophe of Leontes' jealous outburst has occurred. Both Cloten and Autolycus put on the clothes of their counterparts, Posthumus and Florizel, but the effects of their mistaken identities are very different. It almost seems that Shakespeare was experimenting with the possibilities of parody that precedes and of parody that follows the imitated action.

J. H. P. Pafford, the Arden editor of *The Winter's Tale,* suggests that Autolycus "serves as a faint rhythmic parallel to the evil in Leontes in the first part of the play." Pafford makes very clear the distinction between the degrees of evil: "On the stage the crimes of Autolycus are hardly felony at all; they are primarily tricks. . . . [Whereas Leontes] is enveloped in black madness and is incompetent . . . [Autolycus] has a sunny roguish competence."[10] This seems to me to be an important distinction. There is a sense in which Autolycus replaces Leontes, much like the "understudy" function that Cloten fulfills for Posthumus. Both Cloten and Autolycus are onstage substitutes for figures who are absent and who are apparently more significant.

Autolycus's first song about the "sweet o' the year," when the birds' songs accompany his tumbling in the hay with his "aunts," directly contrasts the "winter's tale" that resulted from suspected sexual tumbling in Sicilia. Autolycus has tumbled in another way, from the service of Prince Florizel (who is soon to appear attired like Golden Apollo, disguised as a "poor humble swain" [IV.iv. 30-31]); and Leontes has certainly fallen out of service to Apollo when he denies Apollo's oracle (III.ii.140). Autolycus stresses his search for reinstatement from time to time, and finally influences the plot's conclusion because of his desire to regain favor with his master:

> I am courted now with a double occasion: gold and a
> means to do the Prince my master good; which who knows
> how that may turn back to my advancement?
>
> (IV.iv.833-35)

Autolycus's self-conscious announcement of his role, following the conclusion of the carefree song in which he promises "my account I well may give" (IV.iii.21), might remind us of Leontes' previous announcement of *his* role as royal cuckold:

Go play, boy, play. Thy mother plays, and I
Play too, but so disgrac'd a part, whose issue
Will hiss me to my grave: contempt and clamor
Will be my knell.

(I.ii.187-90)

Autolycus tells us that "My father nam'd me Autolycus, who being, as I am, litter'd under Mercury, was likewise a snapper-up of unconsider'd trifles" (IV.iii.24-26); he then proceeds to demonstrate how well he plays his assigned role by snapping up the trifle of the Clown's purse.

The style of Autolycus's performance far transcends the negative vibrations that would ordinarily be set in motion by the victimizing of the heroine's adoptive brother. Because we know the Clown is foolish, we cannot consider him strong support for Perdita's fortunes, but he is ostensibly of her party and is carrying the money for the purchases she has ordered. Therefore we are at least minimally on his side. I would suggest that the manipulation of the audience's sympathies in this scene is similar to that employed in the Sicilian scenes earlier. There, we wanted Hermione's honor to be defended against Leontes' accusations; here, we want Perdita's plans to be protected. The Clown, as the displaced victim for Perdita, becomes a comic parallel to Hermione, and their attackers deserve our condemnation. But neither Leontes nor Autolycus actually alienates us entirely. This is partially because of mitigating factors that derive from other characters' limitations: in Leontes' case, Paulina's shrewish harrassment provides mitigation, and in Autolycus's, the Clown's own inadequacies mark him as "a prize." We are caught between applauding Autolycus's cleverness as a rogue and worrying about the results of the Clown's aborted marketing mission. What keeps us from becoming too involved with the Clown's plight? One answer is that parody contains our reaction. The Good Samaritan scene undergoes parodic reenactment with the Clown standing in for the Good Samaritan.[11] But what prevents us from inferring that the allusion is seriously intended is the inadequacy of both the victim and the helper in this highway robbery. The Clown has already displayed his pragmatic distance from tragic event in the discovery scene of the abandoned Perdita and the devoured Antigonus: "I'll go see if the bear be gone from the gentleman and how much he hath eaten" (III.iii.128-30). He has acquired a sister and some prosperity, but he remains an objective fool who may either submit to or offer indignities to the human situation. Thus, he is an appropriate victim for Autolycus's refined skills as a "snapper-up of unconsider'd trifles."

Aside from the Good Samaritan parody, this scene may parody scenes within the play. Does Autolycus's groan, "O that ever I was born!" (IV.iii.50), remind us of another victim we have witnessed earlier? No exact imitation exists, but suggestive parody may. The posturing of Autolycus echoes Leontes' protestations of pain: "I have drunk, and seen the spider" (II.i.45), and "Nor night, nor day, no rest" (II.iii.1). The difference, as is characteristic of parody, is *between* the levels of enactment. The parallel reminds us of the vast differences between significant and silly actions. Leontes no less than Autolycus falsely sees himself as a victim. Leontes has convinced himself that Polixenes has violated his honor; Autolycus's false plea as victim literalizes Leontes' false plea as cuckold. The difference is that Autolycus knows he is controlling and manipulating others with his illusion, whereas Leontes succumbs to his own deluded creations.

A further level of the imitation exists: Autolycus is both his own attacker and victim; so is Leontes. They create imaginative realities that victimize themselves. Again, the difference between the original and the imitation is that Autolycus *knows* he is playing both parts. Leontes has to learn that he is.

The ballads that Autolycus offers to the country naifs at the sheep-shearing festival delight his audience not only because they deal with "such delicate burthens of dildos and fadings, 'jump her and thump her,'" etc. (IV.iv.194-95), but also because he assures them that these fantastic aberrations—"a usurer's wife [who] was brought to bed of twenty money-bags at a burthen" and a woman who "was turn'd into a cold fish for she would not exchange flesh with one that lov'd her" (IV.iv.263-80)—are true, and have been testified to by witnesses as well. The audience in the theater is delighted for other reasons: that these pastoral figures could believe in the "truth" of these monstrous exaggerations is a comic absurdity. Yet this awareness parallels another that has not seemed funny to us: although these ballads that advise sexual license and the following of unnatural appetites are comically and obviously

false, they imitate Leontes' vision of corruption in Sicilia.[12]
Leontes has accepted his illusion as truth, just as Mopsa, Dorcas,
and the Clown accept the false illusions of Autolycus's ballads. In
both situations, the false illusion hypnotizes those who accept it.
Leontes' vision leads him to deny the truth of the oracle and also
leads to the loss of his wife and both children; Autolycus boasts
of pinching plackets and gelding codpieces of their purses while
his "herd" was "senseless . . . admiring the nothing of it" (IV.iv.
608-13). The suggestions of castration and sterility in both situations are the result of unreasonable fascination with sexual aberrations.

Autolycus, like Falstaff, requires much to be said in his behalf,
but I will make only one more point, about his silence in the final
scenes of the play. He is not present at the reconciliation of the
two kings or the recognition of Perdita and has to hear these
events reported by the three Gentlemen. They suggest that "such
a deal of wonder is broken out within this hour that ballad-makers
cannot be able to express it" (V.ii.23-25); and Autolycus, the
ballad-maker, tacitly agrees. If he is present at the revelation of
Hermione's statue, we hear nothing from him. His absence from
both these scenes of wonder underscores the difference in the
quality of the illusions that he has fabricated and the illusion of
Hermione's resurrection, where the positive values of art's recreative power are explored. Autolycus thus absorbs some of the disordering aspects of Leontes' disturbed imagination from the first
of the play; and, by containing disorder through comic inconsequence, he provides an undersong which contrasts with and makes
more credible Leontes' release from false illusion.

Autolycus's silence in the final scene of wonder contrasts
markedly with Caliban's statement of wonder when he sees the
finely attired court group and recognizes his true master in his
ducal clothing: "O Setebos, these be brave spirits indeed!/ How
fine my master is!" (V.i.261-62). Caliban's response obviously
parodies Miranda's "O brave new world/ That has such people
in't" (V.i.183-84); both Caliban and Miranda are looking at a
company that includes the criminal and unrepentant Antonio
and his less than regenerated conspirator Sebastian. But a significant point is that Caliban singles out his former master, against
whom he has been plotting throughout the play, to recognize as
wondrously fine. Probably as much to Prospero's surprise as to

ours, Caliban voluntarily promises to "be wise hereafter,/ And seek for grace" (V.i.295-96).

Clifford Leech has suggested that Prospero's resumed ducal clothing converts Caliban and thus provides an ironic comment on the trappings of the world.[13] But it is just as possible that Caliban, freed from the imposed aesthetics of Prospero's mind, sees clearly for himself what is rightly purposed from Prospero's resumption of his ducal role in the world. Caliban's perception of what *is* possibly goes even further than Miranda's innocent perception of what may be; nor is he simply overwhelmed by glittering clothes. When the "glistering apparel" (IV.i.193.s.d.) was laid in his path, unpersoned, as temptation to visual splendor, Caliban rejected it in favor of his homicidal pursuits. Only Stephano and Trinculo allowed that line full of glittering cloth to delay them; Caliban was clearly aware of the trap. When Trinculo exclaims, "Look what a wardrobe here is for thee!," Caliban cautions him to "Let it alone, thou fool, it is but trash" (IV.i.223-34).[14]

It seems that in a providentially oriented world, even unregenerate natures may recognize the intended concordance between a man's clothes and his duty. To suggest that Caliban, like Miranda, is "taken in," is to miss the point of Prospero's emergence as a human being in the play. This *is* a beauteous company, not necessarily because of the glitter of courtly attire, but because the wearers now understand and accept what their garments imply. They no longer abstain from their obligations to the robes of office, though Antonio no doubt will try. But Prospero's ironic " 'Tis new to thee" (V.i.184) does not totally control the final vision of the play.

Caliban, after all, has reenacted Antonio's earlier resistance to Prospero's control, and in more directly destructive terms. His plot continues the original exile of Prospero taken to its extremity in planned assassination. Because this plan is directed and acted out by an obviously deformed creature, distinct from the deceptively splendid Antonio, Caliban bears the burden of that entire conflict within the play proper and contains it through comic inconsequence. Whereas Antonio remains silent at the play's end, Caliban speaks of recognition, repentance, and recovery in words that have tremendous impact. Prospero's prescience apparently did not include this conversion.

There are many ways in which Caliban performs parodic actions, only a few of which I have noted here. Prospero's interruption of the masque that celebrates his daughter's engagement fully realizes the antimasquelike function of Caliban:

> *Enter certain* Reapers, *properly habited: they join with the Nymphs in a graceful dance, towards the end whereof Prospero starts suddenly, and speaks; after which, to a strange, hollow, and confused noise, they heavily vanish.*
>
> Pros. *[Aside.]* I had forgot that foul conspiracy
> Of the beast Caliban and his confederates
> Against my life. The minute of their plot
> Is almost come.
>
> (IV.i.138 s.d.-124)

In this case the antimasque is dramatized through Caliban's working out of his plot. The abrupt breaking off of ceremony here reserves more wonder for the final revelation that includes in it the exposed and controlled forces of darkness.

The burdens that all three of these antimasquelike figures carry are physical, philosophical, musical, and even priapic. They exert dramatically an energy, sexual and physical, that the figures they parody do not generate in themselves. Leontes, Posthumus, and Prospero are all somewhat austere figures in their demands for appropriate sexual expression. While Hermione is holding hands with Polixenes in a generous and friendly way, while Imogen unwittingly grants the villain Iachimo the rights to her chaste and privy chamber, while Miranda offers her innocence and love to Ferdinand, who is watching with skeptical eyes? Not only do Leontes, Posthumus, and Prospero become jealous observers, we in the audience become a little suspicious too. But with Autolycus (and the Bohemian Shepherd) we can consider "behind-door-work" as normal and tolerable human behavior; or with Cloten and Caliban we can assume the violability of a maid, and then readjust the romantic idealisms expressed by main characters toward a moderate perspective that mitigates excessive anxiety about either extreme. Cloten, Autolycus, and Caliban are able to carry disordering forces through their containing parodies for Posthumus, Leontes, and Prospero, who cannot afford to bear the burden, but who need a burden to complete their song.

Cymbeline's *Debt to Holinshed: The Richness of III.i*

Joan Warchol Rossi

Traditional scholarship informs us that *Cymbeline*'s historical thread is merely ornamentation. Most recently, Geoffrey Bullough has stated that *"Cymbeline* belongs to a definite tradition of plays in which a faint historical flavour was given to romantic material by the use of names and incidents from the Chronicles"; while he admits that the chronicle material is important, he concludes that the chief contribution of the setting is to "add epic atmosphere to a plot of domestic intrigue."[1] Because Shakespeare's later and better-known romances have a timeless and placeless quality, many scholars assume that *Cymbeline* must also follow this non-historical pattern—a premise which denies *Cymbeline* its individuality as well as the possibility of its unique construction.[2] I suggest that, far from providing only a convenient "epic" context, the story of Cymbeline, Britain, and Rome in Holinshed's *Chronicles of England, Scotland, and Ireland* suggested to Shakespeare several strands of his play and may even have provided the germ of its romantic plot.

Although Shakespeare deals directly with the historical matter in III.i, this scene has generated confusion over precisely where Shakespeare stands in relation to his characters' actions and values. Past interpretation has usually labeled the speeches of the Queen, Cloten, and Cymbeline as conventional inspired nationalism.[3] But does the structure of the scene itself bear out this conclusion? An analysis of III.i gives rise to several puzzling questions and leads to the conclusion that, throughout the scene, Shakespeare systematically undermines the conventional attitudes expressed at the outset.

Lucius begins the ceremonial scene by viewing Cymbeline's refusal of tribute as a failure to follow the tradition instituted by both nations' immediate forefathers: neither Caesar nor Cassibelan is long dead, yet Cymbeline has ignored the contract they had made between Rome and England. Lucius's request for tribute is immediately rejected by the Queen and Cloten. The Queen begins by appearing to be concerned with tradition: she says to Cymbeline: "Remember, sir, my liege,/ The kings your ancestors" (III.i.16-17). But her real concern surfaces immediately; she emphasizes "the natural bravery of [our] isle" (III.i.18) and the island's hazardous natural defenses which destroyed Caesar's fleet. We catch glimpses of a delight in destruction behind her account of boats sucked "up to th' topmast" (line 22) or "Like egg-shells . . . crack'd/ . . . 'gainst our rocks" (lines 28-29). She who in I.v has gathered flowers for poison here revels in nature's destructive powers. We should indeed be apprehensive about nationalism so expressed.

Cloten joins his mother in rejecting any bond or sense of fealty between Britain and Rome: "Britain's a world/ By itself, and we will nothing pay/ For wearing our own noses" (lines 12-14). He insists that might is the sole basis for sovereignty: "Our kingdom is stronger than it was at that time; and . . . there is no moe such Caesars" (lines 34-35). An important part of this warrior code is its all-or-nothing aspect: "you shall find us in our saltwater girdle. If you beat us out of it, it is yours; if you fail in the adventure, our crows shall fare the better for you; and there's an end" (lines 79-82). Those who view Posthumus's assertion that England will not pay "any penny tribute" (II.iv.20) as an indication that Shakespeare approves Cloten's delight in Britain's increased military strength[4] do not consider the fact that this similarity points up an uncomfortable parallel between the two characters. Like Cloten, Posthumus is an all-or-nothing man in his wager with Iachimo: "Only thus far you shall answer: if you make your voyage upon her and give me directly to understand you have prevail'd, I am no further your enemy; she is not worth our debate. If she remain unseduc'd . . . you shall answer me with your sword" (I.iv.157-63). Both characters demonstrate a destructive inflexibility.

Cymbeline responds to Lucius's evocation of bonds and tradition in still another way, by appealing to the ancient British laws which Roman law had replaced. Establishing the ancient laws had made Mulmutius great; Cymbeline intends to achieve greatness

himself by restoring those laws. (However, what Cymbeline reveals of his understanding of law suggests only a limited potential
for success. His insistence on the letter of parental and penal law
without sensitivity to the spirit behind these laws has driven his
daughter from him and will later allow him to order the execution
of a long-lost son.) Another reason for Cymbeline's refusal
emerges as the scene progresses. After formally declaring war,
Lucius adds a private note of thanks and courtesy, which Cymbeline seems to take as a signal for a relaxation of ceremony. He
drops the royal "we" from his speech, addresses Lucius by his
first name, and reveals a pragmatic reason for his denial of tribute:

> I am perfect
> That the Pannonians and Dalmatians for
> Their liberties are now in arms, a president
> Which not to read would show the Britains cold.
> So Caesar shall not find them.
>
> (Lines 72-76)

If, as past scholarship would have it, Shakespeare is trying to move
his audience to nostalgic nationalism, why does he allow his scene
to degenerate from romantic rhetoric to practical politics? Why
does he undercut the motives of the Queen, Cloten, and Cymbeline if theirs is the right position? The answers may lie in a close
look at Shakespeare's source material.

In the *History of England* the material Holinshed offers for
Cymbeline's time has a definite bias in favor of Rome and of
peace. The first version of Cymbeline's reign that appears in the
Chronicles is standard, taken mainly from Fabyan: Kymbeline
"was brought vp at Rome, and there made knight by Augustus
Cesar, vunder whome he serued in the warres, and was in such
fauour with him, that he was at libertie to pay his tribute or not.
Little other mention is made of his dooings, except that during
his reigne, the Sauiour of the world our Lord Iesus Christ the
onelie sonne of God was borne of a virgine."[5] The second and
richer account that appears is culled from the Roman histories
and maintains the pro-Roman bias as well. Here Augustus is a
reluctant adversary; the Britons have refused to pay tribute
immediately upon the death of Julius Caesar, but Augustus "was
contented to winke" for ten years. When he finally does outfit
an expedition for Britain, he is delayed by rebellions elsewhere

three times. It is important to note that these rebellions do not, as they do in Shakespeare, directly influence the British to refuse tribute; they occur at least ten years after Caesar's death and actually prevent Rome from warring with Britain. The passage in the *Chronicles* continues: "But whether this controuersie which appeareth to fall forth betwixt the Britains and Augustus, was occasioned by Kymbeline, or some other prince of the Britains, I haue not to auouch" (1:480). This statement indicates that blame for the controversy lies with the Britons—a situation echoed in Shakespeare's play. But the *Chronicles* tend to exonerate Kymbeline, who "chieflie was loth to breake with them, because the youth of the Britaine nation should not be depriued of the benefit to be trained and brought vp among the Romans, whereby they might learne both to behaue themselues like ciuill men, and to atteine to the knowledge of feats of warre" (1:480).

Shakespeare also rearranges the facts to explore the implications of the "libertie" that the *Chronicles* attribute to Kymbeline. In the play, Rome immediately demands Britain's neglected tribute and declares war upon the British refusal. Not until the end of the play is Cymbeline "at libertie to pay his tribute or not." His decision to pay after he has won not only the right to refuse but the freedom to sever all Roman ties and to make Britain, in Cloten's phrase, "a world/ By itself" emphasizes the play's focus on the voluntary restriction of freedom necessary to all enduring human bonds.

According to Holinshed, British ambassadors appear at Rome offering friendship, and tribute is prudently set, to be gathered with great care so as not to provoke a rebellion. The impression of Rome as peace-lover and peace-keeper is very strong here. But there is also something else. While this second account does not allude to Christ's birth during Kymbeline's reign, the final paragraph implies that the Hand of God actually helped Rome to achieve world peace: "But whether for this respect, or for that it pleased the almightie God so to dispose the minds of men at that present, not onelie the Britains, but in manner all other nations were contented to be obedient to the Romane empire" (1:480). The divine impulse is here connected with the goals, influence, and atmosphere of Rome.

Much that leads to peace in Holinshed's accounts becomes, in contrast, motive for war in Shakespeare's play. In III.i Cymbeline begins by condemning Caesar's ambition and the yoke of subjection which does not become the "warlike" Britons. Insisting that Britain should resist foreign tyranny, he appeals to the memory of Mulmutius Dunwallow as justification for this war. If we turn to the *Chronicles,* we find that, curiously, Mulmutius was noted for his devotion to peace. He was "a right worthie prince. He builded within the citie of London then called Troinouant, a temple, and named it the temple of peace: the which . . . was the same which now is called Blackwell hall, where the market for buieng and selling of cloths is kept" (1.451). Cymbeline's appeal to the memory of a peace-loving monarch when he is about to provoke a war is thus ironically short-sighted. Perhaps Shakespeare recognized a similar irony in the degeneration of Mulmutius's temple of peace into a marketplace, in the transformation of philosophic concerns into questions of buying and selling. Cloten, probably named after Mulmutius's father, has a marketplace mentality: he will fight before paying something for nothing (III.i.42-45). Similarly, the play's mercantile imagery may well have had its inspiration in the *Chronicles'* attribution to Mulmutius of the appointment of "weights and measures, with the which men should buy and sell" (1.451). And the temple's new character as a clothing outlet may well have suggested the play's clothing imagery. In going out of his way to include Mulmutius, Shakespeare may be providing a clue to what stimulated him to build his romance upon this particular piece of history.

Cymbeline's final off-the-record argument reverses another of his predecessor's motives for peace in Holinshed's account. Like Holinshed's king, Cymbeline admits his fealty to Augustus Caesar:

> Thy Caesar knighted me; my youth I spent
> Much under him; of him I gather'd honor,
> Which he to seek of me again, perforce,
> Behooves me keep at utterance.

> (Lines 69-72)

But, unlike Kymbeline, he then rejects that fealty in order to pursue more "honor." The failure to recognize a golden opportunity to strike while Rome is weakened by its attempts to subdue the Dalmatians and the Pannonians would "show the Britains cold." Shakespeare here deliberately manipulates his chronicle sources to make Cymbeline follow the lead of the barbaric nations.

The concern with what "becomes" a warlike people, the pursuit of "honor," and the concern with how the Britons would "show" reveal a motivation considerably less than idealistic. Cymbeline has a Hotspur-like concern for plucking up honor, an obsession which blinds him to the greatest breach of honor—the breaking of the fealty bond.

Thus a careful examination of Holinshed's *Chronicles* suggests that the dramatic function of III.i is far richer than we might otherwise think. Reading a little further in Holinshed may also explain Shakespeare's inclusion of certain other strands. Holinshed's account of the Roman Claudius's landing to quell a British rebellion in which "the backes of the Britains in stead of a shield . . . showed to the persecutors" (1.484) might easily have suggested to Shakespeare the Hay episode from the *History of Scotland*. Shakespeare had certainly encountered this episode in the Scottish history a few years earlier, for the Hay story is sandwiched between the accounts of Donwald and the murder of Duncan on which he had drawn for *Macbeth*. Hay, a poor husbandman, and his two young sons find themselves in the midst of a battle between the Scots and the Danes. They join the Scottish cause, and, as the Scots begin to lose the battle and flee the field, Hay and his sons "placed themselues ouerthwart the lane" and "beat them backe whome they met fleeing." These efforts rally the Scots and turn the tide of the battle so that the Danes are ultimately defeated. The parallels between the Hay episode and the actions of Belarius, Guiderius, and Arviragus are striking and obvious. We find a similar parallel in Holinshed's second account of Claudius's landing in England. This recounting of the rebellion adds the story of Hamo, a Roman Posthumus-prototype, who changed his armor for that of a Briton. The reversal, at least, suggests Posthumus's shift from Roman to British warrior.

In adapting the pro-Roman view of the *History of England* to his own purposes, Shakespeare had to reject the view of the *History of Scotland*.[6] Here again the *Chronicles* refer to Kymbeline's reign as a peaceful one. But whereas in the English annals the rebellions occurring during the reigns of Guiderius and Arviragus are condemned as "breach[es] of peace" caused by "pride," the Scottish account seems to approve the defying of a Rome significantly different in character from that of the earlier English history. This Rome is a crafty and malicious manipulator.

Kymbeline's son Arviragus becomes a Roman pawn, forsaking the interests and ethical code of his people. Upon his ascent to the throne, Arviragus "vpon some priuate displeasure" puts away his wife Voada, sister of the Scottish king Caratake, and marries Genissa, a Roman. Although any Englishman who had lived during or shortly after the reign of Henry VIII might be expected to tolerate the marital whims of a king, the *Chronicles* nonetheless strip Arviragus of the one possible excuse for this behavior: he already has "faire issue" by Voada, a son and two daughters whom he intends to disinherit. Lacking the justification of a need to establish legitimate succession, his behavior becomes heinous. *The History of Scotland* repeats three times that the Britons are vehemently opposed to his deeds. The account adds, however, that these deeds had been counselled by the Roman, Aulus Planctius, for political purposes, "thereby to breake all friendship and aliance betwixt the Britaines and the Scots, to the end that in no case of rebellion they should ioine their powers togither" (5.62). But Arviragus occasions a British rebellion instead, and he is forced to seek Claudius's help to quell it. The pro-Voada forces are overthrown, but there immediately follows a more organized and larger rebellion by Lancastershire, Yorkshire, and Darbyshire. The "Britains" (and here the term excludes the king) prepare to battle "the Romans & Aruiragus, who went about to bring them wholie vnder seruile subiection and thraldome of the same Romans" (5.62). Caratake adds the support of Scotland to the anti-Arviragus forces. There is a tremendous battle; both sides fight with equal valor and because of heavy losses quit the field.

After the battle, Arviragus acknowledges his error in turning against his own people, changes sides, and joins his countrymen "to recouer the intire estate" and expel the Romans. His Roman wife Genissa "being at the same season great with child, tooke such thought for this reuolting of hir husband, that trauelling before hir time, she immediatly died therwith" (5.64). Arviragus is once again completely British, having severed his treacherous political and marital ties to Rome, and the remainder of the war becomes a typical Britain-Rome conflict in which Britain is valiant yet is defeated by a supernatural force. Vespasian arrives on the island, takes command of the well-disciplined Roman troops, and marches against the Britons. There is a fierce battle but fortune, not Roman superiority, is Britain's only enemy.[7] Arviragus tries to commit suicide, but he is prevented by his servants "that hee might be reserued yet vnto some better fortune" (5.65). Arviragus resigns himself and England to Roman dominance, considering "how by reason of this great discomfiture, it was vnpossible to resist the Romane puissance" (5.65). He sends an offer of peace. Vespasian responds with full but not unconditional pardon: "Aruiragus seeing no other remedie, came in vnto Vespasian, according to his appointment, and vpon his submission was pardoned of all his trespasse, and placed againe in the kingdome" (5.65). Nobles, even whole towns are included in the pardon, but Vespasian asks that hostages be delivered "for the better assurance of their loialtie in time to come" (5.65).

Although the *History of Scotland*'s account of Kymbeline and his sons is told from a viewpoint not shared by Shakespeare, it might be well to note that this account came replete with a broken marriage. Indeed, it may not be going too far to suggest that Arviragus's marital difficulties in Holinshed's Scottish version may have given Shakespeare his first hint for the Posthumus-Imogen plot. Although this account has never been cited as a source, direct or indirect, for *Cymbeline,* some of the parallels and similarities of incident are tantalizingly suggestive: the mixture of marriage, politics, and poor judgment; the sudden change of perception and acknowledgement of error by the king; the sudden and fortuitous death of the Roman (that is, wicked) second wife-queen, taking with her the unborn rival claimant to the throne; the matter of hostages and pardon; the influence of a higher power (fortune) in the battle; the final capitulation to Rome. Given Arviragus as the pawn of the devious Roman, Aulus Planctius, Shakespeare needed only to go one step further to make Posthumus the pawn of the devious Renaissance Italian Iachimo. He thereby echoes both of the attitudes towards Rome expressed in the *Chronicles*: the paternal guiding influence in the *History of England* is attributed to classical Rome, the crafty manipulation in the *History of Scotland* to Renaissance Italy. Such evidence at least counters the theory that Shakespeare first settled on the romantic Boccaccio plot and then looked for a convenient "historical" framework. Shakespeare may in fact have first considered history and found within his historical material the suggestions of a romance which he later developed. Serious consideration of the *Chronicles* as a major influence certainly helps in understanding the dramatic intention of III.i and may even do much to explain Shakespeare's combination of disparate elements in his play, for he could have found the rudiments of such a combination in Holinshed's accounts.

8

Tragic Structure in The Winter's Tale: *The Affective Dimension*

Charles Frey

To judge by the classifications of plays in the First Folio, Shakespeare's colleagues, if not Shakespeare himself, thought *The Winter's Tale* and *The Tempest* comedies and *Cymbeline* a tragedy. Of *Pericles,* it seems, they scarcely thought at all, for that play was omitted from their collection. Only after two hundred and fifty years of study were the four plays identified as written consecutively and late in Shakespeare's career. When, about a century ago, scholars began to term the plays "romances" and then even to group them, in collected editions, under that separate heading, they opened a brilliant chapter in Shakespearean interpretation. Not only did the generic label "romance" suggest that there were significant correlations among the plays—correlations which might set them off from all the rest in the fashion that "problem" plays or "Roman" plays are sometimes set off—but also the focus upon romance suggested the special relevance of a literary tradition invested with awesome age, universality, and power.

Romance, the dominant mode of fiction-making numbering among its heroes Odysseus, Alcestis, Apollonius of Tyre, the knights of Charlemagne and Arthur, protagonists of Spenser, Sidney, Greene, Cervantes, and thousands more, usually tells, of course, the elemental story of journey and, sometimes, of return. Return, forgiveness, and reconciliation are much stressed in Shakespeare's romance, and those who, like Edward Dowden, first applied the term did so to suggest the plays' aura of post-tragic acceptance and benign spirituality:

Characteristics of versification and style, and the enlarged place given to scenic spectacle, indicate that these plays were produced much about the same time. But the ties of deepest kinship between them are spiritual. There is a certain romantic element in each. They receive

contributions from every portion of Shakspere's genius, but all are
mellowed, refined, made exquisite; they avoid the extremes of broad
humour and of tragic intensity; they were written with less of passionate concentration than the plays which immediately precede them,
but with more of a spirit of deep or exquisite recreation.[1]

Today, while we are grateful for the insights of an earlier age into
Shakespeare's recreative spirit of romance, we may doubt that he
eschewed "tragic intensity" or that he wrote these plays with less
than "passionate concentration." We are, indeed, rediscovering
for ourselves both the seriousness and craft of romance, and we
are finding in the vaults of Shakespeare's late plays both dark
chambers to be explored and curious treasures that may defy the
light.

One speaks of dark chambers, because in each Shakespearean
romance a motive power of plot arises from the mind's fascination
with familial taboo. *Pericles* opens upon the theme of incest.
Posthumus Leonatus, in *Cymbeline,* and Leontes, in *The Winter's
Tale,* both accuse their wives of adultery. Posthumus himself
was bred in Cymbeline's bedchamber and yet secretly married
Imogen, making himself thus "poison to Cymbeline's blood."
Prospero says of his usurping brother: "he was/ The ivy which
had hid my princely trunk,/ And suck'd my verdure out on't"
(I.ii.85-87). These perceptions of over-close relations in the plays,
relations that threaten the place of potency of each hero, may be
associated with a loss of power to procreate sons, for in each play
the ruler who conceives a daughter is bereft of wife and any sons
he may already have. Perhaps a king in a patrilineal society who
sires a daughter is deemed guilty of less than ideal potency and
hence subject to usurpation. Or perhaps, as *Pericles* suggests, the
sad function of a daughter who is an only child, at least in the
world of romance, is not to stay at home where her father may
find her sexually tempting but instead to travel into strange lands
and there win a husband—preferably, it turns out, the son of her
father's chief enemy to whom her father can now be reconciled.

Whether or not we understand its origins, separation of wives
and daughters from husbands and home remains a chief feature
of Shakespearean romance, and some sort of familial over-
closeness, real or imagined, often initiates the action. We need to
explore more fully how the romances portray man's mistrust and
mistreatment of woman and with what dramatic impact. In *The*

Winter's Tale, the jealousy of Leontes and its consequences are made manifest through a passionate concentration of forms that reach, surely, that tragic intensity Dowden denied to the romances.

During the first three acts of *The Winter's Tale,* Leontes appears four times and each time does the same thing: he denounces Hermione or her surrogate, Paulina, and is rebuked by representatives of his court. To be more precise, in a theme with little variation, Leontes four times expresses his misogyny, separates mother from child, and confronts indignant bystanders. Even if the play were dumb show, this reenacted emblem of blighted affection would work deep into the consciousness of spectators.

During his first appearance onstage (I.ii), Leontes watches Hermione as she holds Polixenes' hand; they withdraw from him, and soon he dismisses Mamillius. His violent argument with Camillo follows. In the third scene, he comes upon Hermione and Mamillius, pulls the boy from her, forces them to separate exits, and faces the rebukes of Antigonus and the lords. The fifth scene shows the king attacking and dismissing Paulina and banishing Perdita in the arms of her defender, Antigonus. In the seventh scene, the trial scene, Leontes attacks Hermione, loses Mamillius and her, and suffers the stinging rebuke of Paulina.

The purpose of this reduplicating structure is not primarily to advance the plot, nor is it to explore the motivations of the king. It serves instead to amplify the dimensions of his nightmare and to demonstrate in wider ambit the consequences of his condition. An audience will persist in finding Leontes mad, but will find it harder and harder to ignore the implications of that madness. His idiom spawns violence, and the audience sees an increasingly violent series of expulsions:

> Bear the boy hence.
>
> (II.i.59)
>
> Away with her, to prison!
>
> (II.i.103)
>
> Go, do our bidding; hence!
>
> (II.i.125)
>
> Leave me solely; go.
>
> (II.iii.17)

> Away with that audacious lady!
>
>   (II.iii.42)
>
> Hence with her, out o' door!
>
>   (II.iii.68)
>
> Will you not push her out?
>
>   (II.iii.74)

As the audience hears Leontes conceive his jealousy, accuse Hermione, debate Paulina, and conduct the trial, it also sees him rejecting advice, dismissing women, losing company, being left alone, so that, while he orally projects an image of alienated man, he iconographically enacts the part as well.

Many of the exits away from Leontes, moreover, are lingering and pointed. Twenty-five lines elapse between his first command to Mamillius—"Go, play" (I.ii.187)—and the completed exit. Nearly as many form the interval between his dismissal of Hermione and her exit, and then the queen delivers a pointed withdrawal speech:

> Who is't that goes with me? . . .
> . . . .
> . . . . Do not weep, good fools,
> . . . .
> . . . . this action I now go on
> Is for my better grace. Adieu, my lord,
> I never wish'd to see you sorry, now
> I trust I shall. My women, come, you have leave.
>
>   (II.i.116-24)

When Paulina brings the infant Perdita to Leontes at night, the entire scene becomes a drawn-out portrayal of the king's physical repulsion. Paulina's final speech points graphically to what must be happening onstage:

> I pray you do not push me, I'll be gone.
> Look to your babe, my lord, 'tis yours. Jove send her
> A better guiding spirit! What needs these hands?
> You, that are thus so tender o'er his follies,
> Will never do him good, not one of you.
> So, so. Farewell, we are gone.
>
>   (II.iii.125-30)

Even the announcement of Mamillius's death is put in terms of withdrawal, departure:

> *Servant.*   O sir, I shall be hated to report it!
>   The Prince your son, with mere conceit and fear
>   Of the Queen's speed, is gone.
> *Leontes.*   How? gone?
> *Servant.*   Is dead.
>   (III.ii.143-45)

In the tragic part of the play, all the Leontean scenes are presented in specific terms of "going." Not only does Leontes physically repel Hermione, Mamillius, Polixenes, Camillo, Paulina, Perdita, and Antigonus, he also seeks to disengage himself from the very ongoing nature of life. His is a cold spirit of negativism. Brooding like the winter on a procreative past that brought with life a knowledge of death—"when/ Three crabbed months had sour'd themselves to death" (I.ii.102)—Leontes expresses his fear of time through hatred of sex, a hysterical misogyny, and obsessive threats of death.

The attitude toward sex is plain enough: "Go to, go to!/ How she holds up the neb! the bill to him!" (I.ii.182-83). One thinks of Lear's "The wren goes to't, and the small gilded fly/ Does lecher in my sight" (IV.vi.112-13). For Leontes as well, the going-to of sex has become horribly repulsive; affection "stabs" and "infects," "revolted" wives are "sluiced" by paramours, the flax wench "puts to," his sheets are "spotted." But, unlike Lear, Leontes keeps his vision of sexual corruption within a relatively narrow focus; all the blame is heaped on women. Misogyny is his distinctive accent:

>   women say so—
>   That will say any thing . . . .
>   (I.ii.130-31)

>   O thou thing!
>   (II.i.82)

>   She's an adultress.
>   (II.i.78)

>   He dreads his wife. . . . a callat
>   Of boundless tongue . . . .
>   (II.iii.80 . . . 91-92)

> I ne'er heard yet
> That any of these bolder vices wanted
> Less impudence to gainsay what they did
> Than to perform it first.
>
> (III.ii.54-57)

Suiting the word to the action, he four times stands across from a woman whom he attacks for "going" and whom he then causes to "go" from the stage.

It is crucially important to realize that such sex-combat or rejection of women organizes the entire visual structure of the play's first half. Once we grasp the pattern, much that remains falls into place. Leontes' rejection of women accompanies his attempt to be self-sufficient, to protect his oft-mentioned "heart," to be the "center," and to found his "faith" only upon himself. He will not share the creative process with anyone else. He seeks to be the sole dispenser of life and death, to run the show:

> Is this nothing?
> Why then the world and all that's in't is nothing.
>
> (I.ii.292-93)

> you may as well
> Forbid the sea for to obey the moon
> As or by oath remove or counsel shake
> The fabric of his folly, whose foundation
> Is pil'd upon his faith, and will continue
> The standing of his body.
>
> (I.ii.426-31)

> if I mistake
> In those foundations which I build upon,
> The centre is not big enough to bear
> A schoolboy's top.
>
> (II.i.101-3)

> There is no truth at all i' th' oracle.
>
> (III.ii.140)

Leontes' faith is founded where it should not be, in himself alone. When he denies the oracle, he openly presumes against the godhead, denies his created status. As king he has perhaps some reason to become trapped in divine analogy, but as man, dependent upon woman in order to play his part in creation, he cannot be self-sufficient. He cannot promise life by himself. He can only

threaten death. And when he banishes woman, his becomes equally an idiom of death:

> give mine enemy a lasting wink.
>
> (I.ii.317)
>
> Commit them to the fire!
>
> (II.iii.96)
>
> The bastard brains with these my proper hands
> Shall I dash out.
>
> (II.iii.140-41)
>
> for the fail
> Of any point in't shall not only be
> Death to thyself but to thy lewd-tongu'd wife.
>
> (II.iii.170-72)
>
> Look for no less than death.
>
> (III.ii.91)

Shakespeare's reduplicating structure thus forces the audience
to hear and see, remember and anticipate, the one strikingly
obsessive act on Leontes' part, that is, rejection and expulsion
of women, kin, and company, together with threats of death. In
many ways, Leontes shows himself caught in the quintessential
winter's tale, enacting the title of the play, unable to see ahead
to "this coming summer," looking back in anguish to a time when
lambs frisked in the sun. He has become the lion in winter, old
man winter, the character in Mamillius's story ("a sad tale's best
for winter") who "dwelt by a church-yard" of graves. Our penul-
timate image of him in the tragic portion of the play is as a man
caught in the deepest winter of despair. After announcing Hermione's death, Paulina, at least momentarily, denies Leontes the
power of effective repentance:

> A thousand knees,
> Ten thousand years together, naked, fasting,
> Upon a barren mountain, and still winter
> In storm perpetual, could not move the gods
> To look that way thou wert.
>
> (III.ii.210-14)

Shakespeare's materializing imagination will immediately produce
a wintry storm and present onstage the violent death of Antigonus.

An audience watching and weighing the four pulsations of madness outlined here should find, during a well-directed and well-acted performance, that Leontes' storm perpetual is regularly if briefly interrupted by a still small voice. All four of the king's scenes are crowded, loud, violent, rhetorically flamboyant. Each is self-fragmenting as exits are made away from Leontes. Hatred and death are the topics, fear and alienation the results. This deepening human winter is in essence the plot. But there is a counterplot.

The counterplot consists of the four relatively brief moments when Leontes is offstage. They are: (1) the conversation of Camillo and Archidamus in the first scene, (2) the meeting of Camillo and Polixenes at the end of the second scene together with the abbreviated tale of Mamillius at the beginning of the third scene, (3) Paulina at the prison in the fourth scene, and (4) the messengers returning from Delphos in the sixth scene. What the audience sees when Leontes is onstage is opposition leading to static isolation. What it sees when he is offstage is cooperation leading to the forward movement of a pair. Archidamus turns from fending off imagined accusations to agreeing with Camillo in the hopes of the young Mamillius; the two counsellors pass across the stage in final amity. After Leontes reveals his jealousy, Camillo meets Polixenes, and they decide to escape together. We see them pass across the stage as friends. Paulina, in the prison, gathers Emilia to her purpose and exits with her. Cleomenes and Dion marvel at their Delphic journey and hasten forward to court.

Leontes, like the last season of the year, appears to look back and view all the generative goings-on of life as repugnant and ineffectual delays against death: "go to," "go, play," "go rot," "go," he says continually. The actors in the small, interstitial scenes are cast in a wholly different perspective. They look forward to *going* forward, and they grasp hopefully at generative continuity and renewal. Archidamus and Camillo forecast the great "going" of the play itself, the summer visit to Bohemia, and they see that the promise of youth freshens old hearts. Polixenes and Camillo find faith in each other by concentrating upon hereditary gentleness and honor, the regenerating opposites of that "hereditary imposition" noted earlier in the play. Polixenes speaks of "our parents' noble names,/ In whose success we are gentle" (I.ii.393-94). Camillo says: "by the honor of my parents, I/ Have utt'red truth" (I.ii.442-43), and Polixenes concludes: "Come, Camillo,/ I will respect thee as a father, if/ Thou bear'st my life off" (I.ii.460-62). In the four brief scenes, the audience can hear brave and hopeful redefinitions of the human family. Not only do the counsellors take physic from the prince and not only do the fleeing men find a certain family identity or bond between themselves, but also Paulina manages to absolve Perdita of inherited taint by stressing that she shares the higher and more universal parentage of us all:

> You need not fear it, sir.
> This child was prisoner to the womb, and is
> By law and process of great Nature thence
> Freed and enfranchis'd.
>
> (II.ii.56-59)

And, finally, as the little scenes take us further and further from Leontes' court and closer to the journey of the play itself, we experience a wider perspective upon the generative continuum that binds us together. The messengers sense that they have journeyed to the quick of nature: "The climate's delicate, the air most sweet,/ Fertile the isle" (III.i.1-2). Privileged to glance upward toward higher powers and to hear the "voice o' th' oracle,/ Kin to Jove's thunder" (III.i.9-10), they gain intimations of a new birth in the "event o' th' journey":

> When the oracle
> (Thus by Apollo's great divine seal'd up)
> Shall the contents discover, something rare
> Even then will rush to knowledge. Go; fresh horses!
> And gracious be the issue!
>
> (III.i.18-22)

This "going," unlike the goings that leave Leontes self-enclosed, rushes toward hope of issue. The whole image is one of birth as the seal gives way, the contents are discovered, and what is rare bursts forth. All four of the non-Leontean scenes thus have to do with accepting and indeed welcoming the progress of generation that makes life ongoing. Carefully opposed and interposed, as they are, against the blustering wrath of the king's scenes, these four moments invite the spectators to recall and anticipate a more sane idiom of praise, prayer, and hope. In them it is hinted that the red blood may someday reign in the winter's pale.

In the light of these scenic contrasts and their implications, we can better understand the theatrical force of *The Winter's Tale* in its tragic portion. The four scenes in which Leontes mis-defines Hermione or Paulina are all statue scenes. In each, he points an accusatory finger at a woman, centrally observed, and charges her with artifice and deceit. Hermione "plays"; she hangs "like her medal" about Bohemia's neck. Leontes sees his wife in terms of an art object, like a statue, to be examined by by-standers: "You, my lords,/ Look on her, mark her well" (II.i.64-65). He takes all for show: "Praise her but for this her without-door form" (II.i.69). He lives in a world of deceitful appearances. Earlier he had confessed: "I am angling," "I play too." Thinking of himself as "a very trick/ For them to play at will" (II.i.51-52), he complains that others laugh at him and "make their pastime" at his sorrow. His scenes with Hermione and Paulina have a staged quality. He forgets his lines and responds as would an actor: "O, I am out" (II.i.72). He thinks that Paulina was "set on" by Antigonus. He refuses, in other words, to accord to either of these women any sincerity, or stable inward faith. Believing that all is artifice and play, he seizes the role of artificer and playmaker. The trial scene is intended to be his masterpiece; there too Hermi-one stands like a statue in central isolation. "My life stands in the level of your dreams" (III.ii.81), she tells Leontes. It is a terrible truth. Leontes has become caught up in the nightmare of unfaith. To him, others lack reality; he thinks of them as being cold as dead men (II.i.151-52), past all shame (III.ii.84). In the play's final scene, he will help to wake a statue, but now he treats the living woman as if she were sleeping marble. When Hermione swoons and appears to die, Paulina aptly challenges Leontes to see if he "can bring/ Tincture or lustre in her lip, her eye,/ Heat outwardly or breath within . . ." (III.ii.204-6). The king, of course, can perform no such creative act; indeed he himself sinks to a shamed and still impotence.

We think of Shakespeare primarily as a verbal artist, forgetting his amazing power to enthrall us with sheer pictographic debate. Leontes at first out-Herods Herod, rising through a crescendo of furious gestures, secretly and then openly denouncing Hermione, striding forward to taunt among the spectators "many a man" with cuckoldry, pointing Hermione offstage, forcing Paulina's exit, stalking around the infant Perdita, plucking Antigonus's beard, striking the oracle from the hand of his astonished officer.

Yet all this happens in a dream of disrelation. The spectators, who have witnessed and suffered under the four assaults of tyrannical madness, must long, surely, for counterviolence, for revenge. It comes, of course, swiftly and, as often, perhaps even too harshly. When the panic-stricken messenger rushes in to shout that Mamillius is dead, when Hermione falls senseless, then Leontes halts in the very act of blaspheming Apollo and stands still at last, reduced now to silence, sculpted into the image of mortified man. And now the dialectical alternation of jealousy and trust is broken as Paulina begins to blast and purge the king's accumulated guilt. As Polixenes, on hearing of Leontes' suspicion, thought of Judas who "did betray the Best" (I.ii.419), so Paulina tells Leontes: "thou betrayedst Polixenes" (III.ii.185). It was a "damnable" act. That and the attempted corruption of Camillo were "trespasses." Even a "devil" would have repented before casting out Perdita. Following Leontes' contrast between Camillo's glistering "piety" and his own "black" deeds, Paulina's tirade (III.ii.175-214) smacks of exorcism. Here is an energetic and sustained recognition of the king's madness and a convincing rejection of it as well, a theatrically impressive and satisfying purgation.

A sense of sacred purgation at the close of the trial scene is entirely appropriate. When Leontes asks pardon for his "great profaneness" against the oracle (III.ii.154), we see that profaneness has been the overriding horror of the play. In *The Winter's Tale,* as in all the romances, Shakespeare shows the nothingness of life lived on the thin lateral line of the secular, where friendship and kinship may be thought to serve self-interest rather than the purposes of a higher order, "great creating nature." All the romances depict dramatic epiphanies when divine powers make themselves manifest and creatures on this worldly plane are reminded of the towering forces which intersect and influence their little linear lives. The halting steps which Leontes, with Paulina's help, now can take toward the "chapel" in furtherance of his penetential vows only hint at the vast journey to be taken by the play toward knowledge of a wide creation in which human love is seen to play its fruitful part. It will be a journey toward knowledge of "the gods themselves" in their full immanence and toward a capacity on all sides to respond when Paulina at last commands: "It is requir'd/ You do awake your faith" (V.iii.94-95). But that journey, to be successful, must not be lightly undertaken, and it is the burden of the play's tragic portion to make its audience hunger for the community and comfort of awakening faith. Through the intensity of Leontes' angry doubt and the antithetical structuring of scenes playing that doubt off against nascent belief, Shakespeare has caused *The Winter's Tale* to carry its often painful but always instructive burden supremely well.

9

The Restoration of Hermoine in The Winter's Tale

David M. Bergeron

On first seeing Hermione in V.iii, standing, in the words of the Folio stage direction, "like a Statue," we may be struck by this seeming cold pastoral that teases us out of thought as doth eternity. But under the guidance of Paulina, the singing master of Leontes' soul, the artifact of Hermione becomes the reality of the woman presumed dead for sixteen years. Small wonder, then, that readers, spectators, and critics have all responded to this startling event, which is unique in all of Shakespeare. Others have suggested the possibility that this renewal of Hermione was not in the earliest version of the play; I support their conjectures and then suggest dramatic and historical sources that may have affected Shakespeare's final design of the play, and consider the nature of the statue of Hermione. My argument is admittedly hypothetical, resting on debatable suppositions, but I believe that it is plausible.[1] I hope that one may finally be able to say of my argument, in the words of Autolycus, "there may be matter in it" (IV.iv.842).

Geoffrey Bullough writes: ". . . looking back over the dialogue, it is obvious that from the moment when Paulina brought news of Hermione's supposed death (III.3.170 ff.) [sic] the intention was to bring her back."[2] But such an intention has seldom proved obvious to most of the play's viewers. We have, I think, every reason to believe that Hermione is dead: Paulina, whom we trust, says that Hermione has died; Hermione's fate is not included in the message of the oracle (III.ii.132-36); Antigonus's vision in III.iii implies a dead Hermione (lines 15-45), and he in fact says, "I do believe/ Hermione hath suffer'd death" (lines 41-42). Certainly the experience of first-time readers or first-time spectators attests to the surprise of finding Hermione alive at the end.

Shakespeare also departs radically from his source, Greene's *Pandosto,* by letting Hermione live. These discrepancies between anticipation and realization, and between play and source, have led a number of people to conclude that somewhere along the line Shakespeare changed his intention and reworked the final act, thereby bringing Hermione to life and somewhat deemphasizing the restoration of Perdita and Leontes.[3]

An additional reason often given for such a conclusion is the evidence—or lack of evidence—of Dr. Simon Forman. The play was probably written in early 1611, and we know for a fact that Forman saw it at the Globe on 15 May 1611. Forman recalls the advent of Leontes' jealousy, the threat to Polixenes, the message of the oracle, the recovery of Perdita, and her restoration to her father; but the rest is silence—not a word about Hermione's revival in the final scene. How anyone could witness the statue's coming to life and not report it almost defies explanation. It is very easy and has been fashionable among some simply to dismiss Forman for the quack astrologer that he was and thus brush away his silence on the matter of Hermione.[4] But we know that Forman could be quite precise and meticulous about details, and his reports of *Macbeth* and *Cymbeline,* also seen in 1611, are reasonably full and accurate.[5]

Pointing out that Forman makes no allusion to the statue scene, Frank Kermode observes: ". . . the play may have been without it in its first form."[6] While concluding that on the whole he believes "the restoration of Hermione must have been part of Shakespeare's original plan," Kenneth Muir also allows that "it is possible that Hermione was not restored to life."[7] Acknowledging Shakespeare's departure from his source and the silence of Forman, W. W. Greg writes: "There are also some hints in Acts III and IV both that Hermione is really dead and that the climax of the play was to be the recognition of Perdita, which in the extant version is curiously slurred over. It has been suggested with some plausibility that the last act as we have it is not the original conclusion of the play."

Assuming at least for the sake of my argument that Shakespeare reshaped *The Winter's Tale* after its first version to include the statue scene, what may have influenced him to do so? We need look no farther than the Lord Mayor's Show presented in the streets of London on 29 October 1611; this civic pageant, entitled *Chruso-thriambos: The Triumphes of Golde,* was written by Anthony Munday, a prolific pageant writer. In his several essays on *The Winter's Tale,* Glynne Wickham has drawn links between it and Munday's pageants of 1605 and 1610, but curiously he has never examined the 1611 show. Several critics have called attention to the masque-like nature of the statue scene, without specifying clearly what the masque elements are and to what masque they may correspond. Richard Studing, for example, says only that "the elements of masque are employed to intensify spectacular dramatic experience"; and Inga-Stina Ewbank observes, "When the statue comes alive, it is as though we were witnessing the central movement of a masque, with music as accompaniment."[8] In light of Munday's 1611 civic entertainment, one can with good reason suggest that not only is the statue scene pageant-like in a number of specific ways, but it also contains striking parallels to one particular pageant.

One fact that links Shakespeare and the pageant is, as I have discussed elsewhere, the performance of John Lowin of the King's Men in the role of Leofstane in *Chruso-thriambos.*[9] Lowin participated primarily because he was a member of the Goldsmiths, the guild that sponsored the show and from which the new mayor came. It is thus difficult to imagine that Shakespeare did not know something about the show, just as it has become almost axiomatic that he was familiar with the Kenilworth (1575) and Elvetham (1591) entertainments as evidenced in *Love's Labor's Lost* and *A Midsummer Night's Dream.* Munday's 1611 show has additional importance because it was expected that Queen Anne would witness the pageant.[10]

Common to both *The Winter's Tale* and *Chruso-thriambos* is the presence of a figure called Time.[11] Cyrus Hoy points out that the appearance of Time as the Chorus at the opening of Act IV is a sign of a mannerist style, while Inga-Stina Ewbank observes that Time's speech is written "in a kind of pageant doggerel."[12] Each critic is correct. Certainly the couplets used here by Time are distinguished from Shakespeare's style in the rest of the play, and couplets are the favorite verse form of pageant dramatists. Munday's Time in the 1611 show varies his couplets with occasional examples of rhyme royal stanzas. Each figure carries his emblematic properties, as was common, and each calls attention to them: Shakespeare's Time: "I turn my glass, and give my scene such growing/ As you had slept between" (IV.i.16-17); Munday's: "As thus I turne my Glasse to Times of old."[13] The thrust of Inga-Stina Ewbank's essay is the crucial importance of Time as concept, not just choric figure, in *The Winter's Tale*; he is likewise essential, dramatically and thematically, in Munday's pageant. And this brings us to the most important relevance of the civic show to Shakespeare's play, the connection with the statue scene.

I believe that the 1611 Lord Mayor's Show has incipient dramatic elements that could have suggested to Shakespeare a means of renewing Hermione's life. After Leofstane's speech of welcome at Baynard's castle, the procession moved "to an ancient Toombe or monument, standing in apt place appointed for it" (sig. A3v)— probably somewhere in Cheapside. Unfortunately Munday does not describe this tomb, though we do find a slight description and an actual drawing for his 1616 pageant in which a similar dramatic device appeared.[14] Time and Leofstane are gathered at the tomb where Leofstane reveals that Time has raised him from the grave for this occasion: "See in how short a while a quiet Soule,/ Hid from this world five hundred years and more,/ May be forgetfull of great Times controule,/ . . . / My selfe . . . could tell this worthy Lord,/ Time had reviv'd me, to attend this day" (sig. B2v). This former mayor Leofstane (who represents London's first mayor, Henry Fitz-Alwin) had lain in the grave some five hundred years only to be renewed by Time. Though the pageant characters are gathered around a tomb, their theme is restoration.

This conversation is but the prelude to the actual restoration that occurs, for lying on the tomb (Time says, "Yet heere sleepes one" [B3v]) is Nicholas Faringdon, a fourteenth-century mayor and Goldsmith.[15] Time reviews some of Faringdon's accomplishments, and then calls him from the grave: "Arise, arise I say, good *Faringdon,*/ For in this triumph thou must needs make one" (B3v). The stage direction underscores the theatrical nature of this event: *"Time striketh on the Tombe with his Silver wand, and then Faringdon ariseth."* Faringdon's first words are: "Astonishment and frightful wonder/ Shakes and splits my soule in sunder." This sense of wonder is in keeping with the "resurrection" that we witness, another example of the triumph of time. Beyond wonder there is joy, as Faringdon says: "Joy and gladsome jouissance,/ Doth old *Faringdon* in-trance,/ To heare the tale that *Time* hath told" (sig. B4v). The scene is a mixture of momentary terror and lasting joy, to which Time in *The Winter's Tale* alludes (IV.i.1).

There are, then, several points of contact between this episode in Munday's pageant and Shakespeare's statue scene. One point is the theme of restoration, which has already been fully explored in V.ii, before we witness Hermione's revival. The renewal of father and daughter and the reconciliation of friends sound the note of hopeful joy, a prelude to what is experienced in V.iii. Here Paulina is in charge, and she may be seen as the agent of Time or the analogue to Time of the pageant. She shapes the dramatic structure, and she calls Hermione from ostensible death. Just as in the pageant there is an actual tomb which spectators see, so in the play in Paulina's chapel the visitors find the statue probably on some kind of tomb device. Mysterious things happen in both pageant and play, but they begin with readily seen, tangible stage properties. All attention focuses on Faringdon's tomb in the pageant and on Hermione's statue in the play's final scene. In a memorable theatrical gesture Time summons Faringdon from the tomb, and correspondingly Paulina brings the supposed statue of Hermione to life in a deliberate and distinctive act. Paulina calls out: "Music! awake her! strike!/ 'Tis time; descend; be stone no more; approach" (V.iii.98-99). The halting cadence parallels Hermione's first slow movements as she descends into life from her niche. Shakespeare's treatment is the more profound, which is not surprising, but it is tantalizing to think that the scene could have been inspired by an insubstantial pageant.

Greg suggests that if indeed *The Winter's Tale* was revised, it may have been for the wedding festivities of Princess Elizabeth in early 1613 (the wedding took place on 14 February).[16] Interestingly, two of the masques performed for the occasion contain statue figures which come to life and participate in the festivities: the first antimasque of Beaumont's *Masque of the Inner Temple and Gray's Inn* includes four statues who dance with the nymphs and stars, and Campion's *Lords' Masque* has two sets of four statues which are transformed into women. The renewal of Hermione would fit these dramatic events and correspond in the larger sense to the occasion of the wedding. One should recall that the marriage of Elizabeth came just a few months after the sudden and tragic death of her brother, Henry, Prince of Wales, on 6 November 1612. Within a brief period of time we meet on the national scene "with things dying, . . . [and] with things new-born" (III.iii.113-14). Certainly a *Winter's Tale* that emphasizes the restoration of Hermione would be deemed most appropriate for a court and nation that had suffered much sorrow over Henry's death. Indeed the elegiac outpourings for Henry, penned by such writers as Campion, Webster, Heywood, Davies, Drummond, Tourneur, and Peacham, are rivaled only by those at the death of Queen Elizabeth.[17] Time that tries all has enabled the country to move beyond the tragedy of Henry to the hopeful joy of Princess Elizabeth; it is an actual national paradigm of tragicomedy.

If Shakespeare were influenced by these events of drama and history (or simply by his own imagination) to create the present ending of *The Winter's Tale,* how was the statue of Hermione to be perceived and understood? The pervasive reaction from those on stage is to comment on the life-likeness of the statue. This has been prepared for by the first report of the statue in V.ii.94-108, where we learn that it is "newly perform'd by that rare Italian master, Julio Romano" (lines 96-97).[18] As the Third Gentleman says: "He so near to Hermione hath done Hermione that they say one would speak to her and stand in hope of answer" (lines 100-102). The theater audience is being guided to an acceptance of the statue though its art beguiles nature. Reporting the scene of the restoration of Leontes and Perdita, the Third Gentleman says: "Who was most marble there chang'd color" (line 90)—which in retrospect underscores again how V.ii is the foretaste of the final scene where that which is marble takes on the reality, not just the colors, of life.

When the curtain is drawn and Leontes, seeing the statue, remarks, "Chide me, dear stone, that I may say indeed/ Thou art Hermione" (V.iii.24-25), the dramatic irony is not felt either on stage or in the audience. He notes Hermione's wrinkles, which he did not expect to see, but Paulina has an easy answer (lines 30-32). Perdita would kiss the statue's hand, but Paulina warns her away: "The statue is but newly fix'd; the color's/ Not dry" (lines 47-48). A similar reaction comes when Leontes tries to kiss the statue (lines 79-83). Blood seems to course through its veins; it seems to breathe; the eyes seem to move. Leontes is so far transported by it that "He'll think anon it lives" (line 69). We, too, are doubtless struck by the verisimilitude of the statue. And when the statue begins to move, those watching it are transfixed, become themselves momentarily stone-like. Years after the play was written Henry Peacham, in his 1634 edition of *The Compleat Gentleman,* discusses the value of statues to poets, painters, architects, and all gentlemen: "To Poets for the presentation of Comedies, Tragedies, Masks, Shewes, or any learned scene whatsoever; the properties whereof can neither be appointed nor judged of, but by such as are well seene in statue-craft."[19] Shakespeare has learned the lesson well.

How might an Elizabethan audience have been prepared to accept the qualities of this statue of the "dead" Hermione? Or, what might they have known about funerary sculpture? Certainly Londoners in particular had many opportunities to see funeral statuary. As Eric Mercer points out: "The history of English sculpture between 1553 and 1625 is inseparable from a history of fashions in funeral monuments, upon which most of the sculptural effort of the period was expended."[20] Mercer also demonstrates the increasing attention to a faithful representation of the deceased person's physical traits; in the early seventeenth century there was a new concern "for the human form and a greater freedom of pose than before."[21] Even before the curtain is pulled to reveal Hermione, the audience would expect the statue, on the basis of their own experience, to be life-like. It is especially interesting, in light of Mercer's comments, to recall Leontes' first words upon seeing Hermione: "Her natural posture!" (V.iii.23). She is not, as Wickham says, "in *pious* posture" reminiscent of earlier traditions,[22] but more relaxed, more natural.

But Wickham is right to focus on some idea of "effigy" for the presentation of Hermione. He suggests that she stands on a tomb in a niche: "It would then be quite clear to the audience that Hermione was not rising like Lazarus . . . from within the sarcophagus, but that the already life-like effigy was translating itself from the semblance of painted stone to life indeed."[23] Elsewhere Wickham points to the carving of the marble statues of Elizabeth and Mary Stuart ordered by James in 1605, the statues to be placed on tombs in Westminster Abbey. The work, carried on by Cornelius and William Cure in Southwark, could easily have been witnessed by Shakespeare. Wickham concludes: "The artistry implicit in borrowing the marble memorials to Elizabeth and

Mary, Queen of Scots, from real life and incorporating them into the statue scene in Paulina's chapel . . . is dazzling."[24] Though surely what he suggests is plausible, I would modify Wickham's certainty by opening another possibility.

Elizabethans would have been familiar with the custom of carrying atop the coffin a manikin-like representation or effigy of the deceased so designed as to be a faithful rendition of the person. In the case of kings, this can vividly illustrate the symbolism of the king's two bodies, the effigy being the sign of kingship that survives while the mortal remains are in the coffin.[25] Such an effigy was constructed for Elizabeth's funeral as indicated, to cite but one example, in the Lord Chamberlain's Records: "Item for x yardes of crimson sattin to make a Robe for the representation [i.e., effigy] at xvjs the yard viijli."[26] In 1606 when King Christian of Denmark came for a visit, one of the things he went to see in Westminster Abbey were the effigies of some seven sovereigns and spouses which had been newly "repayred, robed and furnished at the King's Majestie his charge."[27] One thinks perhaps of Hermione's statue "now newly performed."

If Shakespeare revised *The Winter's Tale* as I have postulated, the memory of Prince Henry's effigy would be fresh. Again the Lord Chamberlain's Records illustrate the procedure; the figure was to be jointed so that it would be moved "to sundrie accions first for the Carriage in the Chariot and then for the standinge and for settinge uppe the same in the Abbye." The Records also indicate a payment of £ 10 to "Abraham Vanderdort for the face and hands of the Princes representation being very curiouslie wrought . . . ."[28] Great care was expended on the exposed hands and face while the rest of the artificial body was clothed in the regal garments. A contemporary account of Henry's funeral illustrates the use of this flexible effigy: "Munday, the 7. of *December*, (the Funerall day) the representation was layd upon the Corps, and both together put into an open Chariot, and so proceeded."[29] Though Hermione's statue is clearly meant to be stone, this custom of funeral effigy provides another reason why Elizabethan audiences would have expected realistic qualities in the statue and how from the great state funerals witnessed by thousands they would have understood the concept of a lifelike representation.

Whatever led Shakespeare to construct the scene in which

Hermione comes to life, he has provided us with a rare moment in the theater, fusing stage and theater audience in a common experience of wonder and, as some critics would have it, miracle. The wasteland of tragedy is behind, and the comic possibilities lie ahead much greater than Leontes had any reason to expect. Suffering and death are overcome by a penance that is efficacious and by a life ever renewing. In this sense the play responds in part to the tragic problem of *King Lear*; and it is instructive to contrast Lear's illusions that are shattered in his final scene with Leontes' most fanciful illusions which are rendered valid as the paradox resolves of a Hermione who seems to be art imitating life but is in fact life imitating art. One of the final tests of Leontes is the test of faith, as Paulina says: "It is requir'd/ You do awake your faith" (V.iii.94-95). The scene up to the movement of the statue illustrates that faith is the substance of things hoped for, the evidence of things not seen.

The First Gentleman in V.ii says: "Every wink of an eye some new grace will be born . . ." (lines 110-11); and measured against the yardstick of time in this play, the animation of Hermione the statue occurs as in the twinkling of an eye. The grace of reunion and redemption gains life here. Or to put it all in the words of another writer whose works were newly translated and published in 1611:

> Behold, I shew you a mysterie: we shall not all sleepe, but we shall all be changed,
>
> In a moment, in the twinckling of an eye, at the last trumpe, (for the trumpet shall sound, and the dead shall be raised incorruptible, and we shall be changed.)
>
> . . . then shall be brought to passe the saying that is written, Death is swallowed up in victorie.
>
> O death, where is thy sting? O grave, where is thy victorie;
>
> (I Corinthians 15: 51-52, 54-55)

10

Immediacy and Remoteness in
The Taming of the Shrew *and* The Winter's Tale

Charles R. Forker   *Tempest*

> the Bard
> Was sober when he wrote
> That this world of fact we love
> Is unsubstantial stuff:
> All the rest is silence
> On the other side of the wall;
> And the silence ripeness,
> And the ripeness all.
>   (W.H. Auden, *The Sea and the Mirror*)

When Shakespeare makes Julio Romano's statue mysteriously descend from its pedestal and live again as Hermione, he does more than dramatize the regenerative theme of *The Winter's Tale.* Tantalizing interplay between art and nature is not merely a perennial concern of pastoral (and therefore of the romances as a group) but a continuing preoccupation in Shakespearean drama from the earliest to the latest plays. But, as G. Wilson Knight among others has noticed,[1] this scene resonates with an other-worldly suggestiveness and bears a visionary emphasis peculiar to the final phase of Shakespeare's dramaturgy. Listen to Paulina:

> As she liv'd peerless,
> So her dead likeness, I do well believe,
> Excels what ever yet you look'd upon,
> Or hand of man hath done; therefore I keep it
> [Lonely] , apart. But here it is; prepare
> To see the life as lively mock'd as ever
> Still sleep mock'd death. Behold, and say 'tis well.
> I like your silence, it the more shows off
> Your wonder; but yet speak. First, you, my liege;
> Comes it not something near?

. . . .

> It is requir'd
> You do awake your faith: then, all stand still.
> . . . .
>   Music! awake her! strike!
> 'Tis time; descend; be stone no more; approach;
> Strike all that look upon with marvel. Come;
> I'll fill your grave up. Stir; nay, come away;
> Bequeath to death your numbness; for from him
> Dear life redeems you. You perceive she stirs.
> Start not; her actions shall be as holy, as
> You hear my spell is lawful. Do not shun her
> Until you see her die again . . . .
>
>   (V.iii.14-106)

With a ritualism and solemnity that owe much to the court masque, the dramatist here offers us a theatrical emblem of consciousness expanding, of perception enlarging its context. Identifying first with Leontes' guilt and restricted awareness, then with the amazement of the assembled onlookers, the audience at the Globe observes a show within a show: Paulina, as presenter, draws a curtain and magically transforms what appears to be stone and paint into flesh and blood. The comparatively remote figure behind the curtain steps forward to join those who had gazed upon her as a thing apart, and as Paulina urges the king and his companions to "awake [their] faith," she speaks past the Sicilians and their guests to stretch the perceptivity of Londoners. Life emerges out of art (a kind of death in Shakespeare's metaphor), but the life in question is "some sixteen years" older than it was, and the reanimation of Hermione is shadowed by the consciousness that all life, which includes art, is subject to limitations of time and physical decay, yet is mysteriously evocative of larger and unseen realities. The rhythm so movingly suggested here—the progression outward from art to life to eternity, from the remoteness of the inert statue through the more immediate and human joy of reunion to the sense of miracle which lies beyond mere sense experience and strangely fuses remoteness with immediacy—may serve as a paradigm for approaching an important aspect of technique and significance in Shakespeare's next play, *The Tempest.*

By way of clarifying the poet's procedure in what may well have been his final unaided drama, let us first consider a play that lies at the opposite end of his career, *The Taming of the Shrew.* All the early comedies of Shakespeare, no less than the late plays, are notable for inventive and varied experiments with conventional material; all, too, toy in their different ways with the elusive relativity of the artificial and the natural, the more remote and the more immediate. *The Taming of the Shrew,* however, is an extreme example of this engrossment, most obviously because it is Shakespeare's only play to present itself by means of an induction which is fully dramatic in its own right. In *The Taming* the playwright conducts his viewers through an elaborate series of gradations or strata which seem peculiarly designed not only to span the gulf between the audience's sense of ordinary life and the farcically simplified world of Katherine and Petruchio, but also to call attention to the artistic conventions and processes by which dramatic illusion is achieved. It is as though Shakespeare were asking us with one voice willingly to suspend our disbelief while inviting us with another to admire his professional skills as a technician of the theater.

The play commences at a level of naturalism not far removed from that of the groundlings. The audience observes Christopher Sly, a drunken tinker, collapse near the door of a tavern from which he has just been expelled by the hostess; too deep in his cups to be more than feebly hostile, he shrugs, "let the world slide" (Ind.i.5-6), and soon passes out. At this point an anonymous lord and his hunting party enter to the sound of horns and invent an interior comedy into which Sly is to be thrust as the chief focus of attention. Life is to be converted into art. Transported to a country house, dressed in finery, and pampered with luxuries which include paintings, music, and theatrical entertainment, "the beggar" is induced to "forget himself" and mistake "a flatt'ring dream or worthless fancy" (Ind.i.41-44) for reality. To amuse the lord as well as those who have paid their pennies on the Bankside, the actor playing Sly exchanges a more immediate identity for a more remote one, and the tinker's psychological confusion at the sudden shift is explained to him ironically as the effect of a dream; the drunken sleep of a few hours (mere minutes in literal playing time) is fictionalized à la Rip van Winkle into a slumber of fifteen years. The lord supports Sly's illusion and further enriches the comedy by casting his boy page in the role of the victim's wife, and by exciting Sly's sexual instincts with pictures of mythological subjects, which, for the sophisticated, represent yet a further degree of remoteness from actuality but for Sly are the immediate enticements of pornography.

After the bibulous tinker has been carried off stage and before he awakens into the illusory world which has been prepared for him, Shakespeare complicates the relationship between drama and life still further by introducing a troupe of itinerant players, one of whom the hospitable lord, like Hamlet in a similar situation, remembers from a former visit. The actor's role on another occasion ("a farmer's eldest son" who "woo'd the gentlewoman so well" [Ind.i.84-85] is recalled, and the stage-managing lord ironically enlists the visiting players as supporting audience for the deception of Sly. They must be careful not to smile at the absurdity of the peasant's new situation and so break the illusion that is so artfully being constructed around him. Already within the induction Shakespeare involves us in a teasing confrontation of mirror with mirror. A theater audience watches an actor in the role of a peer assume the function of dramatist-producer, who imposes his own identity upon an actor, who plays a tinker, who in turn is married to a boy actor playing a page-boy dressed as a lady.

Once Sly has settled into the false identity—and he accepts it with minimal protest—the induction defines three levels of engagement (or detachment). As the clever inventor of a complex joke, the lord remains as much as possible on the periphery of the action to observe the comic effects of his handiwork; Sly obtusely occupies the center, unable to preserve any psychological distance from the immediacy of his experience. The page-boy mediates between these extremes, being almost equally involved in both: with the aid of an onion he feigns tears of joy for Sly's recovery from protracted sleep, while secretly laughing with his stage-managing master at the gullibility and ignorance of the man he is teaching to address him as "Madam." Moreover, we learn that the actor who plays the tinker-lord is to be solemnly attended by other actors, playing actors, who, from the nobleman's point of view, will be simulating off-stage behavior and therefore dealing in illusion, but who, in Sly's distorted vision, will merely appear to be performers who have not yet donned their makeup and costumes.

Having drawn us progressively into this Pirandello-like maze,

Shakespeare now extends the process by having the strolling players perform *The Taming of the Shrew* for the benefit of a triple audience—the paying public at the Globe, the members of the lord's household, and Sly himself as a sixteenth-century *bourgeois gentilhomme.* Making himself comfortable to enjoy the show from his position "aloft," the beringed tinker unconsciously echoes his own words at the tavern door before succumbing to alcoholic oblivion: "Come, madam wife, sit by my side, and let the world slip, we shall ne'er be younger" (Ind.ii.142-44). A flourish of trumpets announces the play even as the horns had signaled the entrance of the lord and his fellow huntsmen. During the first scene of the comedy proper Sly struggles to concentrate on Lucentio's arrival at Padua and Baptista's plan to tie the marriage of his younger daughter to that of his elder. But before long the novice playgoer, heavy with boredom and more drink, is nodding off again. Although a stage direction indicates that Sly and others of his train continue to *"sit and mark"* (I.i.253), at least during part of the succeeding action, the characters of the induction take no further part in the play. It seems clear that these actors soon disappear unobtrusively—probably to reappear below in new roles, as the multiplying complications of the intrigue require. Our last impression of Sly is not unlike our first: as sleep dissolves the reality of the ale-house and enables the lord to supplant it with a manor house, so the reality of the manor house yields to a street in Padua as Sly once again "let[s] the world slip." Since Shakespeare resolutely fails to close the frame so self-consciously erected (a procedure radically different from that of the inferior *Taming of a Shrew*), he would seem to encourage us to look upon the cleverly linked love stories of Bianca and Katherine as coterminous with an elaborate dream—a dream which, in the manner of dreams, combines a sense of strangeness and contrivance with a sense of the natural.

Translated from London to Padua by way of Warwickshire, we discover that the interaction of artifice with naturalness is just commencing. For the sake of exposition, Lucentio and his servant Tranio acquaint us in stiffly manner verse with what they already know of their own origin, history, and reason for coming to a famous university city; then they stand aside to witness the entrance of Baptista, his daughters, and the suitors who are competing for Bianca's hand—a procession which Tranio describes as "some show to welcome us to town" (I.i.47). Romantically smitten at the first sight of Bianca, Lucentio abandons his role as passive spectator and enters the competition as a participant; but in order to get the better of his rivals, he exchanges clothes with his servant, who now becomes his surrogate, and then assumes the further disguise of Cambio, a tutor to Baptista's daughters, that he may have easier access to the object of his affection. Mask conceals mask; Lucentio plays a role within a role. Here we have the theme of the "supposes," which Shakespeare borrowed from Ariosto (via Gascoigne), and the mistaken identities now proliferate to make a dizzying pattern of complication as the different levels of awareness and ignorance interact. In a remarkable addition to the source story, Hortensio, a second suitor, also masquerades as a tutor, taking the name of Licio; and a wandering pedant is induced under false colors to pose as Lucentio's father, only to cause general consternation when confronted by the real father.

Only after the plot of physical disguises and substitutions has begun does Shakespeare introduce us to Petruchio, so that we reach the earthier and more verisimilar of the contrasting love actions at a more remote point of the narrative sequence. Of course, the taming process itself involves the assumption of a tyrannical role to elicit the genuine good sense and capacity for devotion that lie hidden behind Katherine's unnatural facade of aggression. Petruchio teaches his new spouse to know herself by grossly exaggerating her own assumed behavior, by giving her back a distorted reflection of her own willfulness. Until this truth dawns upon her, she understandably thinks of him as a ruthless manipulator of people for theatrical sensation: "Belike you mean to make a puppet of me" (IV.iii.103). Not for nothing is the motif of dress so strenuously emphasized on both sides of the relationship. When Petruchio astonishes the wedding guests by his grotesquely inappropriate apparel ("so unlike yourself" [III.ii.104], in Tranio's phrase), the madcap bridegroom points to the difference between costume and wearer: "To me she's married, not unto my clothes" (III.ii.117). And after Kate has been frustratingly denied the fashionable wardrobe which would support her egotistic self-conception, she must rest content with "honest mean habiliments" and be told that " 'tis the mind that makes the body rich" (IV.iii.170-72). When Kate learns to enter into the game of role-playing which Petruchio initiates, when she can symbolically accept fantasy as truth by admitting that the sun is the moon, she demonstrates a new imaginativeness, unselfishness, and humility that fulfill rather than inhibit her deepest longings. The final episode in which Kate wins the wager for her husband and bests her two companion brides in the contest of obedience serves as a dramatic illustration of how role-playing and integrity, wifely submission and independence of spirit, can be harmoniously reconciled in a single personality. Shakespeare has carried the notion of assumed identity from the superficial level of practical jokes in the induction and of narrative intricacy in the "supposes" plot to the deeper plane of character development and psychological self-realization.

The Taming of the Shrew is typical of Shakespeare's early work not only for its obsession with technical virtuosity, but also for its buoyant confidence in the capacity of dramatic art to penetrate surfaces and expose truth. The comedy takes us by degrees through a sequence of reflecting mirrors, or, to put it another way, into a succession of Chinese boxes that evokes the concept of infinite regression. Shakespeare's layered construction almost suggests analogy with the raked and deeply receding perspective stages of Serlio's description in which the spectator's eye was drawn ever backward toward the vanishing point. Indeed it is not unlikely that Ariosto's *I Suppositi,* the original of Shakespeare's subplot, was actually performed on such a stage in the early 1500s. *The Taming* invites a progressive immersion in illusion, a step-wise movement from comparative realism to comparative artifice, from the more immediate to the more remote, but in a paradoxically circular way that endows the final object of this distancing with the emotional power and immediacy of lived experience. By the end of the play Katherine and Petruchio seem more English than Italian, and when they discard their assumed roles of virago and tamer, yielding to each other with genuine affection ("Why, there's a wench! Come on, and kiss me, Kate" [V.ii.180], they step forward as the characters nearest to us spatially and psychologically. Such a procedure, a sort of dramatic counterpart to Gerard Manley Hopkins's "inscape," says much about Shakespeare's faith in both the means and validity of mimesis.

If *The Taming of the Shrew* directs our attention to the satisfactions of art imitating life, *The Tempest* reverses that perspective. Here the breaking of illusion rather than its creation is Shakespeare's theme, and emergence out of the world of shadows and images is often accompanied by wistfulness or sadness. Even the sordid Caliban, with a melancholy eloquence beyond his normal range, speaks of beautiful dreams that cannot be sustained: "The clouds methought would open, and show riches/ Ready to drop upon me, that when I wak'd/ I cried to dream again" (III.ii. 141-43). It is no accident that *The Tempest* suggests more links with *King Lear* than with the merry comedies written earlier. Prospero, too, knows about the inadequacy of dreams and illusions. Master dramatist that he is, he grows to an awareness that his "so potent art" is but "rough magic" (V.i.50). He breaks his staff and drowns his book, that he may rejoin common humanity with all its unaesthetic flaws. By forgiving his enemies and freeing Ariel, he frees himself from God-like isolation and the compulsion to order reality in accordance with his own private vision of it. Actual life is more painful and untidy than its image on the stage, but it is also more important. Prospero teaches us to mark this truth, and to remember with him that man occupies an uneasy middle ground between the consoling images which he himself creates and those profounder realities beyond his ken of which he himself may be but a crude reflection.

Shakespeare assists our sense of widening perspectives by confining the stage action proper within uncharacteristically classical limits of time and space. Much of what occurs or has occurred off stage must therefore be presented indirectly through narration, a technique that italicizes the relation between informant and informer, and so, by extension, between audience and play. Prospero fussily peppers the long history of his tribulations to his daughter with such interjections as "Dost thou attend me?" (I.ii.78), "Thou attend'st not!" (I.ii.87), and "Dost thou hear?" (I.ii.106). In tandem with characters inside the play whose worlds are being expanded, our imaginations are invited to range outward from a present and local center to embrace "the dark backward and abysm of time" (I.ii.50) and Claribel's wedding at Tunis, as well as the promise of "calm seas, auspicious gales" (V.i.315) and Miranda's marriage at Naples. The method suggests the movement of concentric circles forming around a disturbance in water.

In contrast to the prolonged opening of *The Taming of the Shrew* with its playfully reflexive sense of overlap between art and nature, *The Tempest* plunges us instantly, *in mediis rebus,* into an illusion of maximal immediacy. The shipwreck scene, with its noise, confusion, and apocalyptic fear, is the most naturalistic of the entire play. With the seamen and their passengers we are made to feel intensely the moments that precede death: "All lost! To prayers, to prayers!" . . . "Mercy on us!"—/ "We split, we split!"—"Farewell, my wife and children!"—/ "Farewell, brother!" . . . "The wills above be done! but I would fain die a dry death" (I.i.51-68). The valedictory note on which the play closes is already present in embryo. But by scene ii, we have discovered with Miranda that our gullible senses have deceived us, and that what we took for reality was in fact only a theatrical illusion created by the necromantic art of a magician: "No more amazement. Tell your piteous heart/ There's no harm done" (I.ii.15-16). Almost from the start, then, Shakespeare alerts us to distrust our eyes and ears and to think of life as more mysterious and inclusive than any rendering of it can possibly be, however convincingly presented.

Having instructed us that the tempest was no tempest, Prospero, with the assistance of a metamorphic or invisible Ariel, proceeds to observe the characters under his control as they pursue particular illusions, and to symbolize the nature of these pursuits by various expressions of art—songs, shows, visions, "glistering apparel," masques. Whether these illusions be guilty or innocent—whether they involve the desire for power (like Antonio's, Sebastian's, Stephano's, or Caliban's plots to murder and usurp), or misapprehension about survival (like Alonso's and Ferdinand's belief in each other's death), or the contemplation of perfection (like Caliban's "voices" and "sweet airs, that give delight and hurt not" [III.ii.136-38], Gonzalo's "golden age" [II.i.169], or Miranda's "brave new world" [V.i.183])—all are seen to be comically impotent, naive, or partial. Gilded dreams or distorted fantasies are as little to be relied upon as the "drollery" of unnatural shapes that appear and disappear so suddenly or the banquet that Ariel causes to vanish with a clap of his harpy wings, as trivial in the long run as the "frippery" with which Prospero decoys the drunken butler and his silly mate.

Prospero's most beautiful symbol of illusion is the masque

presented to solemnize the betrothal of Ferdinand and Miranda. It is a dramatic form which represented for Elizabethans not only the ultimate in expensive and ephemeral artifice but also a unique continuity between performer and observer, since, typically, the court masque enlarged its perimeter at the end to embrace members of the audience as participants. Here Shakespeare gathers to a head the ambiguities of nature and art, immediacy and remoteness, that irradiate the entire play and provide that strange sense of new vistas opening out that every student of *The Tempest* has felt. Again the paradoxes of the play-within-the-play are exploited; we return, as Tillyard has noticed,[2] to the principle of infinite regression—Prospero deputizing Ariel to produce a show in which Globe actors, pretending to be spirits, act out the roles of couplet-chanting goddesses, who, in turn, conjure up a still more remote world of "cold nymphs" and "bachelors" (IV.i. 66-67), the idealized, pastoral counterparts of Ferdinand and Miranda.

But in context the dramatic thrust of the masque is less centripetal than centrifugal. Like the statue scene in *The Winter's Tale,* it moves outward from a greater to a lesser remoteness. Iris refers directly to the guests of honor, to "this man and maid" (IV.i.95); Juno speaks of "this twain" (IV.i.104) and then joins Ceres in direct address to the lovers: "Honor, riches, marriage-blessing,/ Long continuance, and increasing,/ Hourly joys be still upon you" (IV.i.106-8). Actors playing actors move forward to involve an onstage audience; fictional characters bless relatively less fictional ones. Prospero observes the masque and the couple's reaction to it from a position still further detached, rather as the anonymous lord observes Sly's reception of *The Taming,* but suddenly a more immediate reality shatters the prepared illusion. Thoughts of Caliban's "foul conspiracy" rouse Prospero from the pleasures of art and prompt his famous aria on revels ending and spirits melting into thin air. The great showman's comment on the fading of the insubstantial pageant with its reverberant pun on "the great globe itself" (IV.i.153) movingly reinforces the old trope of life as a play, of art appropriating nature by dissolving into it. It is a theme inherent in the very genre of the masque.

The concluding lines of Prospero's great speech bear a double significance, both tragic and comic: "We are such stuff/ As dreams are made on; and our little life/ Is rounded with a sleep" (IV.i.

156-58). In the most obvious sense, the sleep referred to is a metaphor for death, consciousness of which suffuses *The Tempest*
in a hundred details from the first until the final scene. In this
reading life is merely the raw material out of which men manu-
facture their illusions, and death marks the inevitable end of the
show. Such a conception recalls Macbeth's despairing image of the
"walking shadow, a poor player,/ That struts and frets his hour
upon the stage,/ And then is heard no more" (V.v.24-26). But
Hamlet considered a more metaphysical possibility: "For in that
sleep of death what dreams may come,/ When we have shuffled
off this mortal coil,/ Must give us pause" (III.i.65-67). Prospero
also seems to glimpse a Christian Neoplatonic continuum, to hint
that the stage illusion merely shades into a higher form of itself,
behind which simulacrum a transcendent Playwright benevolently
observes and superintends his own Creation. As the "baseless
fabric" of the masque appears to man, so man's "little life" may
seem to God and those few visionary souls who, like Lear, can
"take upon [them] the mystery of things/ As if they were God's
spies" (V.iii.16-17). Death may be conceived as an end or a beginning, as a final exit or as "a sea-change/ Into something rich and
strange" (I.ii.401-2). Point of view is all-important. To the unregenerate Antonio a sleeping Alonzo suggests a dead Alonzo.
But for the actual sleepers of the play (Alonzo, Gonzalo, Miranda,
the Boatswain, even perhaps Caliban), slumber is restorative and
life-affirming.

The view of human existence, *sub specie aeternitatis,* as God's
theater and men as his actors was, of course, a Renaissance commonplace, and Shakespeare fortifies the analogy throughout *The
Tempest* by a system of recurrences that implies the Providential
Artist as a shaper of events. Miranda's wedding echoes Claribel's;
Alonzo and his party relive Prospero's "sea-sorrow" (I.ii.170); the
abortive attempt on the King of Naples' life is patterned on a
similar conspiracy against the Duke of Milan. To borrow a phrase
from Antonio, "what's past is prologue" (II.i.253).

The extraordinary humility which *The Tempest* conveys has
much to do with this implied contrast between celestial and
human planes of creativity. The expanding sense of reality which
the vanishing masque had symbolized now takes place, not as a
show, but as a swelling in the hearts of sinful men:

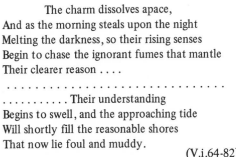

The charm dissolves apace,
And as the morning steals upon the night
Melting the darkness, so their rising senses
Begin to chase the ignorant fumes that mantle
Their clearer reason . . . .

. . . .
. . . . Their understanding
Begins to swell, and the approaching tide
Will shortly fill the reasonable shores
That now lie foul and muddy.
                                                    (V.i.64-82)

And Shakespeare completes the rhythm of withdrawal from illusion established in the masque by carrying it a step further in the epilogue. As mythological deities had come forward to join the lovers, so Prospero, having now "discased" himself, comes forward to join us: "Please you draw near" (V.i.319). The semi-tropical island melts into thin air, and we are invited to free its most commanding presence from the prison of the stage, even as he has just freed Ariel. The magician becomes a mere duke again, exchanging the robe of the conjurer for rapier and cloak. The demigod, with distant resonances of the Word being made flesh, unites himself to the world which he had held in sway. The artist abandons his contemplative cell to reenter the mainstream of political and social life, his charms "o'erthrown," his strength "most faint" (Epilogue, lines 1-2), and "Every third thought" his "grave" (V.i.312). As Prospero begs our prayers and applause, we become freshly aware that the Duke of Milan is one of King James's Servants and that, in turn, the actor beneath his splendid costume is but one more specimen of humankind who, like us, needs love and hopes for grace. In the very act of dissolving our illusions Shakespeare poignantly invokes suggestions of a transcendental vision that makes their loss tolerable, even comic. A merely human art must shrink almost to nullity when the frame of reference is dilated to accommodate the artifice of eternity. And we, like Ferdinand as he confronts the disappearing masque, are bidden by the very nature of the enlarged context to "be cheerful" rather than "dismay'd" that "Our revels now are ended" (IV.i.147-48).

We must be careful not to overgeneralize or unduly simplify

the contrasting attitudes toward illusion which *The Taming of the Shrew* and *The Tempest* so conveniently focus for us. If Shakespeare moved away from a youthful and self-assured embrace of the artist's enterprise in the early comedies toward a riper, more self-abnegating view of it in the romances, the exact route of this journey would be forbiddingly difficult to map. We can think of too many intermediate plays in which the ambiguous relation of truth to illusion not only frustrates our powers of definition but contributes, as nothing else could, to a rich diversity of witty, realistic, romantic, cynical, idealistic, comic, and tragic effects. The dreamers of *A Midsummer Night's Dream* may awake from a bewildering night in the forest to a reassuring sense of clarified directions and fortified identities, but they do so in a context which suggests that love, like art, cannot breathe in too skeptical or rationalistic a climate; and, significantly, it is the fairies, not the mortals, to whom the playwright assigns the final speeches. *A Midsummer Night's Dream* promulgates the idea that at least in some departments of life what the imagination creates or transfigures may claim a certain priority over mere fact. Yet a chronicle play like *Henry V* can shift this emphasis importantly. The Prologue who attempts eloquently to "work" on our "imaginary forces," transporting us from the "wooden O" of the Globe to the "vasty fields of France," sounds curiously embarrassed about the gulf between theatrical illusion and the historical grandeur it attempts to mirror; and so he grows defensive about the inadequacies of his medium, depreciating the actors as "crooked figure[s]," "ciphers to this great accompt," or "flat unraised spirits that hath dar'd/ On this unworthy scaffold to bring forth/ So great an object" (Prologue, lines 5-18). And the epilogue to *All's Well That Ends Well* also underscores the disjunction between a dramatic character and the player who has just enacted him, for only seconds on the stage separate the King of France's offer to dower Diana's marriage from his plea to the audience for applause: "The king's a beggar, now the play is done; / All is well ended, if this suit be won,/ That you express content . . ." (Epilogue, lines 1-3).

Various degrees of aesthetic engagement and disengagement are common in Shakespeare, and his plays encourage us to remark the difference.[3] The brittle sophisticates of *Love's Labor's Lost* maliciously relish the failure of theatrical illusion to sustain itself in the pageant of the Nine Worthies; and the mockery is easy enough when a timid curate such as Sir Nathaniel tries to recreate Alexander the Great or the diminutive Moth takes on the role of Hercules. But here the satire is aimed at artistic pretension in a play that stresses assumed postures as impediments to emotional honesty; nor have Berowne and his companions yet learned the magnanimity and need for empathy that Duke Theseus in a parallel situation enjoins upon Hippolyta: "The best in this kind are but shadows; and the worst are no worse, if imagination amend them" (*Midsummer Night's Dream*, V.i.211-12). Shakespeare's Claudius cannot afford such aloofness as the snobbish young critics of *Love's Labor's Lost* express. For that guilt-ridden regicide, theatrical performance has the devastating impact of a confrontation with the inner self; Hamlet's *Murther of Gonzago*, an ingeniously double illusion which reenacts the crime at the same time that it adumbrates the punishment, becomes unbearable to the King of Denmark for reasons precisely contrary to those which make *The Nine Worthies* unacceptable to the King of Navarre.

The composite figure who bids us farewell at the end of *The Tempest*—a magician, a duke, an actor, and finally just a man—seems to gather together some of these earlier perspectives and symbolizes for the audience both commitment to and disengagement from theatrical art. The unassuming plainness, the almost painful intimacy of the epilogue's tetrameter couplets, stylistically so different from Prospero's more symphonic utterances, suggests a fresh identity, as though the subject of a portrait had stepped from its own frame and had to some extent appropriated the persona of the painter. And yet the speaker is not merely an actor who has shed his role nor wholly a surrogate for Shakespeare, for he continues to speak of Naples and of his Milanese dukedom. One foot, so to say, remains inside the frame. After expanding our whole concept of illusion and reality to take in metaphysical horizons, the dramatist deliberately blurs or fuses the strata discriminated earlier and thereby produces an effect which is intensely personal, human, and specific at the same time that it is profoundly general and philosophic. Somewhat as Chaucer's Parson at the end of *The Canterbury Tales* raises the level of discourse from that of a particular English journey to that of the pilgrimage of the soul, so Shakespeare's Prospero at a like juncture directs our attention away from the dramas that playwrights make to the universal drama in which all men have their exits and their entrances. As the Parson's words shade into Chaucer's, preparing us, as it were, for the Retraction, so Prospero's words shade into Shakespeare's, preparing us for the dramatic silence that was soon to follow. Inevitably the new emphasis brings a shift in tone. We move from a concern with aesthetic problems to a sense of life whose very inclusiveness reorders priorities, orients us away from the sophistications of art toward the deepest of simplicities. The mood is one that mingles nostalgia and love for what is being abandoned with a quickened awareness of the peace that passeth all understanding.

The Tempest thus raises once more the issue debated so charmingly in *The Winter's Tale* on the relation of art to nature. Prospero, and the dramatist behind him, understands well enough the doctrine of Polixenes as illustrated in the discussion of horticultural grafting. He knows how "art . . . does mend Nature," how indeed in one view of the matter "art itself is Nature" (*Winter's Tale,* IV.iv.95-97). Had Shakespeare lost faith in the mimetic power and importance of drama, he could hardly have gone on to write *Henry VIII* and possibly *The Two Noble Kinsmen.* Nevertheless, in the final phase of his career he was breaking away from the kind of stage illusion that has allowed A. C. Bradley and many others to treat Hamlet, Othello, Macbeth, and King Lear almost as if they were living persons. And the effect which Prospero's epilogue seems designed to evoke is emotionally closer to Perdita's innocent distrust of art than to Polixenes' more sophisticated embracement of it. A rereading of *The Taming of the Shrew* in conjunction with *The Tempest* may serve to remind us that as Shakespeare approached the end of his highly experimental and successful career as an illusionist, he came finally to prefer simplicity before Heaven to virtuosity before men.

11

Where the Bee Sucks: A Triangular Study of Doctor Faustus, The Alchemist, *and* The Tempest

David Young

Discussions of *The Tempest* customarily take as their context the body of Shakespeare's work, especially the group of late plays known as the romances. A different perspective may be illuminating: a look at *The Tempest* in the context of English drama as it had developed during Shakespeare's career, especially as seen by contrasts in the work of Christopher Marlowe and Ben Jonson. Such an approach encourages closer attention to the way the play is rooted in its proper soil, the theater of its time. Stage magic was a familiar tradition from the 1580s on, and to ignore its meanings in performance, its peculiarly theatrical dimension, is to overlook something that Shakespeare himself could by no means ignore.

To place together for consideration three great plays of magic— *Doctor Faustus,* written and performed around 1592; *The Alchemist,* composed some eighteen years later, in 1610; and *The Tempest,* written very shortly thereafter, probably in 1611[1] —is not to pretend that other magic plays did not exist on the Elizabethan and Jacobean stages (they were plentiful), nor is it to claim that Shakespeare had the two earlier plays particularly in mind as he sat down to write his. My emphasis here is rather on the achievements of the drama as Shakespeare had known them at the outset of his career, and as they had come to be seen and understood by its close. The grouping of these three plays helps to highlight what was necessarily a much more generalized sense of the matter in its time.

There is a further logic to this triad: because the plays use magic, an art or science inevitably connected with illusion, as central situation and leading theme, they invite comparison, especially on the metaphoric ground where we see the magician as an artist and consider the implications of what is said and thought about illusion in relation to the theater in particular and art in general. To have said this, though, is to be struck by the vivid contrast between *Doctor Faustus* and *The Alchemist.* The two plays seem polar opposites in their views of magic. If there is some validity in connecting Faustus with his creator, and his magic with the theater's dependence on illusion, surely those links have been decisively broken in *The Alchemist,* where the magician Subtle is no better than a sordid charlatan. The difference is informative, however, precisely because it is a measure of the extent to which Jonson thought he was helping to change and reform the theater. Instead of ranging around the known world, *The Alchemist* is set carefully in contemporary London. Instead of portraying the supernatural in the form of devils and angels, the play cultivates a robust empiricism. Instead of placing human appetite in a context where its failure is tragic and grandiose, Jonson exposes it to comic scrutiny and calls it folly. Both Jonson and Marlowe shared the Renaissance interest in man as a protean creature, but Jonson scaled him down from a fabulous, mythic being to the unstable man in the street he could observe by sauntering out of his theater. In this respect, it was entirely appropriate that *The Alchemist* should portray magic by sharply defining its limits. There is room for the Queen of Faery to appear on Jonson's stage, but he takes care that we know she is Dol Common dressed in fancy clothes. And his magician Subtle is not so distant from Jonson after all in his role as manipulator, along with Face, of the spectrum of human folly. Jonson would take pride not in the kind of lyric outbursts of ambition and anguish that allow us to link Faustus with Marlowe, but rather in the dexterity with which the comic tricksters spin the web of comic design. Master plotters all! Jonson's vantage point, like his sense of timing, is ultimately superior to Subtle's, but so is Marlowe's to Faustus's. Both playwrights seek a perspective which will include a fairly full knowledge of the strengths and weaknesses of those branches of illusory art known as theater and magic.

In and around the transformation of dramatic models and artistic values suggested by the contrast of *Faustus* and *The Alchemist,* Shakespeare's own career as a playwright had taken shape. I should like to suggest that *The Tempest* represents Shakespeare's attempt, casual or deliberate, to retain and even restore what was expansive and thrilling about Marlowe's theater, while acknowledging and accepting many of the changes engendered by Jonson's artistic example. If this hypothesis has validity, it will help us to understand how it can be said that Shakespeare's art is a profound combination of the conservative and the innovative. It will also shed some light on the romances as a group, and it may well clarify some things that are puzzling about *The Tempest.* My consideration of these plays will be divided into three key areas: that of language, its use and misuse; that of dramatic decorum; and that of illusion, the claims that theater may or may not make to represent what is real by means that are unreal, or at least illusory. I will conclude with a comparative discussion of their staging.

In a play about magicianship, words will tend to have a heightened potency. Spells, charms, and conjurations are all demonstrations of the idea that there might be a special language, or use of language, that unleashes hidden powers and gives the knowledgeable user an extraordinary control over reality. What is often present as a mild suspicion is raised to an assertion of certainty. Language in *Doctor Faustus* is exciting because it has a mysterious force that is continually confirmed by its poetry, and that finds its most specific realization when Faustus learns to conjure. After some instruction from Cornelius and Valdes—which books to take to a solitary grove and the "words of art" he will need—Faustus draws his magic circle, anagrammatizes Jehovah's name, and is ready to summon Mephistophilis by speaking Latin. The results are instantaneous, and the irony that surrounds Faustus's delighted reaction, "I see there's virtue in my heavenly words" (I.iii.27), is characteristic of the play. The phrase will come to have a different meaning when we know what really brought Mephistophilis, but the potency of language will still hold good; it may not bring authority to the magician, but it will place him in severe jeopardy. When the devils hear someone "rack the name of God," Mephistophilis admits, they react promptly and eagerly (I.iii.47).

The basic movement for Faustus is from potency to impotence. The secrets of astronomy may be "graven in the book of Jove's high firmament" (III.Prologue.3), but he never really learns to read them, as his magic sinks more and more to the level of

self-indulgence and horseplay. At the end words fail him altogether, as the most eloquent pleas only emphasize his futility,
and he offers at the last to burn his books. But the failure in
Faustus is a failure of man rather than of language.

What a different verbal realm we have in *The Alchemist*! If
language has power, it is mostly the power of obfuscation. Subtle's
career may faintly parallel Faustus's as he outsmarts himself
through the pride of manipulation, but he has been summoning
gulls rather than devils, and his fall is just a soft thump over the
back wall. The proto-Miltonic poetry that characterized Marlowe's
play and hero is replaced by a wonderful babel of cant, rhetoric,
slang, and jargon. Learning is present, but usually as some kind of
wild fustian. And language is less a penetration of reality than a
way of misapprehending both self and world. In *Faustus* we are
invited to share a wonder at the power and mystery of language
that Jonson, in his turn, takes to be naive, though he personifies
it expressively in Mammon. His wonder is at the amazing variety
of verbal junk that can litter the human landscape, and his magician knows that language is power only insofar as our naiveté
about its control of reality can be exploited. Jonson's own artistic
ideals seem to lean toward a healthy skepticism about linguistic
potency; like Subtle and Face, he must know folly and knavery
thoroughly if he is to portray them accurately, and that includes
understanding how deeply the possibilities of error have invaded
the phenomenon of human speech.

At first glance, *The Tempest* may seem simply a reversion to the
attitudes behind Marlowe's play: a soaring and eloquent poetry
abounds, and the magician's learning is a source of his ability to
command the elements, as demonstrated by his stream of orders
to Ariel and in his review of his career, which tells us that he has
"call'd forth the mutinous winds" and that "Graves at my com-
mand/ Have wak'd their sleepers, op'd, and let 'em forth/ By my
so potent art" (V.i.48-50). But there is more to the matter than
this. In the first place, Prospero's potent art is less risky and more
clearly *his* than was the case with Faustus. He gives it up voluntarily and takes his leave in a fashion that is more like Subtle's
scramble over the back wall than Faustus's descent into hell-
mouth. Language in *The Tempest* is not a power whose ultimate
uses are fenced off for divine prerogative; it is, like language in
The Alchemist, a human phenomenon, subject less to damnable

presumption than to the varieties of foolish misuse. The ship-wreck, with its shouting, cursing, and desperate commands, is our introduction to this play's verbal universe. Soon after we hear Caliban reminding Prospero, "You taught me language, and my profit on't/ Is, I know how to curse. The red-plague rid you/ For learning me your language" (I.ii.363-65). Language in *The Tempest* is double-edged, a privilege *and* a burden, sharing some of the wonder at its power that we can associate with Marlowe, and some of the knowledge of its limits and misuses that we see in Jonson. From the gabble of the clowns, through the combinations of idealism and cynicism among the courtiers, through the comic but touching innocence of Miranda and Ferdinand, to the fantastic but quirky eloquence of Prospero, the play presents a mixed and complex sense of language that helps to place it near Jonson's in time.[2] But the way in which it comprehends Marlowe's sense of language is remarkable. In his epilogue, Prospero asks for applause with an eloquence that has never been matched:

> And my ending is despair,
> Unless I be reliev'd by prayer,
> Which pierces so, that it assaults
> Mercy itself, and frees all faults.
>
> (Lines 15-18)

Frank Kermode quotes Warburton's comment that this "alludes to the old stories told of the despair of necromancers in their last moments, and of the efficacy of the prayers of their friends for them."[3] If so, Shakespeare's audience might well have been meant to remember Faustus, as earlier when Prospero's "I'll drown my book" echoes Faustus's desperate "I'll burn my books." But the issue here is scarcely the same; an actor is asking us for applause. With a straight face he connects the apparently trivial with the apparently serious: "As you from crimes would pardon'd be,/ Let your indulgence set me free" (Epilogue, lines 19-20). That, in miniature, is the world of *The Tempest*.

Turning to the issue of dramatic decorum—the playwright's code of etiquette and aesthetic principle—it seems clear that if Marlowe knew the notions of decorum that Sidney had outlined, he chose to ignore them in *Doctor Faustus*. Sidney had objected to the expansive and casual treatment of time and place, and to the mixing of comic and tragic, "mingling Kings and Clownes . . .

with neither decencie nor discretion."[4] Marlowe's play ranges
over much of Europe, covers a period of more than twenty years,
and mingles moments of grotesque farce with the somber and
lofty effects of tragic poetry. Moreover, if Marlowe had any mis-
givings about the Elizabethan audience's love of spectacle, he concealed them splendidly; no opportunity for pageantry, dancing,
procession, or show is ignored in *Doctor Faustus.* Nor does the
author seem anxious to dissociate himself from the archaic; his
story's origin in the medieval gothic imagination is made very
clear, and there is much in the play to remind us of earlier
morality and miracle dramas where devils appeared to the popping
of fireworks, delighting audiences with the shivers produced by
the yawning jaws of hell. Marlowe's view of the theatrical medium
seems broad and inclusive, little troubled by questions of compati-
bility and appropriateness. And his attitude toward his audience
is perhaps consistent with this; throughout his career he seems to
have felt that their response was more their affair than his. The
prologue to *Tamburlaine* invited spectators to "View but his
picture in this tragic glass,/ And then applaud his fortunes as you
please" (Prologue, lines 7-8). Machiavel, as Prologue to *The Jew
of Malta,* asks on behalf of Barabas the anti-hero, "I crave but this:
grace him as he deserves!/ And let him not be entertained the
worse/ Because he favors me" (Prologue, lines 33-35). The opening
chorus of *Faustus* strikes a note that is similar, if more bemused:
"Only this, gentles: we must now perform/ The form of Faustus'
fortunes, good or bad./ And now to patient judgments we appeal . . ." (Chorus, lines 7-9). There is certainly no great pressure
on the audience for a particular kind of response in this "as you
like it" introduction of dramatic material; Marlowe's detachment
seems genuine.

Jonson is, especially in *The Alchemist,* a study in contrasts.
He is rigorous about the unities of time and place, and exact
about limiting himself to what he considers appropriate to the
genre. His sense of decorum does not allow for spectacle and
pageantry; he will exercise that taste to great effect in his masques,
but only because it is there appropriate to the decorum of the
form. He has no easy association with the theater of the past;
his plays positively bristle with their sense of contemporaneity
and their differentiation from inferior work of predecessors.
Jonson's comedies proceed from such a rigorous sense of the

appropriate use of theater, genre, characterization, tone, and harmony of plot that a great part of their effectiveness lies in our sense of the triumph of self-fulfillment within a sharply defined aesthetic framework.

That quality is enhanced by Jonson's brisk insistence on coming to terms with his audience lest they fail to understand him. His plays regularly contain prologues, inductions, and other material outlining his aesthetic views and berating playwrights who do not conform to them, not to mention audiences who fail to appreciate their superiority. *The Alchemist* has an epistle dedicatory to Lady Mary Worth, complimenting her on her judgment, "which is a Sidney's" (line 11); an address "To The Reader" which complains about plays "wherein now the concupiscence of dances and antics so reigneth as to run away from Nature and be afraid of her is the only part of art that tickles the spectators" (lines 5-7), and which concludes that "it is only the disease of the unskillful to think rude things greater than polished, or scattered more numerous than composed" (lines 30-32); and a prologue announcing the setting of the comedy:

> Our Scene is London, 'cause we would make known,
> No country's mirth is better than our own.
> No clime breeds better matter for your whore,
> Bawd, squire, impostor, many persons more,
> Whose manners, now called humors, feed the stage.
>
> (Lines 5-9)

The prologue also suggests the principles of comic decorum to which the play adheres: ". . . this pen/ Did never aim to grieve, but better men . . . wholesome remedies . . . fair correctives . . . natural follies" (lines 11-23). Jonson, anxious to be clear about his innovations and his artistic precision, is always ready to educate his audience toward what he sees as better taste. One has, reading or seeing his plays, an invigorating sense of his presence and concern. No "as you please" for him!

Jonson's combativeness stemmed partly from the fact that he had not really turned the tide. *The Tempest,* which is not the least bit embarrassed about the concupiscence of dances and antics, about mixing clowns and kings, or about fantastic plots that run away from Nature, is not so much a return to Marlowe's inclusiveness as a reiteration of its continuing strength as a tradition of the English theater. But Shakespeare's modifications of Marlowe's model in the direction of Jonson's values are interesting to observe, especially in *The Tempest,* where the unities of time and place are observed with an uncharacteristic care. Jonson could complain, in the induction to *Bartholomew Fair,* about the ridiculous "servant-monster," but he could not accuse *The Tempest* of jumping around in space or swallowing great chunks of time. Then too, it might be claimed that Jonson's championing of the polished over the rude and the composed over the scattered is reflected in *The Tempest* when we compare it to *Doctor Faustus.* Its unity of tone is as impressive as anything Jonson ever wrote, and its juxtapositions have a sureness of touch that is never jarring or forced. Shakespeare had, I think, no reason to turn his back on Jonson's ideas, but he seems to have been emphatic about wanting the freedom and flexibility that had characterized the stage since he first began to write. D. J. Palmer has said of *Faustus:* "As in *Tamburlaine,* Marlowe evidently conceives the stage as an area liberated from the limitations which nature imposes on the world around; the restraining conditions of probability here seem to be in abeyance, and Marlowe's stage affords scope to realize the gigantic fantasies of his heroes."[5] That seems to be the point in Shakespeare's case; he can and will appreciate the possibilities that inhere in dramatic design when subject to Jonsonian rigor, but he cannot forgo the opportunities that Palmer describes. Jonson can show us Mammon's fantasies, and their frustration. But if there ever was a play that showed us fantasies realizing themselves, it is *The Tempest;* for that, Shakespeare needed to look back to Marlowe. Jonson's tendency as an artist was to reject and refine, and it served him well. Shakespeare's was to accept and synthesize, and it served him even better.

As for the playwright's attitude toward his audience, which should be included in any consideration of dramatic decorum in Marlowe and Jonson, it is difficult to determine in Shakespeare's case; no doubt it lies somewhere between Marlowe's relative indifference and Jonson's almost excessive concern. We sometimes sense an interest on Shakespeare's part in the progressive understanding of his audience and in a possible sharing of the working artist's concerns and interests with his spectators. But what is so explicit in Jonson is, again and again, implicit in Shakespeare. In many ways, *The Tempest* looks back to *A Midsummer Night's*

Dream, where Shakespeare had used discussions of illusion, poetry, and imagination, as well as a play with obtuse actors and spectators, to express some of his values and artistic ideals. The epilogue had invited dissatisfied spectators to consider the whole thing a dream, but that invitation was inevitably ironic since the decision would link the dreamer with the foolish lovers, the befuddled clowns, and the kindly but benighted Theseus. This use of analogy to confirm artistic principles is also present in *The Tempest.* I have argued in another essay on this play that the continual interplay between the roles of actor and spectator as the various magical shows confront the newcomers to the island gradually develops an analogy between the shipwrecked characters and the actual audience.[6] We are perhaps most of all like Ferdinand and Miranda in finding our "presentation" both pleasurable and harmless, and we have the extraordinary privilege of continually visiting backstage, where Prospero and Ariel are busy preparing the next scene or discussing the previous one. The analogy is subtle and often puzzling, not least in the epilogue, where Prospero suddenly announces to us that he is in *our* power, casting us in his role and burdening us, wryly and offhandedly, with his responsibilities. Like the epilogue of *A Midsummer Night's Dream,* the announcement seems tongue in cheek, and not the less disarming for being so. In fantasies begin responsibilities; so it was for Prospero, so it may be for us. The way in which Shakespeare subsumes Jonson's self-consciousness and Marlowe's detachment is fascinating.

We can now return to a more direct consideration of magic by taking up the question of illusion. One of the leading insights of *Doctor Faustus* is revealed by the way in which Faustus, making himself the apparent master of illusory arts, is, in turn, the victim of a larger illusion. His power is gradually shown to be ludicrous and ephemeral, so that even as he is a figure of wonder to less and less impressive examples of the human species, we are learning that he is the victim of a gigantic hoax. This is sometimes demonstrated by the means that the devils choose to distract him, but it is even more emphatically expressed in the grim honesty of Mephistophilis. When we hear the latter say things like "Why this is hell, nor am I out of it" (I.iii.76), and recognize the foolishness of Faustus's response, "Learn thou of Faustus manly fortitude" (I.iii.85), we have a precise measure of the difference between Faustus's illusions and the reality he must sooner or later confront. At times the devils indulge in the showy theatrics that characterize Faustus's ephemeral authority over nature, but we come to feel that they do not really need to, since their power has an actuality that Faustus's magic lacks. A more orthodox playwright might have been eager to go on to suggest that Lucifer's power is ephemeral next to God's, but Marlowe gives the powers of hell dominion and leaves it at that. The magician's supremacy finally has tragic consequences. Like Icarus, like Prometheus, like Lucifer himself, Faustus must descend from the illusion of being a demigod to the reality of being "all torn asunder by the hand of death" (V.iii.7).

Seldom can a magician trafficking in illusion have had such cooperative victims as the clients Captain Face lures to Subtle's establishment in *The Alchemist.* We know from Face's account what a pitiful fellow Subtle has been in the recent past:

> at Pie-corner
> Taking your meal of steam in from cooks' stalls,
> Where, like the father of hunger, you did walk
> Piteously costive, with your pinched-horn nose,
> And your complexion of the Roman wash
> Stuck full of black and melancholic worms,
> Like powder-corns shot at th' artillery-yard.
>
> (I.i.25-31)

And we know he is likely to be so again. Meanwhile, however, like Faustus, he enjoys a charmed supremacy, not least because his customers are such energetic generators of illusion in their own right. When Jonson has warmed us up with Dapper and Drugger as small-time gambler and tabacconist, all too eager to be hoodwinked, he presents his most generous example, Epicure Mammon, whose alchemy transforms the magician's house effortlessly:

> Come on, sir. Now you set your foot on shore
> In Novo Orbe; here's the rich Peru,
> And there within, sir, are the golden mines,
> Great Solomon's Ophir!
>
> (II.i.1-4)

Faced with such an imagination, the illusionist need hardly lift a finger. Jonson has taken an idea faintly present in Marlowe and given it full play: the fact that illusion is largely a function of human appetite—for power, for wealth, for food and sex. That is why the early picture of the hungry Subtle is so crucial, for it is appetite that finally does the tricksters in, as a sense of power makes them overextend their schemes, and greed coupled with lust fosters a struggle for the rich widow, Dame Pliant. Illusion has something of the same double-edged meaning for the magician in *The Alchemist* as in *Faustus,* but it has no mystery or terror, only a kind of marveling glee at the variety and fertility of the human ability to make appetite a god and to generate consequent self-deceptions.

If illusion is relatively easy to encompass in *Faustus* and *The Alchemist,* it is by comparison enormously elusive in *The Tempest.* The point at which it defines itself in the other two plays is precisely the point at which it begins to open up in *The Tempest.* If we can say that Doctor Faustus is the victim of an illusion larger than his own mastery of illusion, we must recognize that there is no Lucifer to oversee Prospero, and that his own consciousness nonetheless includes an aching awareness of illusion reaching out beyond his grasp to characterize the whole fabric of existence. In a sense he is his own Lucifer. And the illusion encompassing him most immediately is of course the theater itself, so that we see him end not by disappearing into the maw of hell but by stepping out of the play proper and, in the person of the actor, bidding farewell to the audience. If we compare him with Subtle, we get similar results. Prospero is successful partly through the folly and error of those he controls, and his story, like Subtle's, is in one sense a virtuoso turn of managed dupery, a staged parade of folly and vice that makes him a kind of playwright. Both Subtle and Prospero can be said to derive large satisfaction from giving others what they deserve and from what might be called the aesthetics of showmanship. But, again, how different is Prospero's consciousness of his magic and himself. He is in touch with genuine power, abuses it as little as possible, appeals to virtue as well as vice in his victims, and gives magic up voluntarily rather than from force of circumstance. The one magician in Renaissance English drama who retired from his magicianship freely prior to Prospero was Greene's Friar Bacon, and it took four deaths to teach him how much responsibility the practice of magic could entail. There is a fair amount of humor in what Prospero says and does—he tends to get played too solemnly—and he is sometimes masked in humours like a Jonson character, but always with a special consciousness of the reality behind the mask that he is at pains to share with us. If the mystery of his profession makes him kin to Faustus and if the comic manipulations and multiple design of his plot remind us of Jonson's practicers, his own consciousness of who he is and of the peculiar nature of his art marks him off from simpler characters. It is as though Faustus was to have simultaneously the roles of Mephistophilis and the Chorus, or as if Subtle also somehow contained the points of view of characters like Surly and Lovewit.

A word about the relation of illusion to metaphor. Marlowe, using material that is obviously fictive—a fable about a German scholar-magician—wants to use a metaphoric base, which his audience will recognize as such, to move toward a reality that is compounded of psychological and spiritual truths. Jonson, though metaphor is important to him (e.g., the whole idea of alchemy), is anxious to avoid the metaphoric base, electing instead the supposition that he can ground his drama in the daily reality known to his audience, arriving at truths through the selection, design, compression, and typification that he values as artistic skills. Shakespeare may have respected the Jonsonian values, but in this regard—and it is an important one if we want to consider drama's relation, as illusion, to reality—he is in Marlowe's camp, where we are in the presence of the fictive, for better or worse, from the very outset.

I hope it is clear that I have not been abasing Jonson and Marlowe so as to elevate Shakespeare. The point is rather to consider the reaction a thoughtful spectator might have had in the theater, watching *The Tempest,* as he compared its outlines, its tones, its procedures, its themes and variations on the familiar, with a classic of some years earlier and a play of extremely recent vintage. Comparing Prospero to Faustus and Subtle may have helped him see more clearly what Shakespeare was doing, and that exercise still holds good. We often note the benefit that Shakespeare's example provided to his contemporaries; we must not forget that the opposite is true also. *The Tempest* is a great play about magic partly because other great plays about magic preceded it, and it is not, therefore, too much to think that

Shakespeare profited from considering those plays, recent and distant, as he sat to compose his own.

There is something peculiarly theatrical about magic, and it would not do to conclude a consideration of these three plays without asking what we can learn from the little we know about their staging, their separate uses of magic's theatricality. What, for example, of *The Tempest* on the stage? While we know that it is an elaborate stage piece, it has associations with no one particular theater. It appears to have played at the Banqueting House at Whitehall, at the Blackfriars, and at the Globe. As such, it must be regarded, like Ariel's vanishing banquet, as a moveable feast. Neverthelsss, there are aspects of its stage magic that seem to be constant, and that have associations both with Marlowe and with Jonson.

Consider first Marlowe's use of the inner stage. It was a favorite focal point, a location that could punctuate the meaning of an individual destiny. In *The Jew of Malta* Marlowe begins and ends with it. Machiavel speaks the opening chorus, then presumably draws the traverse to reveal Barabas "in his counting house, with heaps of gold before him" (I.i.s.d.). At the end, when Barabas has prepared an elaborate device, he is first seen "with a hammer, above, very busy" (V.v.s.d.). Then, as he is caught in his own trap, the stage direction reads "The cable cut, a caldron discovered" (V.v.65.s.d.). He falls through a trap in the gallery and into the waiting cauldron, which is again revealed by means of the traverse. A nice *coup de théâtre,* and more: Barabas ends where he began, in an emblematic setting where hoarded wealth and power have been transformed to suffering and damnation. Marlowe seems to have liked this idea well enough to return to it in *Faustus.* At the opening the Chorus concludes with the line "And this the man that in his study sits" (Prologue, line 28). Again, it seems apparent that he draws the traverse to discover Faustus surrounded, not by gold like Barabas, but by his books. Toward the very end, the Good Angel tells him, "The jaws of hell are open to receive thee," and the stage direction reads "Hell is discovered" (V.ii.112). This was presumably that spectacular stage property known as the hell-mouth, and there is every reason to believe that it was set up in the inner stage and then revealed by means of the traverse. Editors tend to assume that it is covered up again, but it seems to me at least as reasonable to suppose that it remains visible and that Faustus is finally dragged through it by the devils who come to take him away. Again, then, the hero ends as he began, with a great reckoning in a little room.

This intensified, psychological handling of the inner stage is certainly reflected in *The Tempest.* In this case it becomes Prospero's cell, the source from which the whole tale issues, like some gigantic fantasy of the scholar-hermit, and to which it ultimately returns. We do not know whether Prospero and Miranda first enter from the cell, but Prospero begins referring to it almost immediately. As the play goes on, it is the focus of the clowns' attack, the place in which Prospero "discovers Ferdinand and Miranda playing at chess" (V.i.171.s.d.), and finally the lodging into which the whole cast troops, with Prospero remaining behind a moment to speak the epilogue. As with Barabas and Faustus, it has powerful associations with the mind and destiny of the hero, but it becomes, in Prospero's case, a punctuating device for success rather than failure.

We know that the stage these playwrights used had a traditional schema, with hell below the trap and heaven in the upper areas and stage roof. We know too that they could confirm or alter this pattern to suit their purposes. Thus, if *Faustus* were more traditional, the devils would presumably come and go from the trap, and revelations of the divine would appear above. But Marlowe twice brings Lucifer in "above," to witness Faustus's initial conjuring and again to watch his last hours. This gives an emphatic visual emphasis to the hellish dominion mentioned earlier. And if Prospero can be seen as his own Lucifer, then it is surely important that it is he who appears "on the top" (III.iii. 17.s.d.) to supervise and witness the punishment of his enemies.

A related, and more problematic, issue is where Caliban lodges. We know that he started in Prospero's cell and was then ousted after he attempted to rape Miranda. But does he appear from the trap or from the inner stage when Prospero first calls him out? If the former, we have a confirmation of his evil and of Prospero's definition of him as "a born devil" (IV.i.188). But the only stage direction that gives any clue to this is the one that has Caliban replying "within." This tends to suggest that he comes out from the cell in the inner stage; if that is true, Prospero is closer to the truth of Caliban when he says at the end, "this thing of darkness

I/ Acknowledge mine" (V.i.275-76). For better or worse, Caliban is a part of the natural world that Prospero tries to control responsibly; in this context, that is almost the same thing as saying that Caliban is a part of Prospero's mind, an intractable portion of his imagination. As for the trap, its use in *The Tempest* may have been confined to III.iii as a convenient location for the vanishing banquet.[7]

Jonson's setting is of course a house, and only a house. There is manifold use of the possible entrances and exits, but no suggestion that the inner stage or the areas below the trap or up in the galleries have any special meaning.[8] Face, in his disguise as Lungs, the smoky tender of the alchemist's fire, may clamber up from the trap to converse with Mammon, but it does not really matter; the meaning of the stage is too humanized, too far from the *theatrum mundi,* to evoke a hell or heaven. The stage of *The Tempest* is humanized too, but Shakespeare is careful to retain the resonance that the old three-layer stage suggested.

The issue of spectacle on the stage is a curious and troublesome one. Why did Jonson so detest what he called "the concupiscence of dances and antics," the singing and dancing and love of spectacle and pageant so common to the popular stage, when he himself was experimenting with gorgeous and fantastic effects in his court masques? The answer may well lie in his conviction that artistic craft and moral purpose could be joined effectively only when the perimeters of art were sharply defined and clearly understood. A Jonsonian comedy portrays the humours of men and hopes to clarify the understanding of its audience in great part through a consistent verisimilitude. A Jonsonian masque works with materials of fantasy and symbolism, as expressed by mythic and allegorical personages and by song, dance, and spectacle; it hopes to arrive at significant moral configurations for the edification of the court. Any confusion of the two forms would be abhorrent in its undermining of aesthetic principle and moral clarity. Different forms, different audiences, different artistic means: Jonson's rigor about such matters is impressive.

Now consider how the masque works in *The Tempest.* Like a good court masque, it has a specific occasion, the celebration of a royal betrothal, and on its own terms it performs that function consistently. But Prospero's attitude toward it, and its location in the dramatic action of *The Tempest,* alter its meaning. He calls it "another trick," a "vanity of mine Art" (IV.i.37-41), and tells Ferdinand that the spirits are enacting his "present fancies" (IV.i.122). When he breaks it off, remembering that he must deal with Caliban's conspiracy, he reassures Ferdinand by reminding him how unreal it all was. In itself, this might seem a belittling of the masque form; but Prospero goes on to connect the unreality of the masque with the unreality of existence and the illusory fabric of human nature. The mixing and matching of modes and levels of illusion that Jonson would take for artistic inconsistency becomes the means for a philosophical assertion that is breathtaking in its scope. Ferdinand's comment about the masque—"This is a most majestic vision, and/ Harmonious charmingly" (IV.i.118-19)—ought to become our reaction after Prospero's comment on the pervasiveness of illusion, for that speech gathers the diverse elements of the play into a unity and consistency that were quite simply beyond the reach of Jonson's imagination.

Stephen Orgel, writing about the distinction between drama and masque, has this to say:

> A masque is as much a game as a show. The word was often used in the sixteenth century simply to mean masquerade, and the most common way the age had of defining the form was by its inclusion of masked or disguised courtiers. It involves its audience in ways that are impossible for the drama. Not only is it about the court it entertains, but its masquers are members of that audience, and almost always descend and join with it during the central dance, called the *revels.* The drama is properly a form of entertainment, and involves its audience vicariously. The masque is a form of play, and includes its audience directly.[9]

This puts the Jonsonian view very well, but it also indicates why the possibilities of audience involvement suggested by masquerade were irresistible to dramatists less concerned with hard and fast distinctions. Think of Faustus conversing fecklessly with the Seven Deadly Sins who have been brought on to entertain him, or asking the apparition of Helen to make him immortal with a kiss; such "involving of the audience" carries a great deal of meaning. Think of the way Shakespeare had used masking to break down the distinction between vicarious and actual involvement in plays as early as *Love's Labor's Lost* and *Romeo and Juliet.* Then consider how often the distinction between spectator and actor, witness and participant, gets blurred or inverted in *The Tempest.* Shakespeare was not discovering the possibilities that lay in the relation between what Jonson and Inigo Jones were doing at court and what had been the case in the popular theater; he was, rather, continuing a practice which he had valued and understood for some twenty years. And Jonson himself, as the puppet show in *Bartholomew Fair* suggests, did not always find it in his heart to be consistent.

At first the matter of the individual human being may not seem to have much to do with staging. But Marlowe's essentially tragic vision placed the individual at the center and allowed him, in *Faustus,* the fullest consideration. Much of what takes place on his stage is designed to support this emphasis. Concomitantly, Jonson's comic vision cannot allow the single individual such pride of place, and his staging likewise reflects that fact. Marlowe's drama arranges itself naturally around one point of focus, the tragic hero; Jonson's must find other kinds of unity, so that even arch-rogues like Volpone and Subtle must have accomplices like Mosca and Face, and must be part of a dramatic design whose whole is clearly the sum of many parts, a social unit. That is why, for example, Marlowe must begin and end with Faustus, while Jonson can bring in an entirely new character, Lovewit, to help effect his resolution.

Consider how complicated this matter is in *The Tempest.* Prospero seems at least as great a figure as Faustus, and we are tempted to view him as a special version of the tragic hero. But that does not work. Prospero is too complete, too much the stage-manager, to be real in the same way that Hamlet and Macbeth are real. In so far as the whole play seems to be his dream, his vision, his having his way with no significant opposition from man or nature, he tends to be displaced as an individual, so that our attention is turned, as in Jonson, to the intricacy and pleasure of the comic design. A sound magician, as Faustus says, is a demigod, and the more demigodlike Prospero becomes, the less real he is to us in the usual sense of the word.

Put it another way: Faustus must always be the focus of dramatic action, stage-center metaphorically and often literally; Subtle can come and go, as the necessities of trickery call for his

appearance, disguise, and disappearance. Now you see him, now
you don't. Prospero is so much at the center that he takes us
through fantasy, *beyond* tragedy, and begins to displace himself.
So much is the play his—his wish-fulfillment, his responsibility,
his plot—that his character and destiny begin not to matter. Because they mean everything, they begin to mean nothing. Now
you see them, now you don't. As suggested above, Prospero's
way of asking for applause confounds the most serious issues with
the most trivial, until it is not quite clear which is which. This
having it both ways, a quality that Shakespeare seems to have
delighted in as much as any that can be found in his writings, is
what magic most of all means in *The Tempest*. It is real and unreal, serious and frivolous, tragic and comic, the pride of a demigod and the sly nonsense of the sleight-of-hand man. Any good
staging of the play should keep us in touch with the simultaneity
of these possibilities, though that is no easy order. Their difficulty
and elusiveness are represented by Ariel, particularly by the song
that begins "Where the bee sucks, there suck I" (V.i.88). It is
somehow profoundly beautiful and profoundly silly. It may connect poetry and the imagination with the world of nature in an
ineffable way, but it is impossible to say that with certainty.[10] I
cannot imagine it seeming so right in any play other than *The
Tempest*. In that respect it is like Caliban, that "debosh'd fish"
(III.ii.26), like the epilogue, like the masque, like the opening
scene. It is a midnight mushrump, the art of nature or nature of
art. It is one more way of saying that Shakespeare naturally benefited from the jostling theory and practice of playwrights as great,
and as different, as Marlowe and Jonson, but that, being Shakespeare, he benefited in ways that were especially characteristic of
his greatness. How, indeed, should it have been otherwise?

Notes

Full bibliographical information is not included here for those works which also appear in the Selected Bibliography. For abbreviations used, see List of Abbreviations, p. 181. All citations of Shakespeare are from The Riverside Shakespeare, *ed. G. Blakemore Evans et al. (Boston: Houghton Mifflin, 1974).*

CHAPTER 1
"An Overview of Critical Approaches to the Romances"
by Norman Sanders

1. Edward Dowden, *Shakspere: A Critical Study of His Mind and Art* (1875).

2. See Edmond Malone, ed., *Plays and Poems,* 10 vols. (London: J. Rivington & Son, 1790; rpt. New York: AMS); S. T. Coleridge, *Shakespearean Criticism,* ed. T. M. Raysor, 2 vols. (London: Constable, 1930; rpt. London: Dent, 1960, 1961-62); John Payne Collier, ed., *The Works of William Shakespeare,* 8 vols. (London: Whittaker, 1841-53); Alexander Dyce, ed., *The Works of Shakespeare,* 6 vols. (London: E. Moxon, 1857; 2nd ed. in 9 vols., 1864-67; 5th ed. in 10 vols., 1886); and F. J. Furnivall, ed., *Plays and Poems in Quarto,* 43 vols. (London: W. Griggs and C. Praetorius, 1880-91).

3. A. C. Bradley, *Shakespearean Tragedy: Lectures on "Hamlet," "Othello," "Lear," and "Macbeth"* (London: Macmillan, 1904; rpt. New York: St. Martin's); Roy W. Battenhouse, *Shakespearean Tragedy: Its Art and Its Christian Premises* (Bloomington: Indiana University Press, 1969); and Maynard Mack, *"King Lear" in Our Time* (Berkeley and Los Angeles: University of California Press, 1965).

4. Ben Jonson, *Every Man in His Humour,* in *Ben Jonson,* ed. C. H. Herford, Percy and Evelyn Simpson, 11 vols. (Oxford: Clarendon Press, 1925-52), vol. 3; "Ode to Himself," 6:492-93; *Bartholomew Fair,* vol. 6. All citations to Jonson in this article are from the Herford and Simpson edition; the spelling has been modernized.

5. See Samuel Johnson, *Johnson on Shakespeare,* ed. Walter A. Raleigh (Oxford: Oxford University Press, 1908; rev. ed. 1925); John Dryden, *Essays,* ed. William P. Ker, 2 vols. (Oxford: Oxford University Press, 1900); George Bernard Shaw, *Shaw on Shakespeare,* ed. Edwin Wilson (New York: Dutton, 1961); and Lytton Strachey, "Shakespeare's Final Period," in his *Books and Characters* (1922), pp. 47-64.

6. See Elmer Edgar Stoll, *"The Tempest,"* PMLA 47 (1932): 699-726; Gerald E. Bentley, *The Jacobean and Caroline Stage*, 7 vols. (1941-68), and *Shakespeare and His Theatre* (1964); and Harley Granville-Barker, *Prefaces to Shakespeare*, 2 vols. (1946-47).

7. Dowden, *Shakspere*, pp. 402 ff.

8. Strachey, "Shakespeare's Final Period," pp. 47-64.

9. S. Schoenbaum, *William Shakespeare: A Documentary Life* (New York: Oxford University Press, 1975).

10. Howard Felperin, *Shakespearean Romance* (1972), p. vii.

11. J. M. Nosworthy, ed., *Cymbeline* (1955); E. C. Pettet, *Shakespeare and the Romance Tradition* (1949); Frank Kermode, ed., *The Tempest* (1954).

12. See, for example, Eleanor Terry Lincoln, ed., *Pastoral and Romance: Modern Essays in Criticism* (1969).

13. John F. Danby, *Poets on Fortune's Hill: Studies in Sidney, Shakespeare, Beaumont and Fletcher* (1952), p. 103.

14. Samuel Leslie Bethell, *"The Winter's Tale": A Study* (1947), pp. 76, 103.

15. Colin Still, *Shakespeare's Mystery Play: A Study of "The Tempest"* (1921); enlarged as *The Timeless Theme* (1936), pp. 18, 135.

16. G. Wilson Knight, *The Crown of Life: Essays in Interpretation of Shakespeare's Final Plays* (1947), pp. 226-27.

17. D. G. James, "The Failure of the Ballad-Makers," in his *Scepticism and Poetry: An Essay on the Poetic Imagination* (1937) and D. A. Traversi, *Shakespeare: The Last Phase* (1954).

18. Danby, *Poets on Fortune's Hill*, p. 99.

19. For examples, see E.M.W. Tillyard, *Shakespeare's History Plays* (London: Chatto and Windus, 1944), and *The Elizabethan World Picture* (London: Chatto and Windus, 1943); or Alfred Hart, *Shakespeare and the Homilies* (Melbourne: Melbourne University Press, 1934; rpt. New York: AMS Press, 1971); or M. M. Reese, *The Cease of Majesty: A Study of Shakespeare's History Plays* (London: Arnold, 1961).

20. Northrop Frye, *A Natural Perspective: The Development of Shakespearean Comedy and Romance* (1955).

CHAPTER 2
"Romance as Masque"
by Northrop Frye

1. George Puttenham, *The Arte of English Poesie*, ed. Gladys D. Willcock and Alice Walker (Cambridge: Cambridge University Press, 1936), p. 32. Spelling and orthography have been modernized.

2. Francis Bacon, *The Essays,* ed. Clark Sutherland Northup (Boston: Houghton Mifflin, 1936), p. 120.

3. Jonson made these remarks to William Drummond, Scottish author and literary figure, during a walking tour of Scotland in 1618. The remarks are recorded in *Conversations with Drummond* (in *Ben Jonson,* ed. C. H. Herford, Percy and Evelyn Simpson, 11 vols. [Oxford: Clarendon Press, 1925-52], 1:133).

4. All citations of Jonson are from the Herford and Simpson edition cited in the previous note. Spelling and orthography have been modernized.

5. Bacon, *Essays,* p. 119.

6. *A Book of Masques in Honour of Allardyce Nicoll* (Cambridge: Cambridge University Press, 1964).

7. Gertrude Rachel Levy, *The Gate of Horn* (London: Faber and Faber, 1948), especially pp. 167-212; Levy, *The Sword from the Rock* (London: Faber and Faber, 1953).

8. See Northrop Frye, *The Return of Eden: Five Essays on Milton's Epics* (Toronto: University of Toronto Press, 1965), pp. 17-18.

9. Enid Welsford, *The Court Masque: A Study in the Relationship between Poetry and the Revels* (1927), pp. 184 ff.

10. See Northrop Frye, "The Argument of Comedy," in *English Institute Essays, 1948,* ed. D. A. Robertson, Jr. (1949), pp. 58-73.

11. James Shirley, "Love's Cruelty," in *The Dramatic Works and Poems of James Shirley,* ed. William Gifford and Alexander Dyce (London: John Murray, 1833), p. 213.

12. See G. Wilson Knight, *The Shakespearian Tempest* (1932), pp. vii-19.

13. Jonson, *Timber: or, Discoveries,* ed. Herford and Simpson, 8:626.

14. Jonson makes this comment, through the scrivener, in the Induction (line 131) of *Bartholomew Fair* (ed. Herford and Simpson, 6:16).

CHAPTER 3
"Masking and Unmasking in the Last Plays"
by Clifford Leech

1. Mary Renault, *The Mask of Apollo* (New York: Pantheon, 1966).

2. In the title of this paper, the "-k" spelling of "mask" is used in accordance with the practice of E. K. Chambers in *The Elizabethan Stage* ([Oxford: Clarendon Press, 1923], 1:149-212); that usage will allow me to emphasize the link between the masque proper and the use of disguising and undisguising that is to be found almost everywhere in the drama of the time and became strongly influential in Shakespeare's last plays. But when referring to court performances and masque performances elsewhere, together

with their echoes in the drama of the age, I will henceforth use the "-qu-" spelling.

3. John Milton, *Arcades,* in *Complete Poems and Major Prose,* ed. Merritt Y. Hughes (New York: Odyssey, 1957), p. 79, lines 84, 89-90. All citations of Milton are from this edition.

4. *A Book of Masques in Honour of Allardyce Nicoll* (Cambridge: Cambridge University Press, 1964), pp. 8, 139.

5. Ibid., p. 431.

6. In what follows I am indebted to Inga-Stina Ewbank's contribution to *A Book of Masques,* " 'These Pretty Devices': A Study of Masques in Plays," pp. 405-48. Her approach, however, is different from mine.

7. All citations of *The Malcontent* are from the Revels edition, ed. G. K. Hunter (London: Methuen, 1975).

8. See Alfred Harbage, *Annals of English Drama, 975-1700,* revised by S. Schoenbaum (London: Methuen, 1964), p. 88.

9. *A Book of Masques,* p. 431.

10. All citations of *The Duchess of Malfi* are from the Revels edition, ed. John Russell Brown (London: Methuen, 1964).

11. Clifford Leech, *The John Fletcher Plays* (London: Chatto and Windus, 1962), p. 143.

12. *Duchess of Malfi,* ed. Brown, p. xviii.

13. I cannot agree with Brown's suggestion in the Revels edition (p. 107) that it was elsewhere.

14. Ewbank has convincingly suggested in *A Book of Masques* that Ford here owes a debt to Webster and to the appearance of "twelve frantics" in Campion's *The Lords' Masque* of 1613.

15. All citations of *Perkin Warbeck* are from the Revels edition, ed. Peter Ure (London: Methuen, 1968).

16. William Blissett, "Your Majesty is Welcome to a Fair," in *The Elizabethan Theatre IV,* ed. G. R. Hibbard (Toronto: Macmillan, 1974), pp. 80-105.

17. E. A. Horsman, editor of the Revels edition of *Bartholomew Fair* (London: Methuen, 1960), doubts the linking of Leatherhead with Inigo Jones (pp. xvii-xviii), but what has been said above makes it hard to resist.

18. Clifford Leech, *Shakespeare's Tragedies and Other Studies in Seventeenth Century Drama* (1950), pp. 113-14; E. K. Chambers, *William Shakespeare: A Study of Facts and Problems* (Oxford: Clarendon Press, 1930), 1:271,483.

19. *Timon of Athens,* ed. H. J. Oliver, The Arden Shakespeare (London: Methuen, 1959), p. 28.

20. Ibid., p. 100, note.

21. See Clifford Leech, *"Twelfth Night" and Shakespearean Comedy* (1965), p. 78.

22. *A Book of Masques*, pp. 418-19.

23. Clifford Leech, "The Structure of the Last Plays," *ShS 11* (1958), pp. 19-30.

24. T. S. Eliot, "Marina," in *The Complete Poems and Plays: 1909-1950* (New York: Harcourt, Brace & World, 1952), p. 73.

25. All citations of *The Triumph of Peace* are from the edition in *A Book of Masques*.

26. See *A Book of Masques*, p. 280.

27. *Ben Jonson: The Complete Masques*, ed. Stephen Orgel (1969), pp. 186, 206, 213, 224; *Ben Jonson: Selected Masques*, ed. Stephen Orgel (1970), pp. 116, 140; both in The Yale Ben Jonson (New Haven: Yale University Press).

28. Charles Maturin, *Melmoth the Wanderer*, ed. Douglas Grant (London: Oxford University Press, 1972), p. 157.

CHAPTER 4
"Romance and Romanticism"
by Howard Felperin

1. See W. J. Bate, *The Burden of the Past and the English Poet* (Cambridge: Harvard University Press, 1970); Harold Bloom, *The Anxiety of Influence: A Theory of Poetry* (New York: Oxford University Press, 1973); Bloom, *Kaballa and Criticism* (New York: Seabury, 1975); Bloom, *A Map of Misreading* (New York: Oxford University Press, 1975); Bloom, *Poetry and Repression: Revisionism from Blake to Stevens* (New Haven: Yale University Press, 1976). It will become apparent in the course of this essay that the view of literary history expressed in these works is a logical extension of a much more entrenched and uncontroversial conception of modernism, the essential doctrines of which are represented in *The Modern Tradition: Backgrounds of Modern Literature*, ed. Richard Ellman and Charles Feidelson, Jr. (New York: Oxford University Press, 1965).

2. Northrop Frye, *Anatomy of Criticism* (1957), p. 35.

3. Northrop Frye, *A Study of English Romanticism* (New York: Columbia University Press, 1968), p. 20.

4. Introduction to *The Tempest*, ed. Northrop Frye (1959), p. 26.

5. Ibid., p. 18. See also Northrop Frye, *A Natural Perspective*, pp. 141-59.

6. See, for example, G. Wilson Knight, *The Crown of Life: Essays in Interpretation of Shakespeare's Final Plays* (1947); C. L. Barber, "'Thou That Beget'st Him Did Thee Beget': Transformation in *Pericles* and *The Winter's Tale*," *ShS 22* (1969): 59-67; E. M. W. Tillyard, *Shakespeare's Last Plays* (1938); Derek Traversi, *Shakespeare: The Last Phase* (1954); and David Young, *The Heart's Forest: A Study of Shakespeare's Pastoral Plays* (1972).

7. Introduction to *The Tempest*, ed. Frye, p. 20.

8. Harry Berger, "Miraculous Harp: A Reading of Shakespeare's *Tempest*," *ShakS* 5 (1969): 253-83. My own reading of *The Tempest* is deeply indebted to Berger's, one of the few essays to respond to the difficulties presented by the play rather than to the harmonies that the play, as a romance, is supposed to present. Worth citing in this connection is Joseph H. Summers, "The Anger of Prospero," *MQR* 12 (1973): 116-35, in which the problem of Prospero's conduct is raised as a central issue only to be ceremoniously laid to rest, lest it upset orthodox interpretation.

9. This historical scheme is expressed in almost all of Harold Bloom's writing since *The Anxiety of Influence* (New York: Oxford University Press, 1973). See, for example, *Figures of Capable Imagination* (New York: Seabury, 1975), *A Map of Misreading* (New York: Oxford University Press, 1975), and *Poetry and Repression* (New Haven: Yale University Press, 1976).

10. The tendency to read the novella as a study of the psychological and cultural alienation of modern man was no doubt encouraged by T. S. Eliot's borrowing of the line "Mistah Kurtz—he dead" for the epigraph to "The Hollow Men." The influential work of Albert J. Guerard, *Conrad the Novelist* (Cambridge: Harvard University Press, 1958), pp. 32-43, discusses it as "a *Pilgrim's Progress* for our pessimistic and psychologizing age." Other critics have traced its ironic structural parallels to the descents into hell of the *Inferno* and the *Aeneid*, as well as to medieval quest romance. See *Conrad's "Heart of Darkness" and the Critics,* ed. Bruce Harkness (Belmont, California: Wadsworth, 1960). A valuable, though partial, attempt to de-ironize Conrad's fiction by affirming its continuities with older traditions of romance and Romanticism and by questioning its relation to prevailing notions of modernism is to be found in David Thorburn, *Conrad's Romanticism* (New Haven: Yale University Press, 1974). See especially pp. 153-65.

11. Joseph Conrad, *Heart of Darkness,* ed. Robert Kimbrough (New York: Norton, 1963), pp. 4-5. All citations of Conrad are from this edition and are followed by page references.

12. Thomas Warton, *History of English Poetry* (London, 1781), 3:490-97. See René Wellek, *The Rise of English Literary History* (Chapel Hill: University of North Carolina Press, 1941), pp. 192-94. Warton's successor among modern historians of literary modernism is Geoffrey Hartman, who invokes Warton in formulating his view that "the history of English literature since the Renaissance suggests a continuous process of demystification." See particularly "Romantic Poetry and the *Genius Loci*" and "Toward Literary History" in his *Beyond Formalism* (New Haven: Yale University Press, 1970).

CHAPTER 5
"Fathers and Daughters in Shakespeare's Romances"
by Cyrus Hoy

1. Quoted in Geoffrey Bullough, ed., *Narrative and Dramatic Sources of Shakespeare,* 8 vols. (1957-75), 6 (1966): 237.

2. Robert Greene, *Pandosto,* in *Elizabethan Prose Fiction,* ed. Merritt Lawlis (New York: Odyssey, 1967), p. 277.

CHAPTER 6
"Cloten, Autolycus, and Caliban"
by Joan Hartwig

1. See Lawrence J. Ross, "Shakespeare's 'Dull Clown' and Symbolic Music," *SQ* 17 (1966): 107-28.

2. Lawrence J. Ross, in an unpublished lecture delivered in April 1964, " 'A Most Majestic Vision': A Lecture on Shakespeare and *The Tempest,*" discussed these scenes as analogous action which is used for analysis in a comic key. In a discussion more complex than I can indicate in a note, he demonstrated that the comic analogue enacts the essential absurdity of the kind of moral choice made by all of the usurpers in the play. David Young, in a paper delivered at the Shakespeare Association of America meeting in New Haven, March 1975, suggested an interesting parallel between Caliban's "sweet airs" speech and Prospero's "revels" speech, both of which reflect an enlarging and distancing awareness.

3. John Marston, *The Malcontent,* ed. M. L. Wine, Regents Renaissance Drama Series (Lincoln: University of Nebraska Press, 1964). Although Arthur H. Nethercot notes, in his revised edition of *Elizabethan Plays* (New York: Holt, Rinehart, and Winston, 1971), p. 770, n. 4, that this passage is probably an addition, the scene's authorship makes no difference to my point.

4. William Chappell, *Popular Music of the Olden Time* (London, 1855-59), 1:222.

5. Samuel Johnson, *A Dictionary of the English Language 1755* (New York: AMS Press, 1967).

6. Leo Salingar, *Shakespeare and the Traditions of Comedy* (1974), p. 97. In attempting to describe the effects of Aristophanic parody, Salingar admits that Aristophanes' technique "is more than parody." My point is that we do not yet have a word to indicate the concept more clearly than the existent "parody."

7. Passarello in the lines already cited from *The Malcontent,* and Edgar in *King Lear,* III.iv.85-90.

8. *Samuel Johnson on Shakespeare,* ed. W. K. Wimsatt, Jr. (New York: Hill and Wang, 1960), p. 108.

9. For a more detailed examination of the parodic relationship between Cloten and Posthumus and Imogen, see the chapter on *Cymbeline* in my *Shakespeare's Tragicomic Vision* (1972), pp. 70-82.

10. J. H. P. Pafford, ed., *The Winter's Tale* (1965), p. lxxx, including n. 5.

11. See G. Wilson Knight's comments on this parody in *The Crown of Life,* p. 101.

12. Mary L. Livingston, "The Natural Art of *The Winter's Tale,*" *MLQ* 30 (1969): 240-55, has an excellent discussion of the details of Autolycus's ballads and their inverted relationship to the rest of the play's art.

13. In a speech given at the Shakespeare Association of America meeting in New Haven, March 1975.

14. Alan C. Dessen, *Elizabethan Drama and the Viewer's Eye* (Chapel Hill: University of North Carolina Press, 1977), p. 23, hypothesizes that Caliban (as well as Stephano and Trinculo) returns wearing the stolen "glistering" apparel, thus presenting a visual parallel to Prospero. Admittedly, the stage direction is ambiguous in its pronoun "their" [*"Enter* Ariel, *driving in* Caliban, Stephano, *and* Trinculo *in their stolen apparel"* (V.i.255 s.d.)]; but the comments made by Alonso and Prospero after his appearance in the final scene and Caliban's earlier recognition that the glittering clothes are "trash" hardly support the inference that Caliban has redressed himself.

CHAPTER 7
"Cymbeline's Debt to Holinshed"
by Joan Warchol Rossi

1. Bullough, ed., *Narrative and Dramatic Sources of Shakespeare,* 8 (1975): 7, 11.

2. J. P. Brockbank, in "History and Histrionics in *Cymbeline,*" *ShS 11* (1958), p. 43, suggests that echoes of the Brute legend are used to produce an impressionistic historical effect. The *Chronicles,* however, could also have provided a springboard for these echoes, since Holinshed's reference to "the citie of London then called Troinouant" within the Mulmutius material (1:451) does call to mind Britain's ancestry.

3. There are exceptions: Warren D. Smith, "Cloten with Caius Lucius," *SP 49* (1952): 185-94, and D. R. C. Marsh, *The Recurring Miracle: A Study of "Cymbeline" and the Last Plays* (1962), p. 51, do point out the rudeness of Cloten and the self-interested motivation of the Queen.

4. This view is common among critics and historians alike. See, for example, G. Wilson Knight, *The Crown of Life,* p. 136; and A. L. Rowse, *The*

England of Elizabeth: The Structure of Society (New York: Macmillan, 1951), p. 64.

5. Raphael Holinshed et al., *The Chronicles of England, Scotland, and Ireland* (1587), ed. H. Ellis (London, 1807-1808), 1:479.

6. W. G. Boswell-Stone, *Shakespeare's Holinshed: The Chronicle and the Historical Plays Compared* (London: Lawrence and Bullen, 1896), posits that the peaceful embassy from Augustus to Kymbeline recorded in the *History of Scotland* "may have given Shakespeare a hint for the less peaceful mission of Caius Lucius" (p. 9).

7. "But yet would not all that their fierce and desperate hardinesse preuaile, for fortune by fatall appointment being bent to aduance the Romans vnto the dominion of the whole world, shewed hir selfe so fauourable vnto them in this battell, that in the end, though the Britains with the confederats did what lay in men to doo for atteining of victorie, yet were they beaten downe and slaine euerie mothers sonne, a few onelie excepted, which escaped by flight" (5:64-65).

CHAPTER 8
"Tragic Structure in *The Winter's Tale*"
by Charles Frey

1. Edward Dowden, *Shakspere: A Critical Study of His Mind and Art,* 3rd ed., p. 403.

CHAPTER 9
"The Restoration of Hermione"
by David M. Bergeron

1. My argument will avoid such extremes as insisting that *The Winter's Tale* was written for the investiture of Prince Henry as Prince of Wales in 1610 (Glynne Wickham, "Shakespeare's Investiture Play: The Occasion and Subject of *The Winter's Tale,*" *TLS,* 18 December 1969, p. 1456); or of assigning some possible significance to the fact of the sixteen-year gap between the execution of Mary, Queen of Scots, and the accession of her son James I to the English throne (Glynne Wickham, "*The Winter's Tale*: A Comedy with Deaths," in his *Shakespeare's Dramatic Heritage* [1969], p. 265); or of likening Hermione to the Jacobean view of Mary Stuart (Barbara Everett, Letter in *TLS,* 22 January 1970, p. 84).

2. Bullough, ed., *Narrative and Dramatic Sources of Shakespeare,* 8 (1975): 132.

3. See, for example, J. E. Bullard and W. M. Fox, Letter in *TLS*, 14 March 1952, p. 189.

4. For example, J. H. P. Pafford, ed., *The Winter's Tale*, says: "That Forman does not mention the statue scene is no argument that he did not see it" (p. xxvii). It is interesting to note, however, that Pafford does not hesitate to use Forman to substantiate the gloss on IV.ii.4.

5. A. L. Rowse, *Simon Forman: Sex and Society in Shakespeare's Age* (London: Weidenfeld and Nicolson, 1974).

6. Introduction to *The Winter's Tale*, ed. Frank Kermode, in *The Complete Signet Classic Shakespeare*, ed. Sylvan Barnet.

7. Kenneth Muir, "The Conclusion of *The Winter's Tale*," in *The Morality of Art*, ed. D. W. Jefferson (1969), p. 92.

8. Richard Studing, "Spectacle and Masque in *The Winter's Tale*," *EM* 21 (1970): 76; Inga-Stina Ewbank, "The Triumph of Time in *The Winter's Tale*," *REL* 5 (1964): 98.

9. See David M. Bergeron, "Actors in English Civic Pageants," *RenP 1972* (1973), pp. 24-26.

10. *Collections III: A Calendar of Dramatic Records in the Books of the Livery Companies of London, 1485-1640*, ed. Jean Robertson and D. J. Gordon (Oxford: Malone Society, 1954), p. 83.

11. The correspondence of Time in the play and pageant has been noted by only one critic, Pafford, in his Arden edition, p. 168; he does not mention other important connections.

12. Cyrus Hoy, "Jacobean Tragedy and the Mannerist Style," *ShS 26* (1973), p. 65; Ewbank, "The Triumph of Time," p. 91.

13. *Chruso-thriambos* (London, 1611), sig. B3. All citations of the pageant are from this quarto edition.

14. See David M. Bergeron, *English Civic Pageantry 1558-1642* (London: Arnold; Columbia: University of South Carolina Press, 1971), pp. 155-58 and plate 9.

15. Interestingly, Munday could have seen the actual monument to Faringdon in St. Peter's Church, Cheapside; see John Weever, *Ancient Funerall Monuments* (London, 1631), p. 390.

16. W. W. Greg, *The Shakespeare First Folio* (Oxford: Clarendon Press, 1955), p. 417.

17. See Elkin C. Wilson, *Prince Henry and English Literature* (Ithaca: Cornell University Press, 1946); see also David M. Bergeron, "Prince Henry and English Civic Pageantry," *TSL* 13 (1968): 109-16.

18. See Hoy, "Jacobean Tragedy and the Mannerist Style," pp. 65-66 n., for extensive comment on the appropriateness of the reference to Julio Romano.

19. Henry Peacham, *The Compleat Gentleman*, ed. G. S. Gordon (Oxford: Clarendon Press, 1906), p. 110.

20. Eric Mercer, *English Art 1553-1625* (Oxford: Clarendon Press, 1962),

p. 217; see also J. G. Mann, "English Church Monuments, 1536-1625," *Walpole Society* 21 (1932-33): 1-22.

21. Mercer, *English Art,* p. 247.

22. Wickham, "A Comedy with Deaths," p. 265.

23. Ibid.

24. Glynne Wickham, "Romance and Emblem: A Study in the Dramatic Structure of *The Winter's Tale,*" in *The Elizabethan Theatre III,* ed. David Galloway (1973), pp. 94-95; p. 97.

25. See Ernst H. Kantorowicz, *The King's Two Bodies: A Study in Mediaeval Political Theology* (Princeton: Princeton University Press, 1957), pp. 419-37; see also Ralph E. Giesey, *The Royal Funeral Ceremony in Renaissance France* (Geneva: Droz, 1960).

26. Quoted in W. H. St. John Hope, "On the Funeral Effigies of the Kings and Queens of England, with special reference to those in the Abbey Church of Westminster," *Archaeologia* 60, pt. ii (1907): 553.

27. Ibid., p. 567.

28. Ibid., p. 555. A picture of this effigy on the coffin is contained in Henry Holland's *Herwologia Anglica* (1620) (sig. E2) and is reproduced in Wilson's *Prince Henry and English Literature.*

29. *The Funerals of the High and Mighty Prince Henry* (London, 1613), sig. A4.

CHAPTER 10
"Immediacy and Remoteness"
by Charles R. Forker

1. See especially G. Wilson Knight, *The Crown of Life.*

2. E. M. W. Tillyard, *Shakespeare's Last Plays* (1938), p. 80.

3. This issue has frequently been the subject of recent Shakespeare criticism. See especially Maynard Mack, "Engagement and Detachment in Shakespeare's Plays," in *Essays on Shakespeare and Elizabethan Drama in Honor of Hardin Craig,* ed. Richard Hosley (London: Routledge and Kegan Paul, 1963), pp. 275-96, and Anne Righter, *Shakespeare and the Idea of the Play* (1962). Of more specialized relevance are Ejner J. Jensen, "Spying Scenes and the Problem Plays: A Shakespearean Strategy," *Tulane Studies in English* 20 (1972): 23- 40, and Charles R. Forker, "Shakespeare's Theatrical Symbolism and Its Function in *Hamlet,*" *SQ* 14 (1963): 215-29, rpt. in *Essays in Shakespearean Criticism,* ed. James L. Calderwood and Harold E. Toliver (Englewood Cliffs, N.J.: Prentice-Hall, 1970), pp. 441-58. For a valuable study of the problem in relation to Jonson, see Henry E. Jacobs, "Theaters within Theaters: Levels of Dramatic Illusion in Ben Jonson's Comedy" (Ph.D. diss., Indiana University, 1973).

CHAPTER 11
"Where the Bee Sucks"
by David Young

1. In "Two Magian Comedies: *The Tempest* and *The Alchemist*," *ShS* 22 (1960), pp. 47-58, Harry Levin notes that "the conjunction of Jonson and Shakespeare was never closer or more productive than in the successive seasons of 1610 and 1611, when His Majesty's Servants introduced *The Alchemist* and *The Tempest* respectively. It is conceivable that the same actor created the parts of Jonson's criminal mastermind and Shakespeare's wonder-working sorcerer, and it is suggestive that the actors' list for *The Alchemist* was headed by Richard Burbage" (p. 51). Throughout this essay, all citations of Marlowe are from *The Complete Plays of Christopher Marlowe,* ed. Irving Ribner (New York: Odyssey, 1963); citations of Jonson are from *The Alchemist,* ed. Alvin Kernan, The Yale Ben Jonson (New Haven: Yale University Press, 1974).

2. The "quirky eloquence" I speak of may well be a reflection of Shakespeare's willingness to drift from the Ciceronian syntactical preferences of his earlier work to a Senecanism which is not unlike Jonson's. Jonas Barish, contrasting a passage from *1 Henry IV* with "Baroque" examples from Jonson, notes that the latter "reject the figures of balance, parallel, and climax," preferring a language which "moves in streaks and flashes rather than with a steady pulsation" (*Ben Jonson and the Language of Prose Comedy* [Cambridge: Harvard University Press, 1960], pp. 47-48). I do not know whether anyone has studied this trend in Shakespeare, but I must confine myself here to a single example:

> Being once perfected how to grant suits,
> How to deny them, who t' advance, and who
> To trash for overtopping, new created
> The creatures that were mine, I say, or chang'd 'em,
> Or else new form'd em; having both the key
> Of officer and office, set all hearts i' th' state
> To what tune pleas'd his ear, that now he was
> The ivy which had hid my princely trunk,
> And suck'd my verdure out on 't. Thou attend'st not!
> (I.ii.79-87)

I am grateful to my colleague Robert Pierce for calling my attention to the implications of my mention of Prospero's "quirky eloquence."

3. Frank Kermode, ed., *The Tempest* (1954), p. 134.

4. Sir Philip Sidney, "An Apologie for Poetrie," in *Elizabethan Critical Essays,* ed. C. Gregory Smith (London: Oxford University Press, 1904),

1:199. I am assuming that the entire text of *Faustus* is Marlowe's.

5. D. J. Palmer, "Magic and Poetry in *Doctor Faustus*," *CritQ* 6 (1964): 56.

6. David Young, *The Heart's Forest: A Study of Shakespeare's Pastoral Plays* (1972), pp. 154-59 and 189-91.

7. J. C. Adams, in "The Staging of *The Tempest*, III,iii," *RES* 14 (1936): 404-19, conjectures that the table had a stagehand concealed inside, to make the food vanish at the proper moment. See also Kermode's appendix, "*The Tempest* on the Jacobean Stage," pp. 150-55 in his edition cited above.

8. Unless, as William C. Carroll, who read this for me in manuscript, points out, Jonson makes ironic use of the inner stage by stuffing Dapper in the privy—a parodic "hell-mouth"?

9. *Ben Jonson: Selected Masques*, ed. Stephen Orgel, The Yale Ben Jonson (New Haven: Yale University Press, 1970), p. 1.

10. Harry Berger, in "Miraculous Harp: A Reading of Shakespeare's *Tempest*," *ShakS* 5 (1969): 253-83, finds that Ariel's song "reminds me of Plato's familiar comparison of the poet to a honey-gathering bee in the garden of the muses" (p. 255).

A Selected Bibliography on Shakespeare's Romances

LIST OF ABBREVIATIONS

AI	*American Imago*
AmN&Q	*American Notes & Queries*
BSUF	*Ball State University Forum*
CE	*College English*
ContempR	*Contemporary Review* (London)
CR	*Critical Review*
CritQ	*Critical Quarterly*
DUJ	*Durham University Journal*
EA	*Etudes Anglaises*
EIC	*Essays in Criticism* (Oxford)
ELH	*Journal of English Literary History*
ELN	*English Language Notes*
ELR	*English Literary Renaissance*
EM	*English Miscellany*
ES	*English Studies*
ESRS	*Emporia State Research Studies*
Expl	*Explicator*
HAB	*Humanities Association Bulletin*
HLQ	*Huntington Library Quarterly*
JEGP	*Journal of English & Germanic Philology*
MLN	*Modern Language Notes*
M&L	*Music & Letters* (London)
MLQ	*Modern Language Quarterly*
MLR	*Modern Language Review*
MP	*Modern Philology*
MQR	*Michigan Quarterly Review*
N&Q	*Notes & Queries*
NDQ	*North Dakota Quarterly*
NSST	*New Shakespeare Society Transactions*
PMLA	*Publications of The Modern Language Association of America*
PQ	*Philological Quarterly*
PsyR	*Psychoanalytic Review*
REL	*Review of English Literature*
Rendezvous	*Rendezvous: Journal of Arts & Letters*
RenP	*Renaissance Papers* (of the Southeastern Renaissance Conference)

RES	*Review of English Studies*
RR	*Romanic Review*
RS	*Research Studies* (Washington State)
SEL	*Studies in English Literature, 1500-1900* (Rice)
ShAB	*Shakespeare Association Bulletin*
ShakS	*Shakespeare Studies*
ShS	*Shakespeare Survey*
ShN	*Shakespeare Newsletter*
SJH	*Shakespeare-Jahrbuch* (Heidelberg)
SJW	*Shakespeare-Jahrbuch* (Weimar)
SoRA	*Southern Review: An Australian Journal of Literary Studies* (Adelaide)
SP	*Studies in Philology*
SQ	*Shakespeare Quarterly*
TLS	*Times Literary Supplement* (London)
TSL	*Tennessee Studies in Literature*

General Works with Significant Sections on the Romances

1. Arthos, John. *The Art of Shakespeare.* New York: Barnes and Noble, 1964.
2. Bentley, Gerald E. *The Jacobean and Caroline Stage.* 7 vols. Oxford: Clarendon Press, 1941-68.
3. ____. *Shakespeare and His Theatre.* Lincoln: University of Nebraska Press, 1964.
4. Berry, Francis. *Poets' Grammar: Person, Time, and Mood in Poetry.* London: Routledge and Kegan Paul, 1958.
5. Bodkin, Maud. *Archetypal Patterns in Poetry.* London: Oxford University Press, 1934; rpt. 1963.
6. Bradbrook, Muriel C. *The Growth and Structure of Elizabethan Comedy.* London: Chatto and Windus, 1955, 1962.
7. Brower, Reuben A. *The Fields of Light: An Experiment in Critical Reading.* New York: Oxford University Press, 1951.
8. Brown, John Russell. *Shakespeare and His Comedies.* 2nd ed. with new chapter on the last comedies. London: Methuen, 1962.
9. Bryant, Joseph Allen. *Hippolyta's View: Some Christian Aspects of Shakespeare's Plays.* Lexington: University of Kentucky Press, 1961.
10. Bush, Geoffrey. *Shakespeare and the Natural Condition.* Cambridge: Harvard University Press, 1956.
11. Chambers, E. K. *Shakespeare: A Survey.* New York: Hill and Wang, 1958.

12. Champion, Larry S. *Evolution of Shakespeare's Comedy: A Study in Dramatic Perspective.* Cambridge: Harvard University Press, 1970.
13. Clemen, Wolfgang. *The Development of Shakespeare's Imagery.* London: Methuen, and Cambridge: Harvard University Press, 1951.
14. Colie, Rosalie Littell. *Shakespeare's Living Art.* Princeton: Princeton University Press, 1974.
15. Craig, Hardin. "Shakespeare's Development as a Dramatist in the Light of his Experience." *SP* 39 (1942): 226-38.
16. _____. *An Interpretation of Shakespeare.* New York: Citadel, 1948.
17. _____. *The Enchanted Glass: The Elizabethan Mind in Literature.* Oxford: Basil Blackwell, 1950.
18. _____. *A New Look at Shakespeare's Quartos.* Stanford: Stanford University Press, 1961.
19. Cruttwell, Patrick. *The Shakespearean Moment and Its Place in the Poetry of the Seventeenth Century.* London: Chatto and Windus, 1955.
20. Curry, Walter Clyde. *Shakespeare's Philosophical Patterns.* Baton Rouge: Louisiana State University Press, 1937; 2nd ed., 1959.
21. Dowden, Edward. *Shakspere: A Critical Study of His Mind and Art.* London: Henry S. King, 1875; 2nd ed., London: Macmillan, 1876; 3rd ed., New York, 1881; rpt. London: Routledge and Kegan Paul, 1948.
22. Driver, Tom. *The Sense of History in Greek and Shakespearean Drama.* New York: Columbia University Press, 1960.
23. Edwards, Philip. *Shakespeare and the Confines of Art.* London: Methuen, 1968.
24. Ellis-Fermor, Una. *The Jacobean Drama: An Interpretation.* London: Methuen, 1936.
25. Empson, William. *Some Versions of Pastoral.* Norfolk, Connecticut: New Directions, 1950.
26. Evans, Bertrand. *Shakespeare's Comedies.* Oxford: Clarendon Press, 1960.
27. Evans, B. Ifor. *The Language of Shakespeare's Plays.* Bloomington and London: Indiana University Press, 1952.
28. Farnham, Willard. *The Shakespearean Grotesque: Its Genesis and Transformations.* Oxford: Clarendon Press, 1971.
29. Fergusson, Francis. *The Idea of a Theater.* Princeton: Princeton University Press, 1949; rpt. 1968.
30. _____. *Shakespeare: The Pattern in His Carpet.* New York: Delacorte, 1958.
31. _____. "Romantic Love in Dante and Shakespeare." *Sewanee Review* 83 (1975): 253-66.

32. Frye, Northrop. "The Argument of Comedy." In *English Institute Essays, 1948,* ed. D.A. Robertson, Jr. (New York: Columbia University Press, 1949), pp. 58-73.

33. ____. *Anatomy of Criticism.* Princeton: Princeton University Press, 1957.

34. Frye, Roland Mushat. *Shakespeare: The Art of the Dramatist.* Boston: Houghton Mifflin, 1970.

35. Garber, Marjorie B. *Dream in Shakespeare: From Metaphor to Metamorphosis.* New Haven and London: Yale University Press, 1974.

36. Goddard, Harold C. *The Meaning of Shakespeare.* Chicago: University of Chicago Press, 1951.

37. Goldman, Michael. *Shakespeare and the Energies of Drama.* Princeton: Princeton University Press, 1972.

38. Granville-Barker, Harley. *Prefaces to Shakespeare.* 2 vols. Princeton: Princeton University Press, 1946-1947.

39. Greg, W. W. *Pastoral Poetry and Pastoral Drama.* London: A.H. Bullen, 1906.

40. Grene, David. *Reality and the Heroic Pattern: Last Plays of Ibsen, Shakespeare, and Sophocles.* Chicago: University of Chicago Press, 1967.

41. Herrick, Marvin T. *Tragicomedy: Its Origin and Development in Italy, France, and England.* Urbana: University of Illinois Press, 1955.

42. Hobson, Alan. *Full Circle: Shakespeare and Moral Development.* London: Chatto and Windus, and New York: Barnes and Noble, 1972.

43. Holland, Norman N. *The Shakespearean Imagination.* Bloomington and London: Indiana University Press, and New York: Macmillan, 1964.

44. Honigman, E. A. J. *The Stability of Shakespeare's Text.* London: Edward Arnold, 1965.

45. Hoy, Cyrus. *The Hyacinth Room: An Investigation into the Nature of Comedy, Tragedy, and Tragicomedy.* New York: Alfred A. Knopf, 1964.

46. ____. "Jacobean Tragedy and the Mannerist Style." *ShS 26* (1973), pp. 49-67.

47. Hunter, Robert G. *Shakespeare and the Comedy of Forgiveness.* New York: Columbia University Press, 1965.

48. James, D. G. *Scepticism and Poetry: An Essay on the Poetic Imagination.* London: Allen and Unwin, 1937; rpt. New York: Barnes and Noble, 1960.

49. Kermode, Frank. *English Pastoral Poetry: From the Beginnings to Marvell.* London: Harrap, 1952.

50. Kirsch, Arthur C. *Jacobean Dramatic Perspectives.* Charlottesville: University Press of Virginia, 1972.

51. Knight, G. Wilson. *The Shakespearian Tempest.* London: Oxford University Press, 1932; rpt. London: Methuen, 1971.

52. ____. *Neglected Powers: Essays on Nineteenth and Twentieth Century Literature.* London: Routledge and Kegan Paul, 1970. Contains a previously unpublished essay on the romances by T.S. Eliot.

53. Lawrence, W.W. *Shakespeare's Problem Comedies.* London: Macmillan, 1931; rpt. New York: Frederick Ungar, 1960; rpt. Harmondsworth and Baltimore: Penguin Books, 1969.

54. Lea, K.M. *Italian Popular Comedy: A Study in the Commedia dell' Arte, 1560-1620.* Oxford: Clarendon Press, 1934.

55. Leech, Clifford. *Shakespeare's Tragedies and Other Studies in Seventeenth Century Drama.* London: Chatto and Windus, 1950.

56. ____. *"Twelfth Night" and Shakespearean Comedy.* Toronto: University of Toronto Press, 1965.

57. Levin, Harry. *The Myth of the Golden Age in the Renaissance.* Bloomington: Indiana University Press, 1969.

58. Levin, Richard. *The Multiple Plot in English Renaissance Drama.* Chicago: University of Chicago Press, 1971.

59. McFarland, Thomas. *Shakespeare's Pastoral Comedy.* Chapel Hill: University of North Carolina Press, 1972.

60. Mahood, M. M. *Shakespeare's Wordplay.* London: Methuen, 1957.

61. Marx, Leo. *The Machine in the Garden.* New York: Oxford University Press, 1964.

62. Matthews, Brander. *Shakespeare as a Playwright.* New York: C. Scribner's Sons, 1913.

63. Meader, William Granville. *Courtship in Shakespeare: Its Relation to the Tradition of Courtly Love.* New York: King's Crown Press, Columbia University, 1954.

64. Moulton, Richard G. *Shakespeare as a Dramatic Thinker.* New York: Macmillan, 1907.

65. Muir, Kenneth. *Shakespeare's Sources.* 2 vols. London: Methuen, 1957.

66. ____. *Shakespeare as Collaborator.* New York: Barnes and Noble, 1960.

67. ____. *Last Periods of Shakespeare, Racine, and Ibsen.* Detroit: Wayne State University Press, 1961.

68. Murry, J. Middleton. *Shakespeare.* New York: Harcourt, Brace, 1936.

69. Nelson, Robert James. *Play within a Play: The Dramatist's Conception of His Art: Shakespeare to Anouilh.* Yale Romanic Studies: Second Series, no. 5. New Haven: Yale University Press, and Paris: Presses Universitaires de France, 1958.

70. Nicoll, Allardyce. *Shakespeare.* London: Methuen, 1952.

71. Palmer, D. J. *Shakespeare's Later Comedies: An Anthology of Modern Criticism.* Harmondsworth and Baltimore: Penguin Books, 1971.
72. Parker, Marion Hope. *The Slave of Life: A Study of Shakespeare and the Idea of Justice.* London: Chatto and Windus, 1955.
73. Parrott, Thomas Marc. *Shakespearean Comedy.* New York: Oxford University Press, 1949.
74. Phialas, Peter. *Shakespeare's Romantic Comedies: The Development of Their Form and Meaning.* Chapel Hill: University of North Carolina Press, 1966.
75. Quiller-Couch, Arthur. *Shakespeare's Workmanship.* London: Ernest Benn, 1918; rpt. Cambridge: Cambridge University Press, 1931.
76. Quinones, Ricardo J. "Views of Time in Shakespeare." *Journal of the History of Ideas* 26 (1965): 327-52.
77. ____. *The Renaissance Discovery of Time.* Harvard Studies in Comparative Literature, no. 31. Cambridge: Harvard University Press, 1972.
78. Rabkin, Norman. *Shakespeare and the Common Understanding.* New York: Free Press, 1967.
79. Righter, Anne [Anne Barton]. *Shakespeare and the Idea of the Play.* London: Chatto and Windus, 1962; rpt. Harmondsworth and Baltimore: Penguin Books, 1967.
80. Rose, Mark. *Shakespearean Design.* Cambridge: Belknap Press of Harvard University Press, 1972.
81. Salingar, Leo. *Shakespeare and the Traditions of Comedy.* London: Cambridge University Press, 1974.
82. Scott, W. I. D. *Shakespeare's Melancholics.* London: Mills and Boon, 1962.
83. Smith, Homer. "Pastoral Influence in the English Drama." *PMLA* 12 (1897): 355-60.
84. Smith, Marion Bodwell. *Dualities in Shakespeare.* Toronto: University of Toronto Press, 1966.
85. Speaight, Robert. *Nature in Shakespearean Tragedy.* London: Hollis and Carter, 1955; rpt. New York: Collier, 1962.
86. Spencer, Theodore. *Shakespeare and the Nature of Man.* New York: Macmillan, 1942.
87. Spurgeon, Caroline F. E. *Shakespeare's Imagery and What It Tells Us.* Cambridge: Cambridge University Press, 1935; rpt. Boston: Beacon Press, 1958.
88. Stamm, Rudolph. *The Shaping Powers at Work: Fifteen Essays on Poetic Transmutation.* Heidelberg: Carl Winter, 1967.
89. Stauffer, Donald. *Shakespeare's World of Images: The Development of His Moral Ideas.* New York: Norton, 1949.
90. Stoll, Elmer Edgar. *Art and Artifice in Shakespeare.* Cambridge: Cam-

bridge University Press, 1933; New York: Barnes and Noble, 1951.
91. ____. *Shakespeare's Young Lovers*. New York, London, and Toronto: Oxford University Press, 1937.
92. ____. *Shakespeare and Other Masters*. Cambridge: Harvard University Press, 1940.
93. Styan, J. L. *Shakespeare's Stagecraft*. Cambridge: Cambridge University Press, 1967.
94. Taylor, Edward William. *Nature and Art in Renaissance Literature*. New York: Columbia University Press, 1964.
95. Thompson, Karl F. *Modesty and Cunning: Shakespeare's Use of Literary Tradition*. Ann Arbor: University of Michigan Press, 1971.
96. Toliver, Harold E. *Pastoral Forms and Attitudes*. Berkeley: University of California Press, 1971.
97. Van Doren, Mark. *Shakespeare*. New York: Henry Holt, 1939.
98. Velie, Alan R. *Shakespeare's Repentance Plays: The Search for an Adequate Form*. Rutherford: Farleigh Dickinson University Press, 1972.
99. Weisinger, Herbert. "An Examination of the Myth and Ritual Approach to Shakespeare." In *Myth and Mythmaking,* ed. Henry Murray (New York: George Braziller, 1960).
100. Welsford, Enid. *The Court Masque: A Study in the Relationship between Poetry and the Revels*. Cambridge: Cambridge University Press, 1927.
101. West, Robert H. *Shakespeare and the Outer Mystery*. Lexington: University of Kentucky Press, 1968.
102. Whitaker, Virgil K. *Shakespeare's Use of Learning: An Inquiry into the Growth of His Mind and Art*. San Marino, California: Huntington Library, 1953.
103. Wickham, Glynne. *Shakespeare's Dramatic Heritage*. London: Routledge and Kegan Paul, and New York: Barnes and Noble, 1969.
104. Young, David. *The Heart's Forest: A Study of Shakespeare's Pastoral Plays*. New Haven: Yale University Press, 1972.

Studies of Romance and of Shakespeare's Romances

105. Arthos, John. "Shakespeare and the Ancient World." *MQR* 10 (1971): 149-63.
106. Babula, William. *"Wishes Fall Out As They're Willed": Shakespeare and the Tragicomic Archetype*. Salzburg Series in English Literature, The Institut für Englische Sprache und Literatur. Salzburg: Universitat, 1975.

107. Barton, Anne. "Shakespeare and the Limits of Language." *ShS 24* (1971), pp. 19-30.

108. Berry, Francis. "Word and Picture in the Final Plays." In *Later Shakespeare* (no. 113 below), pp. 81-101.

109. Bevan, Elinor. "Revenge, Forgiveness, and the Gentleman." *REL 8* (1967): 55-69.

110. Bland, D. S. "The Heroine and the Sea: An Aspect of Shakespeare's Last Plays." *EIC 3* (1953): 39-44.

111. Bowers, J. L. "The Romances." In *Shakespeare at 400*, ed. R. G. Howarth (Capetown: Department of English, Capetown University, 1965).

112. Brown, John Russell. "Laughter in the Last Plays." In *Later Shakespeare* (no. 113 below), pp. 103-25.

113. Brown, John Russell, and Harris, Bernard, eds. *Later Shakespeare*. Stratford-Upon-Avon Studies 8. London: Edward Arnold, 1966, and New York: St. Martin's Press, 1967.

114. Bullough, Geoffrey, ed. *Narrative and Dramatic Sources of Shakespeare*. Vol. 8. London: Routledge and Kegan Paul, and New York: Columbia University Press, 1975.

115. Byrne, Sister Geraldine. "Shakespeare and The Golden Age." *South Central Bulletin* 30 (1970): 173-75.

116. Childress, Diana T. "Are Shakespeare's Late Plays Really Romances?" In *Shakespeare's Late Plays* (no. 174 below), pp. 44-55.

117. Cutts, John P. *Rich and Strange: A Study of Shakespeare's Last Plays*. Pullman: Washington State University Press, 1968.

118. Danby, John F. *Poets on Fortune's Hill: Studies in Sidney, Shakespeare, Beaumont and Fletcher*. London: Faber and Faber, 1952.

119. Davis, Walter R. *A Map of Arcadia: Sidney's Romance in Its Tradition*. New Haven: Yale University Press, 1965.

120. Dobrée, Bonamy. "The Last Plays." In *The Living Shakespeare*, ed. Robert Gittings (London: Heinemann, 1960), pp. 140-54.

121. Dunn, Catherine M. "The Function of Music in Shakespeare's Romances." *SQ* 20 (1969): 391-405.

122. Edwards, Philip. "Shakespeare's Romances: 1900-1957." *ShS 11* (1958), pp. 1-18.

123. Felperin, Howard. *Shakespearean Romance*. Princeton: Princeton University Press, 1972.

124. Foakes, F. A. *Shakespeare: The Dark Comedies to the Last Plays—From Satire to Celebration*. Charlottesville: University Press of Virginia, 1971.

125. Frey, Charles. "Teaching Shakespeare's Romances." *ShN* 25 (1975): 52.

126. Frye, Northrop. *A Natural Perspective: The Development of Shakespearean Comedy and Romance*. New York: Columbia University Press, 1955; rpt. New York: Harcourt, Brace and World, 1965.

127. ____. *The Secular Scripture: A Study of the Structure of Romance*. Cambridge and London: Harvard University Press, 1976.

128. Gajdusek, R. E. "Death, Incest, and the Triple Bond in the Later Plays of Shakespeare." *AI* 31 (1974): 109-58.

129. Gesner, Carol. *Shakespeare and the Greek Romance*. Lexington: University Press of Kentucky, 1970.

130. Hartwig, Joan. *Shakespeare's Tragicomic Vision*. Baton Rouge: Louisiana State University Press, 1972.

131. Hoeniger, F. David. "Shakespeare's Romances since 1958: A Retrospect." *ShS* 29 (1976): 1-10.

132. Holloway, John. "The Concepts of 'Myth' and 'Ritual' in Literature." Appendix B in his *The Story of The Night: Studies in Shakespeare's Major Tragedies* (London: Routledge and Kegan Paul, 1961).

133. Homan, Sidney R. "*The Tempest* and Shakespeare's Last Plays: The Aesthetic Dimensions." *SQ* 24 (1973): 69-76.

134. Hunter, G. K. "The Last Tragic Heroes." In *Later Shakespeare* (no. 113 above), pp. 11-30.

135. Ingram, R. W. "Musical Pauses and the Vision Scenes in Shakespeare's Last Plays." In *Pacific Coast Studies in Shakespeare*, ed. Waldo F. McNeir and Thelma N. Greenfield (Eugene: University of Oregon Press, 1966), pp. 234-47.

136. Jacquot, Jean. "The Last Plays and the Masque." In *Shakespeare 1971: Proceedings of the World Shakespeare Congress, Vancouver, August 1971*, ed. Clifford Leech and J.M.R. Margeson (Toronto: Toronto University Press, 1972), pp. 156-73.

137. Kermode, Frank. *William Shakespeare: The Final Plays*. Writers and Their Work, no. 155. London: Longmans, Green, 1963.

138. Knight, G. Wilson. *The Crown of Life: Essays in Interpretation of Shakespeare's Final Plays*. London: Oxford University Press, 1947; rpt. New York: Barnes and Noble, 1966.

139. Lascelles, Mary. "Shakespeare's Pastoral Comedy." In *More Talking of Shakespeare*, ed. John Garrett (London: Hodder and Stoughton, 1954; rpt. New York: Theatre Arts Books, and London: Longmans, Green, 1959).

140. Leavis, F. R. "The Criticism of Shakespeare's Late Plays." *Scrutiny* 10 (1942): 339-42; rpt. in his *The Common Pursuit* (New York: G.W. Stewart, 1952; rpt. New York: New York University Press, 1964).

141. Leech, Clifford. "The Structure of the Last Plays." *ShS 11* (1958), pp. 19-30.
142. Lincoln, Eleanor Terry, ed. *Pastoral and Romance: Modern Essays in Criticism.* Englewood Cliffs: Prentice-Hall, 1969.
143. Long, John H. *Shakespeare's Use of Music: The Final Comedies.* Gainesville: University of Florida Press, 1955.
144. Mackail, John William. "The Note of Shakespeare's Romances." In his *Lectures on Poetry* (London and New York: Longmans, Green, 1911; rpt. Freeport, New York: Books for Libraries Press, 1967), pp. 208-30.
145. Marsh, D. R. C. *The Recurring Miracle: A Study of "Cymbeline" and the Last Plays.* Durban: University of Natal Press, 1962; rpt. Lincoln: University of Nebraska Press, 1969.
146. Melchiori, Barbara. " 'Still Harping on My Daughter.' " *EM 11* (1960): 59-74.
147. Mowat, Barbara A. *The Dramaturgy of Shakespeare's Romances.* Athens: University of Georgia Press, 1977.
148. Muir, Kenneth, ed. *Shakespeare Survey 11* (1958). Entire volume devoted to the romances.
149. ____. "Theophanies in the Last Plays." In *Shakespeare's Late Plays* (no. 174 below), pp. 32-43.
150. ____. *Shakespeare Survey 29* (1976). Entire volume devoted to the romances.
151. Nelson, Thomas Allen. *Shakespeare's Comic Theory: A Study of Art and Artifice in the Last Plays.* The Hague and Paris: Mouton, 1972.
152. Nosworthy, J. M. "Music and Its Function in the Romances of Shakespeare." *ShS 11* (1958), pp. 60-69.
153. Oliver, H. J. "Literary Allusions in Jacobean Drama." *Rice University Studies* 60 (1974): 131-40.
154. Peterson, Douglas L. "Tempest-Tossed Barks and Their Helmsmen in Several of Shakespeare's Plays." *Costerus* 9 (1973): 79-107.
155. ____. *Time, Tide, and Tempest.* San Marino, California: Huntington Library, 1973.
156. Pettet, E. C. *Shakespeare and the Romance Tradition.* London and New York: Staples Press, 1949; rpt. London: Methuen, 1970.
157. Proudfoot, Richard. "Shakespeare and the New Dramatists of the King's Men, 1606-1613." In *Later Shakespeare* (no. 113 above), pp. 235-61.
158. Rabkin, Norman. "The Holy Sinner and the Confidence Man: Illusion in Shakespeare's Romances." In *Four Essays on Romance,* ed. Herschel Baker (Cambridge: Harvard University Press, 1971), pp. 33-53.
159. ____. "Shakespeare's Golden Worlds." *MLQ* 35 (1974): 187-98.

160. Ristine, Frank H. *English Tragicomedy: Its Origin and History.* New York: Columbia University Press, 1910.
161. Russell, Patricia. "Romantic Narrative Plays: 1570-1590." In *The Elizabethan Theatre,* Stratford-Upon-Avon Studies 9, ed. John Russell Brown and Bernard Harris (London: Edward Arnold, 1967, and New York: St. Martin's Press, 1968), pp. 107-29.
162. Salingar, L. G. "Time and Art in Shakespeare's Romances." *Renaissance Drama 9* (1966), pp. 3-35.
163. Selzer, Daniel. "The Staging of the Last Plays." In *Later Shakespeare* (no. 113 above), pp. 127-65.
164. Semon, Kenneth J. "Fantasy and Wonder in Shakespeare's Last Plays," *SQ* 25 (1974): 89-102.
165. Sider, John W. "The Serious Elements of Shakespeare's Comedies." *SQ* 24 (1973): 1-11.
166. Smith, Hallett. "Shakespeare's Romances." *HLQ* 27 (1964): 279-87.
167. ____. "Shakespeare's Last Plays: Facts and Problems." *Shakespeare Research Opportunities* 3 (1967): 9-16.
168. ____. *Shakespeare's Romances: A Study of Some Ways of the Imagination.* San Marino, California: The Huntington Library, 1972.
169. Spencer, Theodore. "Appearance and Reality in Shakespeare's Last Plays." *MP* 39 (1942): 265-74.
170. Strachey, Lytton. "Shakespeare's Final Period." In his *Books and Characters* (New York: Harcourt, Brace, 1922), pp. 47-64.
171. Sutherland, James. "The Language of the Last Plays." In *More Talking of Shakespeare,* ed. John Garrett (London: Hodder and Stoughton, 1954; rpt. London: Longmans, Green, and New York: Theatre Arts Books, 1959).
172. Thorndike, Ashley H. *The Influence of Beaumont and Fletcher Upon Shakespere.* Worcester, Massachusetts: Press of O.B. Wood, 1901; rpt. New York: Russell and Russell, 1965.
173. Tillyard, E. M. W. *Shakespeare's Last Plays.* London: Chatto and Windus, 1938; rpt. 1964.
174. Tobias, Richard C., and Zolbrod, Paul G., eds. *Shakespeare's Late Plays: Essays in Honor of Charles Crow.* Athens: Ohio University Press, 1974.
175. Traversi, Derek. *Shakespeare: The Last Phase.* London: Hollis and Carter, 1954, and New York: Harcourt, Brace, 1955.
176. ____. "The Last Plays of Shakespeare." In *The Age of Shakespeare: The Pelican Guide to English Literature 2,* ed. Boris Ford (Harmondsworth, Middlesex and Baltimore: Penguin Books, 1955).
177. Waith, Eugene M. *The Pattern of Tragicomedy in Beaumont and Fletcher.* New Haven: Yale University Press, 1952.
178. Wells, Stanley. "Shakespeare and Romance." In *Later Shakespeare*

(no. 113 above), pp. 49-79.
179. Wickham, Glynne. "From Tragedy to Tragi-comedy: *King Lear* as Prologue." *ShS 26* (1973), pp. 33-48.
180. Wincor, Richard. "Shakespeare's Festival Plays." *SQ* 1 (1950): 219-40.
181. Yates, Francis A. *Shakespeare's Last Plays: A New Approach.* London: Routledge and Kegan Paul, 1975.

Pericles, Prince of Tyre

182. Arthos, John. "*Pericles, Prince of Tyre*: A Study in the Dramatic Use of Romantic Narrative." *SQ* 4 (1953): 257-70.
183. Baker, Harry T. "The Relation of Shakspere's *Pericles* to the George Wilkins's Novel, *The Painfull Adventures of Pericles, Prince of Tyre.*" *PMLA* 23 (1908): 100-118.
184. Barber, C. L. "'Thou That Beget'st Him Did Thee Beget': Transformation in *Pericles* and *The Winter's Tale.*" *ShS 22* (1969), pp. 59-67.
185. Barker, Gerard A. "Themes and Variations in Shakespeare's *Pericles.*" *ES* 44 (1963): 401-14.
186. Bellinger, Alfred R., ed. *Pericles, Prince of Tyre.* The Yale Shakespeare. New Haven: Yale University Press, 1925.
187. Boyle, Robert. "On Wilkins' Share in the Play Called Shakespeare's *Pericles,*" *NSST* 9 (1882): 323-40.
188. Brockbank, J. P. "*Pericles* and the Dream of Immortality." *ShS 24* (1971), pp. 105-16.
189. Bullough, Geoffrey. "*Pericles* and the Verse in Wilkins' *Painfull Adventures.*" *Bulletin de la Faculté des Lettres de Strasbourg,* Hommage à Shakespeare, Numero Special (May-June, 1961), pp. 11-24.
190. Craig, Hardin. "*Pericles* and *The Painfull Adventures.*" *SP* 45 (1948): 600-605.
191. ____. "When Shakespeare Altered His Sources." *The Centennial Review* 8 (1964): 121-28.
192. Cutts, John P. "*Pericles'* 'Most Heuenly Musicke.'" *N&Q,* n.s. 7 (1960): 172-74.
193. ____. "*Pericles* and the Vision of Diana." *AmN&Q* 3 (1964): 21-22.
194. ____. "*Pericles'* 'Downright Violence.'" *ShakS* 4 (1969): 275-93.
195. ____. "*Pericles* in Rusty Armour, and the Matachine Dance of the Competitive Knights at the Court of Simonides." *Yearbook of English Studies* (1974): 49-51.
196. Dickson, George B. "The Identity of George Wilkins." *ShAB* 14 (1939): 195-207.

197. Easson, Angus. "Marina's Maidenhead." *SQ* 24 (1973): 328-29.
198. Edwards, Philip. "An Approach to the Problem of *Pericles.*" *ShS 5* (1952), pp. 25-49.
199. Eggers, Walter F., Jr. "Shakespeare's Gower and the Role of the Authorial Presenter." *PQ* 54 (1975): 434-43.
200. Elton, William. *"Pericles*: A New Source or Analogue." *JEGP* 48 (1949): 138-39.
201. Elze, K. "Notes and Conjectural Emendations on *Antony and Cleopatra* and *Pericles.*" *Englische Studien* 9 (1886): 267-90.
202. Evans, Bertrand. "The Poem of *Pericles.*" In *The Image of The Work,* ed. Bertrand Evans, et al. (Berkeley and Los Angeles: University of California Press, 1955).
203. Felperin, Howard. "Shakespeare's Miracle Play." *SQ* 18 (1967): 363-74.
204. Fleay, F. G. "Notes on the Play of *Pericles.*" *NSST* 1 (1874): 195-209.
205. ____. "Notes on Marina." *NSST* 1 (1874): 238-41.
206. Flower, Annette C. "Disguise and Identity in *Pericles, Prince of Tyre.*" *SQ* 26 (1975): 30-41.
207. Garret, Robert Max. "Gower in *Pericles.*" *SJH* 48 (1912): 13-20.
208. Gearin-Tosh, Michael. *"Pericles*: The Death of Antiochus." *N&Q,* n.s. 18 (1971): 149-50.
209. Goolden, P. "Antiochus's Riddle in Gower and Shakespeare." *RES,* n.s. 6 (1955): 245-51.
210. Gorfain, Phyllis. "Puzzle and Artifice: The Riddle as Metapoetry in *Pericles.*" *ShS 29* (1976): 11-20.
211. Graves, T. S. "On the Date and Significance of *Pericles.*" *MP* 13 (1916): 177-88.
212. Greenfield, Thelma N. "A Re-examination of the 'Patient' Pericles." *ShakS* 3 (1967): 51-61.
213. Harrison, G. B., ed. *Pericles.* The Penguin Shakespeare. Harmondsworth: Penguin Books, 1958.
214. Hastings, William T. "Exit George Wilkins?" *ShAB* 11 (1936): 67-83.
215. ____. "Shakespeare's Part in *Pericles.*" *ShAB* 14 (1939): 67-85.
216. Hoeniger, F. David. "How Significant Are Textual Parallels? A New Author for *Pericles.*" *SQ* 11 (1960): 27-37.
217. ____, ed. *Pericles.* The Arden Shakespeare. London: Methuen, and Cambridge: Harvard University Press, 1963.
218. Howard-Hill, T. H., ed. *Pericles: A Concordance to the Text of the First Quarto of 1609.* Oxford Shakespeare Concordances. Oxford: Clarendon Press, 1972.
219. Hulme, Hilda M. "Two Notes on the Interpretation of Shakespeare's Text." *N&Q,* n.s. 6 (1959): 354-55.

220. Kane, Robert J. "A Passage in *Pericles.*" *MLN* 68 (1953): 483-84.
221. Kau, Joseph. "Daniel's Influence on an Image in *Pericles* and Sonnet 73: An *Impresa* of Destruction." *SQ* 26 (1975): 51-53.
222. Knapp, Peggy Ann. "The Orphic Vision in *Pericles.*" *Texas Studies in Literature and Language* 15 (1974): 615-26.
223. Lake, D. J. "Rhymes in *Pericles.*" *N&Q,* n.s. 16 (1969): 139-43.
224. ____. "Wilkins and *Pericles*–Vocabulary (1)." *N&Q,* n.s. 16 (1969): 288-91.
225. ____. "The *Pericles* Candidates–Heywood, Rowley, Wilkins." *N&Q,* n.s. 17 (1970): 135-41.
226. Long, John H. "Laying the Ghosts in *Pericles.*" *SQ* 7 (1956): 39-42.
227. McIntosh, William A. "Musical Design in *Pericles.*" *ELN* 11 (1973): 100-106.
228. McManaway, James G., ed. *Pericles.* The Pelican Shakespeare. Baltimore: Penguin Books, 1961.
229. Maxwell, J. C., ed. *Pericles, Prince of Tyre.* The Cambridge Shakespeare. London: Cambridge University Press, 1956.
230. Muir, Kenneth. "*Pericles,* II.v." *N&Q* 193 (1948): 362.
231. ____. "The Problem of *Pericles.*" *ES* 30 (1949): 65-83.
232. ____. "A Mexican Marina." *ES* 39 (1958): 74-75.
233. Nathan, Norman. "*Pericles* and *Jonah.*" *N&Q,* n.s. 3 (1956): 10-11.
234. Parrott, Thomas Marc. "*Pericles*: The Play and the Novel." *ShAB* 23 (1948): 105-13.
235. Praetorius, Charles, ed. *Pericles: by William Shakespeare and others. The First Quarto, 1609, a facsimile from British Museum copy c.12.h.5.* London: C. Praetorius, 1886.
236. ____. *Pericles: by William Shakespeare and others. The Second Quarto, 1609, a facsimile from the British Museum Copy, c.34. k.36.* London: C. Praetorius, 1886.
237. Prior, Roger. "George Wilkins and the Young Heir." *ShS 29* (1976): 33-39.
238. Ridley, M. R., ed. *Pericles.* The New Temple Shakespeare. London: J. M. Dent, and New York: E. P. Dutton, 1935.
239. Rolfe, William J., ed. *Shakespeare's History of Pericles, Prince of Tyre.* New York and Cincinnati: American Book Company, 1898.
240. Schanzer, Ernest. "Heywood's *Ages* and Shakespeare." *RES,* n.s. 11 (1960): 18-28.
241. ____, ed. *Pericles, Prince of Tyre.* Signet Classic. New York: New American Library, 1965.
242. Schiffhorst, Gerald J. "The Imagery of *Pericles* and What It Tells Us." *BSUF* 8 (1967): 61-70.
243. Schrickx, Willem. "*Pericles* in a Book-List of 1619 from the English Jesuit Mission and Some of the Play's Special Problems." *ShS 29*

244. (1976): 21-32.
     Scott, William O. "Another 'Heroical Devise' in *Pericles.*" *SQ* 20 (1969): 91-95.
245. Semon, Kenneth J. "*Pericles*: An Order Beyond Reason." *Essays in Literature* 1 (1974): 17-27.
246. Smyth, Albert H. *Shakespeare's "Pericles" and "Apollonius of Tyre": A Study in Comparative Literature*. Philadelphia: MacCalla & Company, 1898; rpt. New York: AMS Press, 1972.
247. Spiker, Sina. "George Wilkins and the Authorship of *Pericles.*" *SP* 30 (1933): 551-70.
248. Steinhäuser, Karolina. *Die Neueren Anschauungen über die Echtheit von Shakespeare's Pericles*. Heidelberg: Carl Winter, 1918.
249. Thorne, William B. "*Pericles* and the 'Incest-Fertility' Opposition." *SQ* 22 (1970): 43-56.
250. Tompkins, J. M. S. "Why *Pericles*?" *RES*, n.s. 3 (1952): 315-24.
251. Waith, Eugene M. "*Pericles* and Seneca the Elder." *JEGP* 50 (1951): 180-83.
252. Warren, Michael J. "A Note on *Pericles*, Act II, Chorus 17-20." *SQ* 22 (1971): 90-92.
253. Welsh, Andrew. "Heritage in *Pericles.*" In *Shakespeare's Late Plays* (no. 174 above), pp. 89-113.
254. Wilkins, George. *The Painfull Adventures of Pericles, Prince of Tyre*, ed. Kenneth Muir. Liverpool: University of Liverpool Press, 1953.
255. Wood, James O. "Humming Water." *N&Q*, n.s. 13 (1966): 293-94.
256. ___. "*Pericles*, I.ii." *N&Q*, n.s. 14 (1967): 141-42.
257. ___. "Notes on *Pericles*, Acts I and II." *N&Q*, n.s. 14 (1967): 142-43.
258. ___. "The Running Image in *Pericles.*" *ShakS* 5 (1969): 240-52.
259. ___. "A Touch of Melanchthon in Shakespeare." *N&Q*, n.s. 18 (1971): 150.
260. ___. "Shakespeare and the Belching Whale." *ELN* 11 (1973): 40-44.
261. ___. "Shakespeare's Hand in *Pericles.*" *N&Q*, n.s. 21 (1974): 132-33.
262. ___. "The Shakespearean Language of *Pericles.*" *ELN* 13 (1975): 98-103.
263. Wylie, Betty J. "Play-Doctoring the Text of *Pericles.*" *ShN* 23 (1973): 56.

Cymbeline

264. Behrens, Ralph. "On Possible Inconsistencies in Two Character

Portrayals in *Cymbeline.*" *N&Q,* n.s. 3 (1956): 379-80.
265. Bond, R. W. "The Puzzle of *Cymbeline.*" In *Studia Otiosa: Some Attempts at Criticism* (London: Constable, 1938), pp. 69-74.
266. Boodle, R. "The Original of *Cymbeline* and Possibly *The Tempest.*" *N&Q* 76 (1887): 404-5.
267. Brockbank, J. P. "History and Histrionics in *Cymbeline.*" *ShS 11* (1958), pp. 42-49.
268. Camden, Carroll. "The Elizabethan Imogen." *Rice Institute Pamphlet: Studies in English* 38 (1951): 1-17.
269. Carrington, Norman Thomas. *"Cymbeline."* Notes on Chosen English Texts. London: J. Brodie, 1954.
270. Colley, John S. "Disguise and New Guise in *Cymbeline.*" *ShakS 7* (1974): 233-52.
271. Corin, Fernand. "A Note on the Dirge in *Cymbeline.*" *ES* 40 (1959): 173-79.
272. Duncan-Jones, E. E. " 'Forlorn' in *Cymbeline* and *I Henry IV.*" *N&Q,* n.s. 4 (1957): 64.
273. Dunn, Hough-Lewis. "Shakespeare's *Cymbeline,* II, v, 15-17." *Expl* 30 (1972): no. 57.
274. Elze, K. "A Letter . . . on Shakespeare's *Cymbeline.*" *Anglia* 8 (1885): 263-97.
275. Foakes, R. A. "Character and Dramatic Technique in *Cymbeline* and *The Winter's Tale.*" In *Studies in the Arts,* ed. Francis Warner. Oxford: Clarendon Press, 1968.
276. Furness, Horace Howard, Jr., ed. *Cymbeline.* New Variorum. Philadelphia: J. B. Lippincott, 1913.
277. Gesner, Carol. *"Cymbeline* and the Greek Romances." In *Studies in English Renaissance Literature Dedicated to John Earle Uhler,* ed. Waldo F. McNeir (Baton Rouge: Louisiana State University Press, 1962).
278. Greenlaw, Edwin. "Shakespeare's Pastorals." *SP* 13 (1916): 122-54.
279. Harris, Bernard. " 'What's past is prologue': *Cymbeline* and *Henry VIII.*" In *Later Shakespeare* (no. 113 above), pp. 203-33.
280. Hoeniger, F. David. "Dowden Marginalia on Shakespeare." *SQ* 8 (1957): 129-32.
281. ____. "Two Notes on *Cymbeline.*" *SQ* 8 (1957): 132-33.
282. ____. "Irony and Romance in *Cymbeline.*" *SEL* 2 (1962): 219-28.
283. Hofling, Charles K. "Notes on Shakespeare's *Cymbeline.*" *ShakS* 1 (1965): 118-36.
284. Hill, Geoffrey. " 'The True Conduct of Human Judgement': Some Observations on *Cymbeline.*" In *The Morality of Art: Essays Presented to G. Wilson Knight by His Colleagues and Friends,*

ed. D. W. Jefferson (London: Routledge and Kegan Paul, 1969), pp. 18-32.

285. Hosley, Richard, ed. *Cymbeline.* Signet Classic. New York: New American Library, 1968.

286. Howard-Hill, T. H., ed. *Cymbeline: A Concordance to the Text of the First Folio.* Oxford Shakespeare Concordances. Oxford: Clarendon Press, 1972.

287. Hunter, G. K. "The Spoken Dirge in Kyd, Marston, and Shakespeare: A Background to *Cymbeline.*" *N&Q*, n.s. 11 (1964): 146-47.

288. Jones, Emrys. "Stuart *Cymbeline.*" *EIC* 11 (1961): 84-99.

289. Kane, Robert J. "'Richard du Champ' in *Cymbeline.*" *SQ* 4 (1953): 206.

290. Keck, Wendell M. "Accounting for Irregularities in Cloten." *ShAB* 10 (1935): 67-72.

291. Kermode, Frank. "*Cymbeline* at Stratford." *TLS,* 5 July 1974, p. 710.

292. Kirsch, Arthur C. "*Cymbeline* and Coterie Dramaturgy." *ELH* 34 (1967): 285-306.

293. Kluge, Walter. "'Fidele's Dirge' in Shakespeare's *Cymbeline.*" *SJW* 103 (1967): 211-22.

294. Knight, G. Wilson. "The Vision of Jupiter in *Cymbeline.*" *TLS,* 21 November 1936, p. 958.

295. Kott, Jan. "Lucian in *Cymbeline.*" *MLR* 67 (1972): 742-44.

296. Matthews, C. M. "The True Cymbeline." *History Today* (November, 1957), pp. 755-59.

297. Meyerstein, E. H. W. "The Vision in *Cymbeline.*" *TLS,* 15 June 1922, p. 396.

298. Moffett, Robin. "*Cymbeline* and the Nativity." *SQ* 13 (1962): 207-18.

299. Mowat, Barbara A. "*Cymbeline*: Crude Dramaturgy and Aesthetic Distance," *RenP 1966,* ed. George Walton Williams. (Spain: Artes Gráficas Soler, for The Southeastern Renaissance Conference, 1967), pp. 39-48.

300. Muir, Kenneth. "A Trick of Style and Some Implications." *ShakS* 6 (1970): 305-10.

301. Nosworthy, J. M. "The Source of the Wager Plot in *Cymbeline.*" *N&Q* 197 (1952): 93-96.

302. _____. "The Integrity of Shakespeare: Illustrated from *Cymbeline.*" *ShS 8* (1955), pp. 52-58.

303. _____, ed. *Cymbeline.* The Arden Shakespeare. London: Methuen, and Cambridge: Harvard University Press, 1955; rpt. 1966.

304. Powlick, Leonard. "*Cymbeline* and the Comedy of Anticlimax."

In *Shakespeare's Late Plays* (no. 174 above), pp. 131-41.

305. Prior, Moody E. *"Cymbeline." SQ* 7 (1956): 111-13.

306. Rees, Joan. "Revenge, Retribution, and Reconciliation." *ShS* 24 (1971), pp. 31-35.

307. Ribner, Irving. "Shakespeare and Legendary History: *Lear* and *Cymbeline." SQ* 7 (1956): 47-52.

308. Richmond, Hugh M. "Shakespeare's Roman Trilogy: The Climax in *Cymbeline." Studies in the Literary Imagination* 5 (1972): 129-39.

309. Rogers, H. L. "The Prophetic Label in *Cymbeline." RES*, n.s. 11 (1960): 296-99.

310. Rudolph, Johanna. *"Cymbeline* und *Fidelio*: Ein Beitrag zur Wechselbeziehung der Künste." *SJW* 108 (1972): 64-80.

311. Scheller, Bernhard. "Die Volkgestalten aus *Cymbeline* im Volkskunstaschaffen." *SJW* 108 (1972): 122-28.

312. Schork, R. J. "Allusion, Theme, and Characterization in *Cymbeline." SP* 69 (1972): 210-16.

313. Schwartz, M. M. "Between Fantasy and Imagination: A Psychological Exploration of *Cymbeline.*" In *Psychoanalysis and Literary Process*, ed. F. C. Crews (London: Cambridge University Press, 1970), pp. 219-83.

314. Shaheen, Naseeb. "The Use of Scripture in *Cymbeline." ShakS* 4 (1969): 294-315.

315. Siemon, James Edward. "Noble Virtue in *Cymbeline." ShS* 29 (1976): 51-61.

316. Smith, Warren D. "Cloten with Caius Lucius." *SP* 49 (1952): 185-94.

317. Stamm, Rudolf. "George Bernard Shaw and Shakespeare's *Cymbeline.*" In *Studies in Honor of T. W. Baldwin*, ed. Don Cameron Allen (Urbana: University of Illinois Press, 1958), pp. 254-66.

318. Stephenson, A. A. "The Significance of *Cymbeline." Scrutiny* 10 (1942): 329-38.

319. Stolzenberg, Grisela von. "Christliche Lehre *Cymbeline* und *The Winter's Tale." Literatur in Wissenschaft und Unterricht* 3 (1970): 87-91.

320. Swander, Homer. *"Cymbeline* and the 'Blameless Hero.'" *ELH* 31 (1964): 259-70.

321. ____. *"Cymbeline*: Religious Idea and Dramatic Design." In *Pacific Coast Studies in Shakespeare*, ed. Waldo F. McNeir and Thelma N. Greenfield (Eugene: Oregon University Press, 1966), pp. 248-62.

322. Thorne, William B. *"Cymbeline*: 'Lopp'd Branches' and the Concept of Regeneration." *SQ* 20 (1969): 143-59.

323. Tinker, F. C. *"Cymbeline." Scrutiny* 7 (1938): 5-20.

324. Warren, Roger. "Theatrical Virtuosity and Poetic Complexity in *Cymbeline." ShS* 29 (1976): 41-49.

325. West, E. J. "Shaw, Shakespeare, and *Cymbeline.*" *Theatre Annual* 8 (1950): 7-24.

326. Wilson, Harold S. *"Philaster* and *Cymbeline.*" In *English Institute Essays, 1951,* ed. Alan S. Downer (New York: Columbia University Press, 1952), pp. 146-67.

327. Woodruff, Neal, Jr. *"Cymbeline."* In *Shakespeare: Lectures on Five Plays,* Carnegie Series in English, no. 4 (Pittsburgh: Carnegie Institute of Technology, 1958), pp. 53-69.

The Winter's Tale

328. Andrews, Michael C. "Sidney's *Arcadia* and *The Winter's Tale.*" *SQ* 23 (1972): 200-202.

329. Barber, Charles. *"The Winter's Tale* and Jacobean Society." In *Shakespeare in a Changing World,* ed. Arnold Kettle (New York: International Publishers, 1964), pp. 233-52.

330. Barber, C. L. See no. 184 above.

331. Bethell, Samuel Leslie. *"The Winter's Tale": A Study.* London and New York: Staples Press, 1947; rpt. London: Folcroft Press, 1970.

332. Biggins, Dennis. "'Exit Pursued by a Beare': A Problem in *The Winter's Tale.*" *SQ* 13 (1962): 3-13.

333. Blissett, William. "The Wide Gap of Time: *The Winter's Tale.*" *ELR* 1 (1971): 52-70.

334. Bonjour, Adrien. "The Final Scene of *The Winter's Tale.*" *ES* 33 (1952): 193-208.

335. _____. "Polixenes and the Winter of his Discontent." *ES* 50 (1969): 206-12.

336. Bowers, R. H. "Autolycus in 1636." *SQ* 11 (1960): 88-89.

337. Brooke, Nicholas. *"The Winter's Tale." DUJ* 57 (1965): 112-13.

338. Bryant, Jerry H. *"The Winter's Tale* and the Pastoral Tradition." *SQ* 14 (1963): 387-98.

339. Bryant, Joseph A. "Shakespeare's Allegory: *The Winter's Tale.*" *SR* 63 (1955): 202-22.

340. Champion, Larry S. "The Perspective of Comedy: Shakespeare's *The Winter's Tale.*" *CE* 32 (1971): 428-47.

341. Clubb, Louise G. "The Tragicomic Bear." *Comparative Literature Studies* 9 (1972): 17-30.

342. Coghill, Nevill. "Six Points of Stage-Craft on *The Winter's Tale.*" *ShS 11* (1958), pp. 31-41.

343. Cottell, Beekman W. *"The Winter's Tale."* In *"Lovers Meeting": Discussions of Five Plays by Shakespeare,* Carnegie Series in English, no. 8 (Pittsburgh: Carnegie Institute of Technology,

1964), pp. 69-82.

344. Cox, Lee Sheridan. "The Role of Autolycus in *The Winter's Tale.*" *SEL* 9 (1969): 283-301.

345. Crupi, Charles. *"The Winter's Tale* and *The Thracian Wonder."* *Archiv fur das Studium der Neueren Sprachen und Literaturen,* 207 (1972): 341-47.

346. Cutts, John P. "Robert Johnson and the Court Masque." *M&L* 41 (1960): 111-26.

347. Duncan-Jones, E. E. "Hermione in Ovid and Shakespeare." *N&Q,* n.s. 13 (1966): 138-39.

348. Egan, Robert. *Drama Within Drama: Shakespeare's Sense of His Art in "King Lear," "The Winter's Tale," and "The Tempest."* New York: Columbia University Press, 1975.

349. Ellis, John. "Rooted Affection: The Genesis of Jealousy in *The Winter's Tale."* *CE* 25 (1964): 545-47.

350. Ewbank, Inga-Stina. "The Triumph of Time in *The Winter's Tale."* *REL* 5 (1964): 83-100.

351. Fergusson, Francis, ed. *The Winter's Tale.* The Laurel Shakespeare. New York: Dell, 1959.

352. Foakes, R. A. See no. 275 above.

353. Fox, Geoffrey Percival. *"The Winter's Tale."* Notes on English Literature. Oxford: Basil Blackwell, 1967.

354. Frye, Dean, ed. *The Winter's Tale.* Dubuque, Iowa: William C. Brown, 1972.

355. Frye, Northrop. "Recognition in *The Winter's Tale."* In *Essays on Shakespeare and Elizabethan Drama in Honor of Hardin Craig,* ed. Richard Hosley (Columbia: University of Missouri Press, 1962), pp. 235-46; rpt. in his *Fables of Identity: Studies in Poetic Mythology* (New York: Harcourt, Brace and World, 1963).

356. Furness, Horace Howard, ed. *The Winter's Tale.* New Variorum Edition. Philadelphia: J.B. Lippincott, 1898.

357. Gourley, Patricia Southard. "'O my most sacred lady': Female Metaphor in *The Winter's Tale."* *ELR* 5 (1975): 375-95.

358. Greenlaw, Edwin. See no. 278 above.

359. Happé, Peter. *Notes on "The Winter's Tale."* London: Ginn, 1969.

360. Hart, Edward L. "A Mixed Consort: Leontes, Angelo, Helena." *SQ* 15 (1964): 75-83.

361. Hartwig, Joan. "The Tragicomic Perspective of *The Winter's Tale."* *ELH* 37 (1970): 12-36.

362. Hellenga, Robert R. "The Scandal of *The Winter's Tale."* *ES* 57 (1976): 11-18.

363. Hoeniger, F. David. "The Meaning of *The Winter's Tale."* *University of Toronto Quarterly* 20 (1950): 11-26.

364. Hofling, Charles K. "Notes on Shakespeare's *The Winter's Tale.*" *PsyR* 58 (1971): 90-110.
365. Holland, Joanne Field. "The Gods of *The Winter's Tale.*" *Pacific Coast Philology* 5 (1970): 34-38.
366. Holt, Charles Loyd. "Notes on the Dramaturgy of *The Winter's Tale.*" *SQ* 20 (1969): 47-51.
367. Honigmann, E. A. J. "Secondary Sources of *The Winter's Tale.*" *PQ* 34 (1955): 27-38.
368. Hotine, Kate. "Shakespeare's *Winter's Tale.*" *ContempR* 211 (1967): 46-48.
369. Howard-Hill, T. H. "Knight, Crane, and the Copy for the Folio *Winter's Tale.*" *N&Q*, n.s. 13 (1966): 139-40.
370. ____, ed. *The Winter's Tale: A Concordance to the Text of the First Folio.* Oxford Shakespeare Concordances. Oxford: Clarendon Press, 1969.
371. Hughes, Merritt Y. "A Classical vs. a Social Approach to Shakespeare's Autolycus." *ShAB* 15 (1940): 219-26.
372. Hutchinson, Peter. "Franz Fuhmann's *Bohmen Am Meer*: A Socialist Version of *The Winter's Tale.*" *MLR* 67 (1972): 579-89.
373. Iwasaki, Soji. "*Veritas Filia Temporis* and Shakespeare." *ELR* 3 (1973): 249-63.
374. Jamieson, Michael. "Shakespeare's Celibate Stage." In *Papers Mainly Shakespearian,* Aberdeen University Studies, no. 147, ed. George Ian Duthie (Edinburgh: Oliver and Boyd for the University of Aberdeen, 1964), pp. 21-39; rpt. in *The Seventeenth-Century Stage: A Collection of Critical Essays,* ed. G. E. Bentley (Chicago: University of Chicago Press, 1968), pp. 70-93.
375. Kaula, David. "Autolycus' Trumpery." *SEL* 16 (1976): 287-303.
376. Kermode, Frank, ed. *The Winter's Tale.* Signet Classic. New York: New American Library, 1963.
377. Lancaster, H. Carrington. "Hermione's Statue." *SP* 29 (1932): 233-38.
378. Laroque, François F. "Feasts and Festivity in *The Winter's Tale.*" *Cahiers Elisabéthains* 6 (1974): 8-14.
379. Lawlor, John. "*Pandosto* and the Nature of Dramatic Romance." *PQ* 41 (1962): 96-113.
380. Lindenbaum, Peter. "The Itinerant Scholar: The Uses of Pastoral in *The Winter's Tale.*" *ShN* 20 (1970): 28.
381. ____. "Time, Sexual Love, and the Uses of the Pastoral in *The Winter's Tale.*" *MLQ* 33 (1972): 3-22.
382. Livingston, Mary L. "The Natural Art of *The Winter's Tale.*" *MLQ* 30 (1969): 340-55.
383. Ludwig, Jay B. "Shakespearean Decorum: An Essay on *The Winter's*

　　　　Tale," *Style* 8 (1974): 365-404.
384.　McCloskey, John C. "Shakespeare's *The Winter's Tale,* I, ii." *Expl* 23 (1965): no. 40.
385.　Martinet, Marie-Madelaine. "*The Winter's Tale* et Julio Romano." *EA* 28 (1975): 257-68.
386.　Matchett, William H. "Some Dramatic Techniques in *The Winter's Tale.*" *ShS 22* (1969), pp. 93-107.
387.　Maveety, Stanley R. "Hermione, a Dangerous Ornament." *SQ* 14 (1963): 485-86.
388.　＿＿＿. "What Shakespeare did with *Pandosto*: An Interpretation of *The Winter's Tale.*" In *Pacific Coast Studies in Shakespeare,* ed. Waldo F. McNeir and Thelma N. Greenfield (Eugene: Oregon University Press), 1966.
389.　Maxwell, Baldwin, ed. *The Winter's Tale.* The Pelican Shakespeare. Baltimore: Penguin Books, 1956.
390.　Meldrum, Ronald M. "Dramatic Intention in *The Winter's Tale.*" *HAB* 19 (1968): 52-60.
391.　Mills, Barriss. "Motivation in *Othello* and *The Winter's Tale.*" *University Review* (Missouri University) 33 (1966): 107-12.
392.　Milward, Peter. "A Theology of Grace in *The Winter's Tale.*" *English Literature and Language* 2 (1964): 27-50.
393.　Moore, John Robert. "Ancestors of Autolycus in the English Moralities and Interludes." *Washington University Studies,* Humanistic Series 9 (1922): 157-64.
394.　Mowat, Barbara Adams. "A Tale of Sprights and Goblins." *SQ* 20 (1969): 37-46.
395.　Mueller, Martin. "Hermione's Wrinkles, or, Ovid Transformed: An Essay on *The Winter's Tale.*" *Comparative Drama* 5 (1971): 226-39.
396.　Muir, Kenneth. ed. *Shakespeare, "The Winter's Tale": A Casebook.* London: Macmillan, 1968, and Nashville: Aurora Publishers, 1970.
397.　＿＿＿. "The Conclusion of *The Winter's Tale.*" In *The Morality of Art: Essays Presented to G. Wilson Knight by His Colleagues and Friends,* ed. D. W. Jefferson (London: Routledge and Kegan Paul, and New York: Barnes and Noble, 1969), pp. 87-101.
398.　Nathan, Norman. "Leontes' Provocation." *SQ* 19 (1968): 19-24.
399.　Neely, Carol Thomas. "*The Winter's Tale*: The Triumph of Speech." *SEL* 15 (1975): 321-38.
400.　Nuttall, A. D. *William Shakespeare: "The Winter's Tale."* Arnold's Studies in English Literature, no. 26. London: Edward Arnold, 1966.

401. Ortego, Phillip D. "*The Winter's Tale* as a Pastoral Tragicomic Romance." *Rendezvous* 5 (1970): 31-34.

402. Pafford, J. H. P. "Music and the Songs of *The Winter's Tale*." *SQ* 10 (1959): 161-75.

403. ____. "*The Winter's Tale*: Typographical Pecularities in the Folio Text." *N&Q*, n.s. 8 (1961): 172-78.

404. ____, ed. *The Winter's Tale*. The Arden Shakespeare. London: Methuen, and Cambridge: Harvard University Press, 1963.

405. Parsons, Natalie. "Shakespeare's Ladies: Paulina in *The Winter's Tale*." *Baconiana* 34 (1950): 228-30.

406. Price, T. R. "The Construction of 'A Winter's Tale.'" In his *Shakespeariana* (London, 1890), pp. 195-207.

407. Proudfoot, Richard. "Directing the Romances: 2. Verbal Reminiscence and the Two-Part Structure of *The Winter's Tale*." *ShS 29* (1976): 67-78.

408. Pulc, I. P. "Shakespeare's *The Winter's Tale*, IV, iv, 112-127." *Expl* 29 (1971): no. 76.

409. Pyle, Fitzroy. "*The Winter's Tale*": *A Commentary on the Structure*. London: Routledge and Kegan Paul, and New York: Barnes and Noble, 1968.

410. Quiller-Couch, Arthur, and Wilson, J. Dover, eds. *The Winter's Tale*. The Cambridge Shakespeare. Cambridge: Cambridge University Press, 1931.

411. Rashbrook, R. F. "*The Winter's Tale*." *N&Q* 192 (1947): 520-21.

412. Rees, Joan. See no. 306 above.

413. Reid, Stephen. "*The Winter's Tale*." *AI* 27 (1970): 263-78.

414. Rittenhouse, David. "A Victorian *Winter's Tale*." *Queen's Quarterly* 77 (1970): 41-55.

415. Rockas, Leo. "Browzing of Ivy: *The Winter's Tale*." *Ariel* 6 (1975): 3-16.

416. Rundus, Raymond J. "Time and His 'Glass' in *The Winter's Tale*." *SQ* 25 (1974): 123-25.

417. Schanzer, Ernest. "Heywood's *Ages* and Shakespeare." *RES* 11 (1960): 18-28.

418. ____. "The Structural Pattern of *The Winter's Tale*." *REL* 5 (1964): 72-82.

419. ____, ed. *The Winter's Tale*. The Penguin Shakespeare. Baltimore: Penguin Books, 1969.

420. ____. "Shakespeare and the Doctrine of the Unity of Time." *ShS 28* (1975), pp. 57-61.

421. Schmitt, Anthony B. "Herbert Beerbohm Tree Produces *The Winter's Tale*." *Ohio State University Theatre Collection Bulletin* 17

(1970): 20-31.

422. Schwartz, Murray M. "Leontes' Jealousy in *The Winter's Tale.*" *AI* 30 (1973): 250-73.

423. Scott, William O. "Seasons and Flowers in *The Winter's Tale.*" *SQ* 14 (1963): 411-17.

424. Shikoda, Mitsuo. "The Pastoral Settings in *The Winter's Tale*: An Interpretation." *Essays and Studies in English Language and Literature* 57 (1970): 39-50.

425. Siegel, Paul N. "Leontes a Jealous Tyrant." *RES,* n.s. 1 (1950): 302-7.

426. Siemon, James Edward. "The Canker Within: Some Observations on the Role of the Villain in Three Shakespearean Comedies." *SQ* 23 (1972): 435-43.

427. ____. "'But It Appears She Lives': Iteration in *The Winter's Tale.*" *PMLA* 89 (1974): 10-16.

428. Sims, James H. "Perdita's 'Flowers o' th' Spring' and 'Vernal Flowers' in *Lycidas.*" *SQ* 22 (1971): 87-90.

429. Smith, Hallett. "Leontes' *Affectio.*" *SQ* 14 (1963): 163-66.

430. Smith, Jonathan. "The Language of Leontes." *SQ* 19 (1968): 317-27.

431. Somer, John L. "Ralph Crane and 'an olde play called Winter's Tale.'" *ESRS* 10 (1962): 22-28.

432. Spencer, Terence J. B. "Shakespeare's Isle of Delphos." *MLR* 47 (1952): 199-202.

433. ____. "The Artistry of Shakespeare's *The Winter's Tale.*" *Eigo Seinen* 116 (1970): 72-77.

434. Stolzenberg, Grisela von. See no. 319 above.

435. Stone, Brian. "*The Winter's Tale.*" *TLS,* 31 October 1975, p. 1299.

436. Studing, Richard. "Spectacle and Masque in *The Winter's Tale.*" *EM* 21 (1970): 56-80.

437. ____. "'That rare Italian Master'—Shakespeare's Julio Romano." *HAB* 23 (1971): 22-26.

438. Tannenbaum, Samuel A. "Textual and Other Notes on *The Winter's Tale.*" *PQ* 7 (1928): 358-67.

439. ____. "The 'Valley' in *The Winter's Tale.*" *ShAB* 7 (1932): 192-93.

440. Taylor, George C. "Hermione's Statue Again: Shakespeare's Return to Bandello." *ShAB* 13 (1938): 82-86.

441. Taylor, John. "The Patience of *The Winter's Tale.*" *EIC* 23 (1973): 333-56.

442. Taylor, Michael. "Shakespeare's *The Winter's Tale*: Speaking in the Freedom of Knowledge." *CritQ* 14 (1972): 49-56.

443. Thorne, James P. "The Grammar of Jealousy: A Note on the Character of Leontes." In *Edinburgh Studies in English and Scots,* ed. A. J. Aitken et al. (London: Longmans, 1971), pp. 55-65.

444. Thorne, William B. "'Things Newborn': A Study of the Rebirth Motif in *The Winter's Tale." HAB* 19 (1968): 34-43.

445. Tinker, F.C. *"The Winter's Tale." Scrutiny* 5 (1937): 344-64.

446. Traversi, Derek A. "A Reading of the Pastoral Scene of *The Winter's Tale.*" In *The Winter's Tale,* ed. Francis Fergusson, The Laurel Shakespeare (New York: Dell Publishing, 1959).

447. Trienens, Roger J. "The Inception of Leontes' Jealousy." *SQ* 4 (1953): 321-26.

448. Uphaus, Robert W. "The 'Comic' Mode of *The Winter's Tale." Genre* 3 (1970): 40-54.

449. Waller, G. F. "Romance and Shakespeare's Philosophy of Time in *The Winter's Tale." SoRA* 4 (1970): 130-38.

450. Warren, Roger. "'Gust' and Poisoned Cups in *The Winter's Tale* and 'Sonnet 114.'" *N&Q,* n.s. 17 (1970): 134-35.

451. Weinstein, Philip M. "An Interpretation of Pastoral in *The Winter's Tale." SQ* 22 (1971): 97-109.

452. White, Christine. "A Biography of Autolycus." *ShAB* 14 (1939): 158-68.

453. Wickham, Glynne. "Shakespeare's Investiture Play: The Occasion and Subject of *The Winter's Tale." TLS,* 18 December 1969, p. 1456.

454. _____. "Romance and Emblem: A Study in the Dramatic Structure of *The Winter's Tale.*" In *The Elizabethan Theatre III,* ed. David Galloway (Hamden, Conn.: The Shoestring Press, and Toronto: Macmillan, 1973), pp. 82-99.

455. Williams, John A. *The Natural Work of Art: The Experience of Romance in Shakespeare's "The Winter's Tale."* Cambridge: Harvard University Press, 1967.

456. Wilson, Harold S. "'Nature and Art' in *The Winter's Tale,* IV, iv, 86ff." *ShAB* 18 (1943): 114-20.

457. Wright, T. "Bohemia's Sea Coast in *The Winter's Tale." Baconiana* 38 (1954): 117-24.

458. Yune, Chung-Un. "'O She's Warm': An Essay on *The Winter's Tale." English Language and Literature* (Seoul), no. 48 (1973): 48-65.

The Tempest

459. Adams, J. C. "The Staging of *The Tempest,* III, iii." *RES* 14 (1936): 404-19.

460. Allen, Don C. *"The Tempest."* In his *Image and Meaning: Metaphoric Traditions in Renaissance Poetry* (Baltimore: Johns Hopkins University Press, 1960; 2nd ed. enl., 1968).

461. Babler, O. F. "Shakespeare's *Tempest* as an Opera." *N&Q* 196 (1951): 30-31.

462. Back, Guy. "Dramatic Convention in the First Scene of *The Tempest.*" *EIC* 21 (1971): 74-85.

463. Bacon, Wallace A. "A Note on *The Tempest*, IV, i." *N&Q* 192 (1947): 343-44.

464. Barber, Lester E. "*The Tempest* and New Comedy." *SQ* 21 (1970): 207-11.

465. Bareham, T. "*The Tempest*: The Substantial Pageant Unfaded." *DUJ*, n.s. 32 (1971): 213-22.

466. Bartenschlager, Klaus. "Shakespeares *The Tempest*: Der Ideale Traum und Prosperos Magie." *SJH* 106 (1970): 170-87.

467. Berger, Harry. "Miraculous Harp: A Reading of Shakespeare's *Tempest.*" *ShakS* 5 (1969): 253-83.

468. Berry, Francis. "Shakespeare's Directive to the Player of Caliban." *N&Q*, n.s. 4 (1957): 27.

469. Boss, Judith E. "The Golden Age, Cockaigne, and Utopia in *The Faerie Queene* and *The Tempest.*" *Georgia Review* 26 (1972): 145-55.

470. Boughner, Daniel C. "Jonsonian Structure in *The Tempest.*" *SQ* 21 (1970): 3-10.

471. Bowen, H. E. " 'I'll Break My Staff . . . I'll Drown My Book.' " *RenP 1961*, ed. George Walton Williams and Peter G. Phialas (Durham: Southeastern Renaissance Conference, 1962), pp. 47-56.

472. Bowling, Lawrence E. "The Theme of Natural Order in *The Tempest.*" *CE* 12 (1951): 203-9.

473. Bradbrook, Muriel C. "Romance, Farewell! *The Tempest.*" *ELR* 1 (1971): 239-49.

474. Brockbank, Philip. "*The Tempest*: Conventions of Art and Empire." In *Later Shakespeare* (no. 113 above), pp. 183-201.

475. Brower, Reuben A. "The Mirror of Analogy: *The Tempest.*" In his *The Fields of Light* (no. 7 above).

476. _____. "The Heresy of Plot." In *English Institute Essays, 1951*, ed. Alan S. Downer (New York: Columbia University Press, 1952), pp. 44-69.

477. Brown, John Russell. *Shakespeare: "The Tempest."* Studies in English Literature, no. 39. London: Edward Arnold, 1969.

478. Bundy, Murray W. "The Allegory in *The Tempest.*" *RS* 32 (1964): 189-206.

479. Bushnell, Nelson S. "Natural Supernaturalism in *The Tempest.*" *PMLA* 47 (1932): 684-98.

480. Campbell, O. J. "Miss Webster and *The Tempest.*" *American Scholar* 14 (1945): 271-81.

481. Carnes, Valerie. "Renaissance Conceptions of Mind, Imagination, and Art in Shakespeare's *The Tempest.*" *NDQ* 35 (1968): 93-103.

482. Cawley, Robert Ralston. "Shakespere's Use of the Voyagers in *The Tempest.*" *PMLA* 41 (1926): 688-726.

483. Chambers, E. K. "The Integrity of *The Tempest.*" *RES* 1 (1925): 129-50.

484. Collins, J. Churton. "Poetry and Symbolism: A Study of *The Tempest.*" *ContempR* 93 (January 1908): 65-83.

485. Coletti, Theresa. "Music and *The Tempest.*" In *Shakespeare's Last Plays* (no. 174 above), pp. 185-99.

486. Coursen, Herbert R., Jr. "Prospero and the Drama of the Soul." *ShakS* 4 (1968): 315-33.

487. Craig, Hardin. "Magic in *The Tempest.*" *PQ* 47 (1968): 8-15.

488. Currey, R. N. "Jonson and *The Tempest.*" *N&Q* 192 (1947): 468.

489. Curry, Walter Clyde. "Sacerdotal Science in Shakespeare's *The Tempest.*" In his *Shakespeare's Philosophical Patterns* (no. 20 above).

490. Cutts, John P. "Music and the Supernatural in *The Tempest*: A Study in Interpretation." *M&L* 39 (1958): 347-58.

491. ____. "Widow Dido: A Note on *The Tempest.*" *AmN&Q* 1 (1962-63): 134-35, 150-52.

492. Davidson, Frank. "*The Tempest*: An Interpretation." *JEGP* 62 (1963): 501-17.

493. De Perott, Joseph. *The Probable Source of the Plot of Shakespeare's "Tempest."* Worcester: Clark University Press, 1905.

494. Devereux, E. J. "Sacramental Imagery in *The Tempest.*" *HAB* 19 (1968): 50-62.

495. Dircks, P. T. "Shakespeare's Use of the Catch as Dramatic Metaphor." *SQ* 24 (1973): 88-90.

496. Ditsky, John M. "Everyman Meets Caliban and Ariel: Mythic Oppositions in Popular Art." *University of Dayton Review* 10 (1973): 33-37.

497. Dobrée, Bonamy. "*The Tempest.*" *Essays and Studies* 5 (1952): 13-25.

498. Draper, John W. "Monster Caliban." *Revue de Littérature Comparée* 40 (1966): 599-605.

499. Driver, Tom. "The Shakespearian Clock: Time and the Vision of Reality in *Romeo and Juliet* and *The Tempest.*" *SQ* 15 (1964): 363-70.

500. Durrant, G. H. "Prospero's Wisdom." *Theoria* 7 (1955): 50-58.

501. Ebner, Dean. "*The Tempest*: Rebellion and the Ideal State." *SQ* 16 (1965): 161-73.

502. Echeruo, M. J. C. "The 'Savage Hero' in English Literature of the Enlightenment." *English Studies in Africa* 15 (1972): 1-13.

503. Eddy, Darlene Mathis. "The Brave Diligence: Harmonies of *The Tempest.*" *BSUF* 16 (1975): 12-25.
504. Egan, Robert. "This Rough Magic: Perspectives of Art and Morality in *The Tempest.*" *SQ* 23 (1972): 171-82.
505. _____. See no. 348 above.
506. Epstein, Harry. "The Divine Comedy of *The Tempest.*" *ShakS* 8 (1975): 279-96.
507. Fahey, Paul. "Prospero and the Critics." *CR* 15 (1972): 113-28.
508. Fain, John Tyree. "Some Notes on Ariel's Song." *SQ* 19 (1968): 329-32.
509. Fairchild, Hoxie Neale. "Emending the Text of *The Tempest.*" *ShAB* 7 (1932): 186-91.
510. Fehrenbach, Robert J. "Performance Dates of *The Tempest* in the 1677-78 Theatrical Season." *N&Q*, n.s. 17 (1970): 217-18.
511. Fiedler, Leslie. "Caliban or Hamlet." *Encounter* 26 (1966): 27.
512. Fitz, L.T. "The Vocabulary of the Environment in *The Tempest.*" *SQ* 26 (1975): 42-47.
513. Fox, Charles O. "A Crux in *The Tempest.*" *N&Q*, n.s. 4 (1975): 515-16.
514. Frank, Mike. "Shakespeare's Existential Comedy." In *Shakespeare's Late Plays* (no. 174 above), pp. 142-65.
515. Fraser, John. "*The Tempest* Revisited." *CR* 11 (1968): 60-78.
516. Freehafer, John. "Shakespeare's *Tempest* and the Seven Champions." *SP* 66 (1969): 87-103.
517. Frye, Northrop, ed. *The Tempest.* The Pelican Shakespeare. Baltimore: Penguin, 1959.
518. Furness, Horace Howard, ed. *The Tempest.* New Variorum. Philadelphia: J. B. Lippincott, 1892.
519. Fyler, Anson C., Jr. "Self-Unification: An Archetypal Analysis of Prospero in Shakespeare's *The Tempest.*" *Hartford Studies in Literature* 3 (1971): 45-50.
520. Gesner, Carol. "*The Tempest* as Pastoral Romance." *SQ* 10 (1959): 531-39.
521. Gilbert, Allan H. "Montaigne and *The Tempest.*" *RR* 5 (1914): 357-63.
522. _____. "*The Tempest*: Parallelism in Characters and Situations." *JEGP* 14 (1915): 63-74.
523. Gillie, Christopher. "*The Tempest.*" *Uses of English* 7 (1955): 37-41.
524. Gohn, Ernest. "*The Tempest*: Theme and Structure." *ES* 45 (1964): 116-25.
525. Goldsmith, Robert Hillis. "The Wild Man on the English Stage." *MLR* 52 (1958): 481-91.

526. Gray, Henry David. "The Sources of *The Tempest.*" *MLN* 35 (1920): 321-30.

527. ____. "Some Indications That *The Tempest* Was Revised." *SP* 28 (1921): 129-40.

528. Grudin, Robert. "Prospero's Masque and the Structure of *The Tempest.*" *South Atlantic Quarterly* 71 (1972): 401-9.

529. Grushow, Ira. "Brave New World and *The Tempest.*" *CE* 24 (1962): 42-45.

530. Hankins, John E. "Caliban and the Bestial Man." *PMLA* 62 (1947): 793-801.

531. Harrison, G. B. "*The Tempest.*" In *Stratford Papers on Shakespeare 1962*, ed. B. W. Jackson (Toronto: W. J. Gage for McMaster University, 1963), pp. 212-38.

532. Hart, Jeffrey P. "Prospero and Faustus." *Boston University Studies in English* 2 (1956): 197-206.

533. Hart, John A. "*The Tempest.*" In *Shakespeare: Lectures on Five Plays.* Carnegie Series in English, no. 4 (Pittsburgh: Carnegie Institute of Technology, 1958), pp. 71-83.

534. Hawkins, Harriett B. "Fabulous Counterfeits: Dramatic Construction and Dramatic Perspectives in *The Spanish Tragedy, A Midsummer Night's Dream,* and *The Tempest.*" *ShakS* 6 (1970): 51-65.

535. Henze, Richard H. "*The Tempest*: Rejection of a Vanity." *SQ* 23 (1972): 420-34.

536. Higgs, Elton D. "Post-Creation Freedom in *The Tempest.*" In *Shakespeare's Late Plays* (no. 174 above), pp. 200-212.

537. Hilberry, Conrad. "*The Tempest*: Act IV." *CE* 23 (1962): 586-88.

538. Hirst, David. *Notes on "The Tempest."* London: Ginn, 1969.

539. Hodgen, Margaret T. "Montaigne and Shakespeare Again." *HLQ* 16 (1952): 23-42.

540. Hoeniger, F. David. "Prospero's Storm and Miracle." *SQ* 7 (1956): 33-38.

541. Hofling, Charles K. "Psychological Aspects of Shakespeare's *Tempest.*" *PsyR* 61 (1974): 375-96.

542. Holland, Norman N. "Caliban's Dream." *Psychoanalytic Quarterly* 37 (1968): 114-25.

543. Horne, David, ed. *The Tempest.* The Yale Shakespeare. New Haven: Yale University Press, 1955.

544. Hotson, Leslie. "Sir Dudley Digges and *The Tempest.*" In his *I, William Shakespeare, Do Appoint Thomas Russell, Esquire* (London: Cape, 1937; rpt. New York: Oxford University Press, 1938).

545. Howard-Hill, T. H., ed. *The Tempest: A Concordance to the Text of*

the *First Folio*. Oxford Shakespeare Concordances. Oxford: Clarendon Press, 1969.

546. Howarth, Robert Guy. *Shakespeare's Tempest. A Public Lecture for the English Association.* Sidney: Australasian Medical Publishing Company, 1936.

547. Hudson, Randolph. "Shakespeare's *The Tempest,* I, ii, 437-441." *Expl* 27 (1969): no. 34.

548. Hunt, John Dixon. *A Critical Commentary on Shakespeare's "The Tempest."* London: Macmillan, 1968.

549. Hutchens, Eleanor N. "The Transfer of Power in *Lear* and *The Tempest." REL* 4 (1963): 82-93.

550. Hyman, Stanley Edgar. "Portraits of the Artist: Iago and Prospero." *Shenandoah* 21 (1970): 18-42.

551. Ingram, William. *"The Tempest* and Plato's *Republic." CEA Critic,* 28 (1966): 11-12.

552. James, D. G. *The Dream of Prospero.* Oxford: Clarendon Press, 1967.

553. Jewkes, W. T. " 'Excellent dumb discourse': The Limits of Language in *The Tempest."* In *Essays on Shakespeare,* ed. Gordon Ross Smith (University Park: Pennsylvania State University Press, 1964), pp. 196-210.

554. Johnson, W. Stacy. "The Genesis of Ariel." *SQ* 2 (1951): 205-10.

555. Jones, H. W. *"The Tempest,* III, i, 13-17." *N&Q* 195 (1950): 293-94.

556. Kermode, Frank, ed. *The Tempest.* The Arden Shakespeare. London: Methuen, and Cambridge: Harvard University Press, 1954.

557. Kittridge, George Lyman, ed. *The Tempest.* Boston: Ginn, 1939.

558. Knights, L. C. *"The Tempest."* In *Shakespeare's Late Plays* (no. 174 above), pp. 15-31.

559. Knox, Bernard. *"The Tempest* and the Ancient Comic Tradition." In *English Stage Comedy,* English Institute Essays 1954, ed. W.K. Wimsatt, Jr. (New York: Columbia University Press, 1955), pp. 52-73.

560. Langbaum, Robert, ed. *The Tempest.* The Signet Shakespeare. New York: New American Library, 1964.

561. ____. *"The Tempest* and Tragicomic Vision." In *The Modern Spirit: Essays on The Continuity of Nineteenth- and Twentieth-Century Literature,* ed. Robert Langbaum (New York: Oxford University Press, 1970), pp. 185-99.

562. Latham, Jacqueline E. M. " 'Standing Water' in *The Tempest* and Joseph Hall's Characters." *N&Q,* n.s. 21 (1974): 136.

563. ____. *"The Tempest* and King James's *Daemonologie." ShS* 28 (1975), pp. 117-25.

564. Laurent, Martha. "Shakespeare's *The Tempest,* V, i, 134-148." *Expl* 22 (1964): no. 65.

565. Lawrence, W. J. "The Masque in *The Tempest.*" *Fortnightly Review* 113 (June, 1920): 941-46.

566. Lawry, Jon S. "'Born to set it right': Hal, Hamlet, and Prospero." *BSUF* 5 (1964): 16-25.

567. Lees, F. N. "*Dido, Queen of Carthage* and *The Tempest,*" *N&Q,* n.s. 11 (1964): 147-49.

568. Levin, Harry. "Two Magian Comedies: *The Tempest* and *The Alchemist.*" *ShS* 22 (1969), pp. 47-58.

569. Levin, Richard. "Anatomical Geography in *The Tempest,* IV.i. 235-238." *N&Q,* n.s. 11 (1964): 142-46.

570. ____. "Elizabethan 'Clown' Subplots." *EIC* 16 (1966): 84-91.

571. Luce, Morton, ed. *The Tempest.* The Arden Shakespeare. Cambridge: Harvard University Press, 1901.

572. Luria, Maxwell S. "Standing Water and Sloth in *The Tempest.*" *ES* 49 (1968): 328-31.

573. McArthur, Herbert. "Tragic and Comic Modes." *Criticism* 3 (1961): 37-45.

574. McCloskey, John C. "Caliban, Savage Clown." *CE* 1 (1940): 354-57.

575. McDowell, John H. "Spectacular Effects in *The Tempest.*" *Theatre Survey* 18 (1972): 46-54.

576. Macht, David I. "Biblical Allusions in Shakespeare's *The Tempest* in the Light of Hebrew Exegesis." *Jewish Forum* (August 1955), pp. 3-5.

577. McLauchlan, Juliet. "Dramatic Convention in the First Scene of *The Tempest.*" *EIC* 21 (1971): 424-26.

578. McNeir, Waldo F. "*The Tempest*: Space-Time and Spectacle-Theme." *Arlington Quarterly* 2 (1970): 29-58.

579. McPeek, James A. S. "The Genesis of Caliban." *PQ* 25 (1946): 378-81.

580. Madsen, William G. "The Destiny of Man in *The Tempest.*" *Emory University Quarterly* 20 (1964): 175-82.

581. Magarey, Kevin. "Dragon into Bat: The Mind and Heart of Mr. Nuttall." *SoRA* 4 (1971): 91-129.

582. Major, John M. "*Comus* and *The Tempest.*" *SQ* 10 (1959): 177-83.

583. Marker, Frederick J. "The First Night of Charles Kean's *The Tempest* —From the Notebook of Hans Christian Anderson." *Theatre Notebook* 25 (1971): 20-23.

584. Markland, Murray F. "The Order of 'The Knight's Tale' and *The Tempest.*" *RS* 33 (1965): 1-10.

585. Mason, Philip. *Prospero's Magic: Some Thoughts on Class and Race.* London: Oxford University Press, 1962.

586. Merton, Stephen. "*The Tempest* and *Troilus and Cressida.*" *CE* 7 (1945): 143-50.

587. Meyers, Jeffrey. "Savagery and Civilization in *The Tempest, Robinson*

Crusoe and *The Heart of Darkness.*" *Conradiana* 2 (1970): 171-79.

588. Milward, Peter. "Gonzalo's 'Merry Fooling.'" *Shakespeare Studies* (Japan) 11 (1975): 28-36.

589. Mowat, Barbara A. "'And that's true too': Structures and Meanings in *The Tempest.*" *RenP 1976,* ed. Dennis G. Donovan and A. Leigh DeNeef (Spain: Artes Gráficas Soler, for The Southeastern Renaissance Conference, 1977), pp. 37-50.

590. Munim, K. M. A. "Reflections on *The Tempest.*" in *Homage to Shakespeare,* ed. Syed Sajjad Husain (Dacca: Dacca University Press, 1965), pp. 52-59.

591. Nakanishi, Masako. "The Structure of *The Tempest.*" *Studies in English Literature* (English Literary Society of Japan) Eng. no. (1971): 169-71.

592. Neilson, Francis. *Shakespeare and "The Tempest."* Rindge, N.H.: R. R. Smith, 1956.

593. Newell, W.W. "Sources of Shakespeare's *Tempest.*" *Journal of American Folklore* 16 (1903): 234-57.

594. Nilan, Mary M. "*The Tempest* at the Turn of the Century: Cross-Currents in Production." *ShS 25* (1972), pp. 113-23.

595. ____. "Shakespeare Illustrated: Charles Kean's 1857 Production of *The Tempest.*" *SQ* 26 (1975): 196-204.

596. Nosworthy, J. M. "The Narrative Sources of *The Tempest,*" *RES* 24 (1948): 281-94.

597. Nugent, Mary Ellen. "Puck and Ariel." *Littérature,* no. 7 (1966): 74-79.

598. Nuttall, A. D. *Two Concepts of Allegory: A Study of Shakespeare's "The Tempest" and the Logic of Allegorical Expression.* London: Routledge and Kegan Paul, 1967.

599. ____. "An Answer to Mr. Magarey." *SoRA* 4 (1971): 255-64.

600. ____. "Two Unassimilable Men." In *Shakespearean Comedy,* Stratford-Upon-Avon Studies 14, ed. Malcolm Bradbury and David Palmer (New York: Crane, Russak, 1972), pp. 210-40.

601. Nuzum, David G. "The London Company and *The Tempest.*" *West Virginia University Philological Papers* 12 (1959): 12-23.

602. Orgel, Stephen K. "New Uses of Adversity: Tragic Experience in *The Tempest.*" In *In Defense of Reading,* ed. Reuben A. Brower and Richard Poirier (New York: E. P. Dutton, 1962), pp. 110-32.

603. Palmer, D. J. *Shakespeare: "The Tempest": A Casebook.* London: Macmillan, 1968.

604. Parsons, Howard. "Shakespeare's *Tempest*: An Emendation." *N&Q* 194 (1949): 121-22.

605. ____. "Shakespeare's *Tempest*: An Emendation." *N&Q* 194 (1949): 303.

606. ____. "Shakespeare's *Tempest*: A Further Emendation." *N&Q* 194 (1949): 424.

607. ____. "Further Emendations in *The Tempest.*" *N&Q* 195 (1950): 74-75.

608. ____. "*The Tempest*: Further Emendations." *N&Q* 195 (1950): 294-95.

609. Pearson, D'Orsay W. "'Unless I Be Reliev'd by Prayer': *The Tempest* in Perspective." *ShakS* 7 (1974): 253-82.

610. Philips, James E. "*The Tempest* and the Renaissance Idea of Man." *SQ* 15 (1964): 147-59.

611. Quiller-Couch, Arthur, and Wilson, J. Dover, eds. *The Tempest*. The Cambridge Shakespeare. London: Cambridge University Press, 1921.

612. Quinn, D. B. "A *Tempest* Allusion?" *SQ* 22 (1971): 78.

613. Rea, John D. "A Source for the Storm in *The Tempest.*" *MP* 17 (1919): 279-86.

614. Reed, Robert R., Jr. "The Probable Origin of Ariel." *SQ* 11 (1960): 61-65.

615. Rickey, Mary Ellen. "Prospero's Living Drolleries." *RenP 1964*, ed. S. K. Heninger, Jr., et al. (Japan: Charles E. Tuttle, for The Southeastern Renaissance Conference, 1965), pp. 35-42.

616. Righter, Anne [Anne Barton], ed. *The Tempest*. The Penguin Shakespeare. Baltimore: Penguin, 1968.

617. Robinson, James E. "Time and *The Tempest.*" *JEGP* 63 (1964): 255-67.

618. Rockett, William. "Labor and Virtue in *The Tempest.*" *SQ* 24 (1973): 77-84.

619. Rohrsen, Peter. "Ein Antikolonialistischer *Sturm.*" *SJH* 108 (1972): 150-69.

620. Ryken, Leland. "The Temptation Theme in *The Tempest* and the Question of Dramatic Suspense." *TSL* 14 (1969): 119-27.

621. Schanzer, Ernest. See no. 407 above.

622. Schorin, Gerald. "Approaching the Genre of *The Tempest*." In *Shakespeare's Last Plays* (no. 174 above), pp. 166-84.

623. Seiden, Melvin. "Utopianism in *The Tempest.*" *MLQ* 31 (1970): 3-21.

624. Semon, Kenneth J. "Shakespeare's *Tempest*: Beyond Common Joy." *ELH* 40 (1973): 24-43.

625. Sewell, Elizabeth. "As I Was Sometime Milan: Prospects for a Search for Giordano Bruno, through Prospero, Coleridge, and the Figure of Exile." *Mosaic* 8 (1975): 127-37.

626. Sherwood, Henry C. *The Tempest*. Notes on English Literature. Oxford, Basil Blackwell, 1973.

627. Shrimpton, Nick. "Directing the Romances: I. Directing *The Tempest.*" *ShS 29* (1976): 63-67.

628. Silhol, Robert. "Magie et Utopie dans *La Tempête.*" *EA* 17 (1964): 447-56.

629. Sisson, C. J. "The Magic of Prospero." *ShS 11* (1958), pp. 70-77.

630. Slater, Ann Pasternak. "Variations within a Source: From Isaiah XIX to *The Tempest.*" *ShS 25* (1972), pp. 125-35.

631. Sloman, Judith, "Dryden, Caliban, and Negative Capability." In *Transactions of the Samuel Johnson Society of the Northwest,* vol. 6 (Calgary, Alberta: Samuel Johnson Society of the Northwest, 1973), pp. 45-57.

632. Smeall, J. F. S. "To Hear Voices in *The Tempest.*" *NDQ* 32 (1964): 23-26.

633. Smith, Denzell S. "Prospero the Shaman." *Rendezvous* 7 (1972): 1-11.

634. Smith, Hallett, ed. *The Tempest: A Collection of Critical Essays.* Twentieth Century Interpretations. Englewood Cliffs: Prentice Hall, 1969.

635. Smith, Irwin. "Ariel as Ceres." *SQ* 9 (1958): 430-32.

636. ———. "Ariel and the Masque in *The Tempest.*" *SQ* 21 (1970): 213-22.

637. Smith, Sharon L. "The *Commedia dell' Arte* and Problems Related to Source in *The Tempest.*" *ESRS* 13 (1964): 11-23 and 38-39.

638. Solomon, Andrew. "A Reading of *The Tempest.*" In *Shakespeare's Last Plays* (no. 174 above), pp. 213-34.

639. Spearing, Anthony C., and Spearing, J. C., eds. *The Tempest.* The Macmillan Shakespeare. London: Macmillan, 1971.

640. Stadler, Verena. "Zur Utopie des Gonzalo in Shakespeare's *Tempest,* II, i, 139-64." *SJH* 104 (1968): 169-78.

641. Still, Colin. *Shakespeare's Mystery Play: A Study of "The Tempest."* London: Palmer, 1921. Enlarged as *The Timeless Theme.* London: Nicholson and Watson, 1936.

642. Stock, Frithjof. "Vom Ariel in Shakespeares *The Tempest* zum Ariel in Goethes *Faust II.*" *Arcadia* 7 (1972): 274-80.

643. Stoll, Elmer Edgar. *"The Tempest." PMLA* 47 (1932): 699-726.

644. Sturgis, Marie H. "Shakespeare's Miranda." *ShAB* 10 (1935): 36-44.

645. Summers, Joseph H. "The Anger of Prospero." *MQR* 12 (1973): 116-35.

646. Tannenbaum, Samuel A. "How Not to Edit Shakspere." *PQ* 10 (1931): 97-137.

647. ———. "Textual Difficulties in *The Tempest*: Old and New." *ShAB* 6 (1931): 148-60.

648. Taylor, A. B. "Shakespeare and the Apes." *N&Q,* n.s. 16 (1969): 144-45.

649. Taylor, George Coffin. "Shakespeare's Use of the Idea of the Beast in Man." *SP* 42 (1945): 530-43.

650. Toma, Sanda. "Remarks on Caliban's Identity." *Analele Universitătii, Bucuresti, Limbi Germanice* 22 (1973): 207-13.

651. Traversi, Derek. *"The Tempest." Scrutiny* 16 (1949): 127-57.

652. Uphaus, Robert W. "Virtue in Vengeance: Prospero's Rarer Action." *Bucknell Review* 18 (1970): 34-51.

653. Urban, Raymond A. "Why Caliban Worships the Man in the Moon." *SQ* 27 (1976): 203-5.

654. Wagner, Emma Brockway. *Shakespeare's "Tempest": An Allegorical Interpretation.* Yellow Springs, Ohio: Antioch Press, 1933.

655. Warren, Roger. "Prospero's Renunciation and Coriolanus's Capitulation." *N&Q,* n.s. 21 (1974), 134-36.

656. Waswo, Richard. "Parables of Civilization: *Sir Gawain and the Green Knight* and *The Tempest." Genre* 6 (1973): 448-61.

657. Waterston, G. Chychele. "Shakespeare and Montaigne: A Footnote to *The Tempest." RR* 40 (1949): 165-72.

658. Way, P. D. L., ed. *The Tempest.* The Alexander Shakespeare. London: Collins, 1974.

659. Weber, Burton J. "The Ordering of *The Tempest." Wascana Review* 10 (1975): 3-20.

660. Weidharm, Manfred. "A Possible Textual Corruption in *The Tempest." N&Q,* n.s. 4 (1957): 335.

661. Welsh, James. "A Misrepresented Reading in Folio *Tempest* 285 (I. ii. 175)." *SQ* 26 (1975): 213-14.

662. West, Robert H. "Ceremonial Magic in *The Tempest.*" In *Shakespearean Essays,* ed. Alwin Thayer and Norman Sanders (Knoxville: University of Tennessee Press, 1964); also appears as Chapter Six in West's *Shakespeare and the Outer Mystery* (no. 101 above).

663. Wickham, Glynne. "Masque and Anti-Masque in *The Tempest." Essays and Studies* 28 (1975): 1-14.

664. Willson, Robert F., Jr. "The Plays within *A Midsummer Night's Dream* and *The Tempest." SJW* 110 (1974): 101-11.

665. Wilson, Harold S. "Action and Symbol in *Measure for Measure* and *The Tempest." SQ* 4 (1953): 375-84.

666. Wilson, John Dover. *The Meaning of "The Tempest."* Newcastle-upon-Tyne: The Literary and Philosophical Society of Newcastle-upon-Tyne, 1936; rpt. Folcroft, Pennsylvania: Folcroft, 1972.

667. Zimbardo, Rose Abdelnour. "Form and Disorder in *The Tempest." SQ* 14 (1963): 49-56.

Contributors

DAVID M. BERGERON (The University of Kansas) is the author of *English Civic Pageantry 1558-1642, Shakespeare: A Study and Research Guide,* and essays in such journals as *Texas Studies in Literature and Language* and *Shakespeare Quarterly.*

HOWARD FELPERIN (The University of Melbourne) is the author of *Shakespearean Romance, Shakespearean Representation,* and numerous essays.

CHARLES R. FORKER (Indiana University) has edited Shirley's *The Cardinal* and Shakespeare's *Henry V;* he is also the author of numerous essays on Renaissance drama in such periodicals as *Shakespeare Quarterly, Shakespeare Studies, Anglia, Modern Language Quarterly,* and *Comparative Drama.*

CHARLES FREY (The University of Washington) is the author of articles on Shakespeare in various journals including *Shakespeare Studies* and *Studies in English Literature.* He has presented papers at meetings of the MLA and the Shakespeare Association of America and has lectured at the Shakespeare Institute of America.

NORTHROP FRYE (The University of Toronto) is the author of numerous milestone studies, including *Fearful Symmetry: A Study of William Blake, Anatomy of Criticism, A Natural Perspective, Fools of Time,* and *The Secular Scripture.*

JOAN HARTWIG (The University of Kentucky) is the author of *Shakespeare's Tragicomic Vision* and essays in such journals as *Journal of English Literary History* and *Texas Studies in Literature and Language.*

CYRUS HOY (The University of Rochester) is the General Editor of the Regents Renaissance Drama Series, the editor of several individual Renaissance plays, and the author of *The Hyacinth Room: An Investigation into the Nature of Comedy, Tragedy, and Tragicomedy,* and of numerous essays and reviews.

HENRY E. JACOBS (The University of Alabama) is the co-author of *An Annotated Bibliography of Shakespearean Burlesques, Parodies, and Travesties,* and the author of articles on Renaissance drama in such periodicals as *Texas Studies in Literature and Language* and *Southern Humanities Review.*

CAROL MCGINNIS KAY (The University of Alabama) is the author of articles and reviews on Shakespeare and drama in *Shakespeare Quarterly, Satire Newsletter, Studies in the Literary Imagination, Studies in Philology, Shakespeare Studies,* and other scholarly journals.

CLIFFORD LEECH (formerly of the University of Toronto) was General Editor of the Revels Plays from 1958 to 1970. He is the editor of *Two Gentlemen of Verona* (Arden), and the author of *The Dramatist's Experience with Other Essays on Literary Theory, Shakespeare's Tragedies and Other Studies in Seventeenth-Century Drama, Tragedy,* and numerous other books and essays.

JOAN WARCHOL ROSSI (The University of Illinois) is a doctoral candidate whose dissertation topic is *Cymbeline.*

NORMAN SANDERS (The University of Tennessee) is the General Editor of the Oxford Standard English Authors edition of Greene, and the editor of *Henry VI, Part 1, Julius Caesar, The Two Gentlemen of Verona* (Penguin), and Greene's *James the Fourth* (Revels); he is the author of articles on Shakespeare and Greene, and numerous reviews, including the annual survey of scholarship in *Shakespeare Survey.*

DAVID YOUNG (Oberlin College) is the author of *Something of Great Constancy: The Art of "A Midsummer Night's Dream," The Heart's Forest: Shakespeare's Pastoral Plays,* and essays on Shakespeare and contemporary poetry.

Index

Acharnians, The (Aristophanes), 15, 18

Aeschylus, 93

Agamemnon (Aeschylus), 93

Albee, Edward, 16

Alchemist, The (Jonson), 150-66, passim

Allegory. *See* Shakespeare, William: Romances, visionary approach to

All's Well That Ends Well, 146

Anatomy of Criticism (Frye), 62

Anne, Queen of England, 127

Anniversaries (Donne), 19

Antimasque: 18-29, 41-49; actors in, 19, 59; in *Bartholomew Fair*, 47-49; as burlesque, 19, 34; cosmology of, 22-25; in *Duchess of Malfi*, 46-47; figures in, 18, 129; imagery in, 25-29; in Jonson, 41; popularity of, 21-22, 42-43; in *Satiromastix*, 45; in *Tempest*, 54-55, 103; in *Two Noble Kinsmen*, 46-47; in *Winter's Tale*, 36-37

Antonio's Revenge (Marston), 44

Antony and Cleopatra, 77

Apple Cart, The (Shaw), 15

Arcades (Milton), 27, 28, 41-42

Ariosto, Lodovico, 139-40

Aristophanes, 13-16, 18, 28-29

Aristotle, 40

Arms and the Man (Shaw), 13

Art versus Nature, 134-38, 140-43, 145, 146-48

As You Like It, 79

Auden, W. H., 134

Back to Methuselah (Shaw), 14

Bacon, Sir Francis, 18, 20, 24, 36

Barber, C. L., 64

Bartholomew Fair (Jonson), 2-3, 47-49, 165

Bate, W. J., 68

Battenhouse, R. W., 2

Beaumont, Francis, 34, 42, 129; and John Fletcher, 87

Beckett, Samuel, 15, 16

Beethoven, Ludwig van, 12

Bentley, G. E., 3

Bethell, S. L., 7

Birds, The (Aristophanes), 14, 15

Black Comedy, 14, 15

Blissett, William, 47-48, 53

Bloom, Harold, 68-69

Bradley, A. C., 2

Brecht, Bertold, 40

"Brief über den Roman" (Schlegel), 60

Brown, John Russell, 47n

Bullough, Geoffrey, 104, 125

Burlesque, 19, 34

"Burnt Norton" (Eliot), 23

Camino Real (Williams), 14

Campion, Thomas, 24, 25, 36, 129, 130

Canterbury Tales, The (Chaucer), 147

Cardenio (ascribed to Shakespeare), 56

Cervantes, Miguel de, 113
Chambers, E. K., 49
Chappell, William, 92
Charles I, King of England, 40, 58
Chaucer, Geoffrey, 33, 147-48
Chekhov, Anton, 14
Cherry Orchard, The (Chekhov), 14
Christian, King of Denmark, 132
Chronicles of England, Scotland, and Ireland (Holinshed), 104, 106-11
Chruso-thriambos: The Triumphes of Golde (Munday), 127-30
Comédie larmoyante, 12
Comedy of Errors, The, 51, 55
Comedy of the absurd, 14, 15
Commedia dell' arte, 11, 15
Compleat Gentleman, The (Peacham), 131
Comus (Milton), 27-28, 42, 47
Confidential Clerk, The (Eliot), 16
Conrad, Joseph, 69-76
I Corinthians, 133
Coriolanus, 50, 77, 82
Cure, Cornelius and William (of Southwark), 131
Cymbeline, 30, 31, 36-38, 52-53, 56, 77, 78, 82, 85-86, 88, 91, 94-97, 104-12, 113-14, 126
Cynthia's Revels (Jonson), 43-44, 58

Danby, John, 6
Dante Alighieri, 24, 63
Davies, Sir John, 37, 130
Dekker, Thomas, 45
Dessen, Alan C., 174n
Detachment, 137, 146, 147. *See also* Remoteness
Dickens, Charles, 12
"Dioce" (Pound), 24
Donne, John, 19
Dowden, Edward: concept of Shakespeare's romances, 4, 113-14, 115; label for Shakespeare's romances, 1
Drummond, William, 19, 130
Duchess of Malfi, The (Webster), 45-47

Ecclesiazusae (Aristophanes), 14
Eliot, T. S., 16, 23, 39, 52, 72
Elizabeth, Princess, 129-30
Elizabethan Drama and the Viewer's Eye (Dessen), 174n
Elizabeth I, Queen of England, 130-32
Elvetham Entertainment, 127
Engagement, 137, 146, 147. *See also* Immediacy
Entertainment: as distinguished from masque, 41-42, 47, 127-28
Every Man in His Humour (Jonson), 2
Every Man Out of His Humour (Jonson), 14
Ewbank, Inga-Stina, 45, 50, 127-28

Faringdon, Nicholas, 128
Faust (Goethe), 31
Faustus, Doctor (Marlowe), 150-66 passim
Felperin, Howard, 5
Fidelio (Beethoven), 12
Fielding, Henry, 12
Fletcher, John, 31, 55. *See also* Beaumont, Francis
Ford, John, 47
Forman, Dr. Simon, 126
Fortunate Isles, The (Jonson), 23, 26
Friar Bacon and Friar Bungay (Greene), 159
Frogs, The (Aristophanes), 14, 15
Frye, Northrop, 9, 61-64, 68, 69, 74
Funerary sculpture, 131-32

Garson, Barbara, 16
Gascoigne, George, 139
Gate of Horn, The (Levy), 24
Gilbert, Sir W. S. and Sir Arthur Sullivan, 12-13
Goethe, Johann Wolfgang von, 31
Goldsmith, Oliver, 12
Gondoliers, The (Gilbert and Sullivan), 13
Granville-Barker, Harley, 3

Greek drama, 40, 93; affinities between Old Comedy and masque, 18-29; Old Comedy versus New Comedy, 11-18
Greene, Robert, 51, 55, 87, 113, 126, 159
Greg, W. W., 126, 129

Hamlet, 40, 51, 57, 77, 79, 147
Heart of Darkness, The (Conrad), 69-76
Henry, Prince of Wales (d. 1612), 129-30, 132
Henry IV, Part II, 57
Henry V, 57, 146
Henry VIII, 31-34, 41, 43, 55, 57, 148
Heywood, Thomas, 130
History of England. See Chronicles of England, Scotland, and Ireland
History of English Poetry (Warton), 76
History of Scotland. See Chronicles of England, Scotland, and Ireland
Holinshed, Raphael, 104, 106-12
"Hollow Men, The" (Eliot), 72
Hoy, Cyrus, 127
Hymenaei (Jonson), 21, 26

Illusion, 40-41, 51, 52, 56-59, 67, 133, 136-48, 150-51, 157-61
Il Penseroso (Milton), 27
Immediacy, as dramatic technique, 135, 136, 137, 139, 140, 142, 143
Importance of Being Earnest, The (Wilde), 13
Ionesco, Eugene, 15
Irony, 33, 34, 40, 43, 49, 50, 55, 57-59, 62, 66-69, 74-76, 108, 130, 136-37
I Suppositi (Ariosto), 139-40

James, D. G., 9
James I, King of England, 19, 20, 21, 26, 27, 40-49, 51, 56, 57, 131, 145

James IV (Greene), 51
Jew of Malta, The (Marlowe), 161
Johnson, Samuel, 93, 97
Jones, Inigo, 21, 24, 49
Jonson, Ben, 2-3, 14, 19-21, 23-28, 30, 32, 35, 36, 41, 42, 54, 57, 59; The Alchemist, 150-66 passim; Bartholomew Fair, 47-49; Cynthia's Revels, 43-44, 58; "Humours" theory, 11-12

Kenilworth Entertainment, 127
Kermode, Frank, 5, 126, 153
King and No King, A (Beaumont and Fletcher), 87
King Lear, 49, 51, 77, 78, 80-83, 97, 133, 141
Knight, G. Wilson, 8, 34, 64, 134
Knight's Tale (Chaucer), 33

Leech, Clifford, 102
Levy, Gertrude Rachel, 24
Lord Chamberlain's Records, 132
Lord Mayor's Show, 41, 126-28
Lords' Masque, The (Campion), 24-25, 36, 129
Love Freed from Ignorance and Folly (Jonson), 19, 26
Lovers Made Men (Jonson), 24
Lover's Melancholy, The (Ford), 47
Love's Cruelty (Shirley), 30
Love's Labor's Lost, 34, 127, 146-47, 165
Lowin, John, 127
Lycidas (Milton), 28
Lyly, John, 41, 51

Macbeth, 29, 51, 77, 109, 126, 144
MacBird (Garson), 16
Mack, Maynard, 2
Magic, 53, 64, 65, 67, 142, 145, 150-66 passim
Magic Flute, The (Mozart), 37-38
Major Barbara (Shaw), 13
Malcontent, The (Marston), 44-45, 50, 92
"Marina" (Eliot), 52

Marlowe, Christopher, 150-66 passim
Marston, John, 44-45, 50, 92
Mary Stuart, Queen of Scots, 131, 132
Mask. *See* Masque
Mask of Apollo, The (Renault), 40
Masque: affinities with romance, 29-30, 32, 34-38; characteristics of, 19, 20-21, 40-43; cosmology of, 22-23, 35; distinction between mask and masque, 169-70n; distinction between masque and drama, 164, 166; as illusion, 40; imagery of, 24-28; major masques, 43-49, 135, 142-44; organizing principle of, 18; for Princess Elizabeth's wedding, 129-30; relation to Shakespeare's romances, 51-59, 63, 83; relation to statue scene in *The Winter's Tale*, 127; in *The Tempest*, 154, 163-65
Masque of Anarchy (Shelley), 33
Masque of Augurs, The (Jonson), 25, 26
Masque of Blackness, The (Jonson), 27, 41
Masque of Flowers, The (Anon.), 24, 43
Masque of Queens, The (Jonson), 27, 41
Masque of the Gypsies Metamorphosed, The (Jonson), 42, 43
Masque of the Inner Temple and Gray's Inn (Beaumont), 42, 129
Maturin, Charles, 59
Measure for Measure, 86, 90
Melmoth the Wanderer (Maturin), 59
Mercer, Eric, 131
Mercury Vindicated from the Alchemists (Jonson), 26
Merry Wives of Windsor, The, 79
Metamorphosis (Ovid), 23
Middleton, Thomas, 44
Midsummer Night's Dream, A, 34, 79, 127, 146, 147, 156-57
Milton, John, 22, 27, 28, 41-42, 47, 63

Molière, Jean-Baptiste, 11-12, 29
Mozart, Wolfgang Amadeus, 37-38
Mucedorus (Anon.), 18
Much Ado About Nothing, 79
Muir, Kenneth, 126
Munday, Anthony, 127-30
Murther of Gonzago (in *Hamlet*), 147
Music, 91-93; in romance and masque, 37-38

"Nativity Ode" (Milton), 27, 28
New Comedy, 11-18, 29, 36, 64-65
Nosworthy, J. M., 5

Oberon (Jonson), 20, 25
"Ode to Himself" (Jonson), 2-3
Odyssey (Homer), 23
Old Comedy, 11, 13-18, 28, 29, 34
Orchestra (Davies), 37
Orgel, Stephen, 59, 164
Othello, 51, 77, 80, 81
Ovid, 23
Oxford English Dictionary, 93

Pafford, J. H. P., 98
Palmer, D. J., 156
Pandosto (Greene), 55, 87, 126
Paradise Lost (Milton), 27
Parody, 12, 15; Autolycus as parodic fool, 98-101, 103; Caliban as parodic fool, 101-03; Cloten as parodic fool, 94-97, 103; definition of, 94; of Good Samaritan parable, 99-100; relationship to "parode," 93
Pastoralism, 134; in Shakespeare's romances, 38; Shakespeare's use of, 6
Peace (Aristophanes), 15
Peacham, Henry, 130, 131
Pericles, 30, 31, 35, 36, 49, 52, 53, 55, 56, 57, 77, 78, 81, 84-85, 88, 113-14
Perkin Warbeck (Ford), 47
Pettet, E. C., 5
Pinafore, HMS (Gilbert and Sullivan), 13

Plain Dealer, The (Wycherley), 40

Plautus, 13

Pleasure Reconciled to Virtue (Jonson), 25

Popular Music of the Olden Time (Chappell), 92

Pound, Ezra, 24

Purgatorio (Dante), 24

Puttenham, George, 14

Remoteness, as dramatic technique, 135, 136, 137, 139, 140, 143

Renault, Mary, 40

Revels, 41-44, 50, 54, 58

Revenger's Tragedy, The (Tourneur), 44

Romance: nature of, 1-2, 113; in *Heart of Darkness*, 69-76; versus Romanticism, 60-64, 68; in *The Tempest*, 64-69. See also Shakespeare, William

Romeo and Juliet, 43, 55, 79, 165

Salingar, Leo, 94

Satiromastix (Dekker and perhaps Marston), 45

Schiller, Friedrich von, 61-62, 68

Schlegel, Friedrich, 60, 68

Schoenbaum, Samuel, 5

Sea and the Mirror, The (Auden), 134

Sex, in *The Winter's Tale*, 117-19

Shakespeare, William. Romances: affinities with the masque, 29-30, 32, 34-38 passim, 51-59, 63, 83; art versus nature in, 134; biographical criticism of, 3-5; as differentiated from comedy, 29-30, 38; New Comedy, in, 36; as opposed to tragedies, 51-53, 77; role of the gods in, 35; romantic comic form in, 29; structural approach to, 5-6; visionary approach to, 6-10. Sonnets, 83. Tragedies, 83-84. Works, *see individual play titles*

Shaw, George Bernard, 13-14, 15, 16

Shelley, Percy Bysshe, 33

Sheridan, Richard Brinsley, 12

Shirley, James, 21, 30, 32, 41, 43, 58

Sidney, Sir Philip, 113, 153

Sir Thomas More (Anon.), 18

Spenser, Edmund, 60, 63, 113

Still, Colin, 8

Stoll, E. E., 3

Strachey, Lytton: concept of Shakespeare's romances, 4

Studing, Richard, 127

Supposes. See I Suppositi

"Sweeny Agonistes" (Eliot), 16

Sword from the Rock, The (Levy, 24

Tamburlaine (Marlowe), 156

Taming of a Shrew, The (Anon.), 138

Taming of the Shrew, The, 57, 78-79, 134, 136-41, 142, 148

Tempest, The, 20, 30, 31, 34-38, 53, 56, 63, 64-69, 70, 77, 78, 88-90, 91-94, 101-3, 113, 135, 141-48 passim, 150-66 passim; criticism by Colin Still, 8

Terence, 13, 29

Three Sisters, The (Chekhov), 14

Tillyard, E. M. W., 64, 143

Timon of Athens, 49-51, 58, 82, 83

Tom Jones (Fielding), 12

Tourneur, Cyril, 130

Tragedies, Shakespeare's, 83-84; as opposed to romances, 51-53; as precursors of romances, 77

Tragedy, Elizabethan, 29

Tragic structure, in *The Winter's Tale*, 113-24

Traversi, D. A., 9, 64

Triumph of Peace, The (Shirley), 21, 41, 43, 58

Troilus and Cressida, 16-17, 18, 34

Twelfth Night, 51

Two Gentlemen of Verona, The, 51, 79

Two Noble Kinsmen, The, 31, 33-35, 42, 45-47, 55, 148

"Uber naive und sentimentalische Dictung" (Schiller), 61-62

Vanderdort, Abraham, 132

Waiting for Godot (Beckett), 15
Warton, Thomas, 76
Webster, John, 45-47, 130
"Well-made play," 12, 15
Westminster Abbey, 131, 132
Wickham, Glynne, 127, 131, 132
Wilde, Oscar, 13, 16

Williams, Tennessee, 14
Winter's Tale, The, 30, 31, 35-38, 50, 53-57, 77-78, 85-88, 91, 94, 98-101, 103, 113-24, 125-35
Wodehouse, P. G., 13
Wycherley, William, 40

You Never Can Tell (Shaw), 13
Your Five Gallants (Middleton), 44

Zoo Story (Albee), 16